Women of Achievement

Madonna

Women of Achievement

Abigail Adams
Susan B. Anthony
Tyra Banks
Clara Barton
Hillary Rodham Clinton
Marie Curie
Ellen DeGeneres
Diana, Princess of Wales
Tina Fey
Ruth Bader Ginsburg
Joan of Arc
Helen Keller
Madonna
Michelle Obama
Sandra Day O'Connor
Georgia O'Keeffe
Nancy Pelosi
Rachael Ray
Anita Roddick
Eleanor Roosevelt
Martha Stewart
Barbara Walters
Venus and Serena Williams

Women of Achievement

Madonna

ENTERTAINER

Hal Marcovitz

MADONNA

Chelsea House
An imprint of Infobase Publishing
132 West 31st Street
New York, NY 10001

Library of Congress Cataloging-in-Publication Data
Marcovitz, Hal.
Madonna: entertainer / Hal Marcovitz.
p. cm. — (Women of achievement)
Includes bibliographical references and index.
ISBN 978-1-60413-859-7 (hardcover)
1. Madonna, 1958—Juvenile literature. 2. Rock musicians—United States—Biography—Juvenile literature. 3. Motion picture actors and actresses—United States—Biography—Juvenile literature. I. Title. II. Series.

ML3930.M26M37 2010
782.42166092—dc22

2010005688

Chelsea House books are available at special discounts when purchased in bulk quantities for businesses, associations, institutions, or sales promotions. Please call our Special Sales Department in New York at (212) 967-8800 or (800) 322-8755.

You can find Chelsea House on the World Wide Web at http://www.chelseahouse.com.

Text design by Erik Lindstrom
Cover design by Ben Peterson
Composition by EJB Publishing Services
Cover printed by Bang Printing, Brainerd, MN
Book printed and bound by Bang Printing, Brainerd, MN
Date printed: October 2010
Printed in the United States of America
10 9 8 7 6 5 4 3 2 1

This book is printed on acid-free paper.

All links and Web addresses were checked and verified to be correct at the time of publication. Because of the dynamic nature of the Web, some addresses and links may have changed since publication and may no longer be valid.

CONTENTS

Becoming Little Eva

As the American pop star Madonna was driven through the streets of Buenos Aires, Argentina, she saw some graffiti that she was not used to seeing in the United States: "GET OUT, MADONNA!" Madonna shuddered at the message. Back home, her fans lined up for hours to buy tickets to her concerts. Her albums sold in the millions. Photographers and tabloid reporters hounded her constantly. In Argentina, however, many people were not as willing to embrace her. As the car neared her hotel, Madonna saw protesters burning a dummy of her in effigy. She thought, "How's that for a welcome?"[1]

It was January 1996. Madonna had arrived in the South American country on a mission to convince President Carlos Menem to permit a movie company to film scenes for the musical *Evita* in the Argentine capital. The film would tell the story of Eva Perón, the immensely popular former first lady of Argentina. Some 40 years after her death, Evita—a term of endearment that means "little Eva"—was regarded by many Argentines as a candidate for sainthood.

And so when they learned that Madonna had been cast to portray their beloved Evita in the film version of what had been a hit Broadway play, many Argentines bristled at the thought. After all, Madonna had risen to popularity as a singer willing to perform edgy and sexually suggestive music. She had few qualms about exposing her body on stage and screen as well as for national magazines. Soon after Madonna was selected for the role, Menem announced that he would bar the movie company from filming in his country. "I am very aware," he told a TV audience, "that the Argentines who still hold Evita as a martyr and saint would not tolerate someone like Madonna portraying her on the screen, a woman who is the embodiment of vulgarity."[2]

WORTHY OF PLAYING EVITA

At the time, the film's cast had gathered at a music studio in London, England, to record the songs that would be featured in the movie. Learning of the president's decision, the film's director, Alan Parker, was despondent. To Parker, the idea of making the movie without filming in Buenos Aires was unthinkable. Parker knew the value of creating the movie on the same streets that Evita had walked as an impoverished young woman in the 1930s and 1940s.

Parker was particularly intrigued by the idea of filming his star on the balcony of the Casa Rosada, the presidential palace in downtown Buenos Aires that overlooks the sprawling Plaza de Mayo. That is where Evita, the wife of President Juan Perón, addressed the people of Buenos Aires, and that is where Parker hoped to film Madonna

During the filming of the movie adaptation of the hit musical *Evita*, Madonna *(center)* performs "Don't Cry for Me Argentina" on the historic balcony of the presidential palace in Buenos Aires, Argentina. After initial reluctance, the government of Argentina was swayed to facilitate the production of the movie by Madonna.

singing "Don't Cry for Me Argentina," the soulful ballad that is the musical's signature song.

Parker called the cast members together and told them that he did not see how the production could continue without the cooperation of the Argentine government. He told them he was thinking about shutting down the film. "This project continues to stumble upon obstacle upon obstacle," he said. "If it's ever finished, it will be a miracle."[3]

At that point, Madonna spoke up. She told Parker and the cast members that she would go to Buenos Aires. She intended to tour the city, study the life of Evita, get to know the people of Buenos Aires, and prove to the Argentines that she was worthy of portraying Eva Perón on film. She planned to meet personally with President Menem. "I can hardly blame them if the 'me' they know is the one they've read about in the newspapers," Madonna said. "I am prepared to disarm all and get them to share their deepest, darkest secrets about Eva."[4]

A few weeks later, Madonna arrived in Buenos Aires to find the people hostile, the weather rainy and unpleasant, and the president unwilling to meet her. She dug in for what she expected would be a visit of several weeks.

CHARMING THE PEOPLE OF BUENOS AIRES

Immediately after arriving, Madonna summoned a hairstylist and directed her to pull her dyed blonde hair into a tight bun at the back of her head in the style worn by Evita. She told another beautician to pluck her eyebrows into thin brown arches. Finally, Madonna inserted brown contact lenses onto her eyes so her eye color matched Evita's.

Whenever Madonna ventured into public, she wore conservative 1940s-style skirts with hemlines that reached nearly to her ankles. She wore little jewelry. Many times, Madonna drew gasps from the Argentines—particularly those old enough to have seen Evita in person. Practically overnight, Madonna had effectively transformed herself into the image of Eva Perón.

Madonna spent the next several weeks touring the city, meeting Argentines who had known Evita, and doing her best to charm the people of Buenos Aires. Soon, the angry crowds she had been seeing were replaced by the more adoring kind that she was more accustomed to seeing. In fact, on a visit to Evita's grave, Madonna had to sneak out of the back entrance of her hotel because the crowds waiting to catch a glimpse of her had grown too big for the police to manage.

And then, on a visit to La Boca, an impoverished neighborhood in Buenos Aires, Madonna—who had been raised a Catholic—entered a church, knelt, and prayed.

Afterward, she said, "I just had an uncontrollable urge to thank God for allowing me to see Buenos Aires and learn about the woman who gave so much love to her people. I'm convinced that President Menem will give us permission to film *Evita* here."[5]

Soon after the visit to La Boca, Madonna received a message: The president would be honored if she would join him for dinner.

DINNER WITH THE PRESIDENT

Madonna would dine with Menem in a presidential retreat on an island in the El Tigre River, accessible only by boat or helicopter. On the evening of the dinner, two security officers arrived at Madonna's hotel to escort her to the island. To avoid the crowds out front, they left through the hotel kitchen, then drove quickly through the Buenos Aires streets until they arrived at a small military airport outside the city. Madonna and the two guards boarded a helicopter and made the short flight to the island, where she saw a large, ornate stone house. The guards told Madonna that the president used the mansion to meet visiting heads of state and other dignitaries. Dressed in an evening gown and mink stole, the singer did her best to keep her clothes unruffled as she stepped out of the helicopter with its rotor blades churning noisily.

Shown into the mansion, Madonna was escorted through a marble foyer decorated with oil paintings and large glass chandeliers and was met by a charming young woman who would serve as translator. After introducing herself, the translator led Madonna into a wood-paneled dining room where three place settings of crystal dinnerware had been set on top of a blue tablecloth. A moment later, President Menem stepped into the dining room. Madonna found him gracious, but the president made it clear that he would not be easy to convince: "There are serious problems today in

Argentina, and I feel a duty to my people to protect the memory of our sainted Evita."[6]

Dinner was served. Madonna found herself doing most of the talking as she told the president of her respect for Evita's story and how she felt emotionally connected to the former first lady. Both had lost a parent at a young age—Evita's father died when she was a child, just as Madonna had lost her mother. And, like Evita, Madonna told the president, she had arrived in a big city—New York—with little money, no friends, and no prospects. Both had persevered, though, and both found success and fame. "Evita is the poor girl who made good, just like me," Madonna said. "She came to Buenos Aires at fifteen to make a career in the movies. I came to New York . . . to make a career in music, and both of us had love affairs with men who helped us achieve our goals."[7]

At the conclusion of the dinner, Madonna gave Menem a tape of her performance of "Don't Cry for Me Argentina," recorded weeks before in London. Menem ushered his guest into the mansion's living room, where he inserted the cassette into a tape player. For the next several minutes, he listened in silence as one of the world's most famous singing voices performed the haunting lyrics to a song that told of a woman's love for her country and the people of Argentina. At the conclusion of the song, the Argentine president rose, walked over to Madonna, and gently kissed her on each cheek. He whispered, "*Suerte, niña*"[8]—a Spanish term that means "Lucky girl." He then left the room.

The two security officers quickly reappeared and escorted Madonna to the helicopter; she was whisked back to Buenos Aires, then driven to her hotel. A few days later, Alan Parker received a phone call from the president's office. The filming could proceed in Buenos Aires, and the film company would be granted access to whatever buildings it needed, including the Casa Rosada.

Girl from Michigan

If you were a student at Adams High School in Rochester, Michigan, in 1972 and wanted to see a good football game, you attended the games played by the school's varsity squad. But if you were more interested in watching electric and scintillating dance moves by the cheerleaders, then you headed for the Adams High junior varsity games.

One of the lead cheerleaders on the ninth-grade squad was Madonna Ciccone, who had incorporated modern dance moves and rock 'n' roll tunes into the squad's performances. It was no secret around Adams High that the varsity cheerleaders were deeply envious of the JV squad and their leader, Madonna. "She was very good, very showy," recalls fellow JV cheerleader Lucinda Axler. "She knew how to draw attention to herself. She had a big mouth and had the moves, too."[1]

Indeed, by the age of 14, Madonna was an incandescent though unpolished performer. A year later, she convinced her reluctant father to let her drop out of piano lessons and take up classical dance. Soon after, Madonna enrolled in the Rochester School of Ballet. The school's owner, Christopher Flynn, recognized her talent. "He was my mentor, . . . everything," Madonna recalled years later. "He understood me."[2]

HER FATHER'S FAVORITE

Madonna Louise Veronica Ciccone was born on August 16, 1958, in Bay City, Michigan, the daughter of Silvio "Tony" Ciccone and Madonna Louise Firkin. Her father, a first-generation Italian American, was the first in his family to attend and graduate from college and her mother was French Canadian. The family lived first in Pontiac, a blue-collar suburb of Detroit, then later moved to a more upscale home in nearby Rochester Hills.

Madonna was the third child and the oldest daughter in what would grow into a family of eight children. As the eldest daughter, she was clearly her father's favorite. "She was spoiled from the very beginning,"[3] claims her younger brother Christopher. Even as a young girl, she loved watching Hollywood musicals while poring through fan magazines, reading over the details of the lives of the stars.

Madonna was very close to her mother, who called her "little Nonnie." The two had a special relationship; her mother had, after all, given her first-born daughter her own name. As a young girl, Madonna recalls sneaking into her parents' bedroom and getting into bed with them so she could snuggle close to her mother. "She was beautiful," Madonna says of her mother, "and very loving and devoted to her children."[4]

When Madonna was five years old, her mother was diagnosed with breast cancer. This once loving and vibrant woman soon grew weary, unable to keep after the children or keep up with the housework. Madonna was too young to understand what was wrong with her mother, but she was well aware that her mother was terribly ill. On one occasion, Madonna recalled growing frustrated when her mother collapsed onto the living room couch, too tired to play with her. "Why are you doing this?" Madonna cried. "Stop being this way. Be who you used to be! Play with me!"[5]

Her mother died a short time later. It was a devastating blow to the young girl, who never quite recovered from the loss. A few years later, her father remarried. As for Madonna, she would grow into a rebellious and impatient teenager, due mostly to an abrasive relationship with her stepmother, Joan. "I had moments of chaos and sometimes I suffered," Madonna recalls. "I mean, my mother died when I was little, and that was difficult for me for a while. . . . I didn't accept my stepmother when I was growing up. In that retrospect I think I was really hard on her."[6]

NO WALLFLOWER

Despite the friction at home, there was no questioning Madonna's talent, particularly as a dancer. After attending a Catholic elementary school, Madonna enrolled as a student at West Junior High School. She gave her first public performance in the seventh grade, singing and dancing in a school talent show. She performed a cover of "Baba O'Riley," a 1971 hit single by The Who. She recalls:

> I had my girlfriends paint my body with fluorescent hearts and flowers. I wore a pair of shorts and a midriff top, and I just went mad. I had a strobe light and black light. I'm sure everyone thought I was insane. It was my first time onstage. That was the beginning of my provocative performances, I guess. I just went

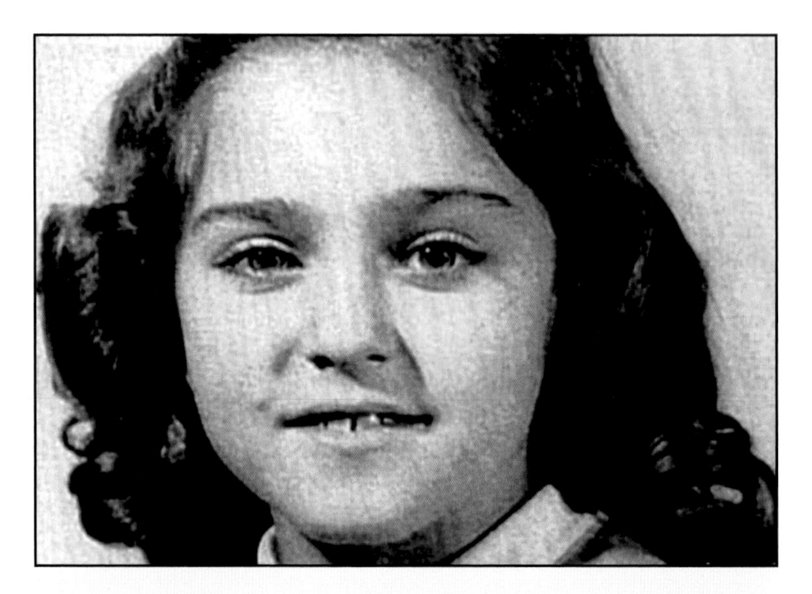

Madonna Louise Ciccone at age nine. Her mother's death when she was just five years old had a profound effect on her life.

> for it. No girls would talk to me after that, and the boys looked at me weird.[7]

At Adams High School, Madonna was a straight-A student and also excelled onstage, consistently winning the lead roles in school plays and musicals, including *My Fair Lady*, *Cinderella*, *The Wizard of Oz*, and *Godspell*. "When the spotlight came on her, she was pure magic," recalls Beverly Gibson, the drama teacher at Adams.

> People paid attention to her; you couldn't take your eyes off her. You often hear about people who become famous being wallflowers. You hear their friends and teachers say, "Oh, I would never have expected her to become famous." Not so with Madonna. There was no way she could ever be anything other than famous at something. I would

> watch her on stage with that vibrant personality and charisma, and think to myself, "Oh, my, it is inevitable, isn't it?"[8]

In the evenings, Madonna took dance lessons at Rochester School of Ballet. Flynn drove his students hard—so much so that after class, their feet were often bleeding. But Madonna was naturally competitive and thrived on the challenge; she soon emerged as Flynn's star pupil. Under Flynn's guidance, Madonna was able to hone her talent as a dancer: She became a disciplined performer able to follow direction but still capable of bringing her own style to her performances. "I feel superior," Madonna said after ballet class one day. "I feel [like] a warrior."[9]

Madonna graduated from Adams High School in 1976 and enrolled in the University of Michigan in Ann Arbor, about 30 miles (40 kilometers) west of Detroit. Flynn also taught at the university and, through his intercession, Madonna was awarded a scholarship to study dance.

Madonna excelled in her classes in Ann Arbor, particularly those taught by Flynn. She brought a lot of raw energy to her performances and pushed herself hard. It was during these early classes at Michigan that something of Madonna's style started emerging: She often showed up for class wearing a torn leotard held together by safety pins. "All these girls would come to class with black leotards and their hair up in buns with little flowers in it," Madonna recalls.

> So I cut my hair really short and I'd grease it so it would be sticking up, and I'd rip my tights so there were runs all over them. Anything to stand out from them and say, "I'm not like you. Okay? I'm taking dance classes and everything but I'm not stuck here like you."[10]

SUMMER IN NORTH CAROLINA

As exhausting as dance classes could be, Madonna aimed to make the most of her time at the university. After sweating through hours of classes all week, Madonna and her classmates would head for the Ann Arbor nightclubs on weekends, where they danced until the early hours of the morning. "She'd drag me out of bed," recalls Whitley Setrakian, who was Madonna's roommate at Michigan.

> I couldn't keep up with her. She was up in the morning and out the door, in class before everyone else, warming up. We'd go out dancing on Saturday nights, up all night dancing very late. She'd be up early warming up if she had a rehearsal on Sunday morning. She was not easy on herself. She lived hard and worked hard.[11]

At the end of Madonna's first year at Michigan, Flynn alerted his star pupil to an exciting opportunity. The world-famous choreographer Pearl Lang intended to recruit 20 promising young dance students for a summer-long project at Duke University in Durham, North Carolina. At the conclusion of the summer, Flynn said, some of the students might be offered full-time jobs as dancers in Lang's New York-based company, the American Dance Center. Madonna needed no further convincing; she soon made plans to head for Durham.

Although just 18 years old, Madonna made the decision to audition for Lang's class without asking her father or stepmother for permission. When Tony Ciccone heard his daughter intended to head for North Carolina on her own, he was infuriated. He made it clear that she would have to find a way to pay for the trip and live on her own in Durham with no help from him.

Flynn came to her rescue. He called friends at Duke University and asked them to lend her a dorm room for the summer. Next, he gave her some money for the bus ticket.

IN HER OWN WORDS

Madonna says she owes much of her success as a performer to Christopher Flynn, her first ballet teacher in Rochester, Michigan. Flynn, who died of AIDS in 1990, was first to recognize her talent and helped hone her ability as a dancer. She recalled in an interview:

> When I was in the tenth grade I knew a girl who was a serious ballet dancer. She looked really smarter than your average girl but in an interesting, offbeat way. So I attached myself to her and she brought me to a ballet class, and that's where I met Christopher Flynn, who saved me from my high school turmoil. . . .
>
> I really loved him. He was my first taste of what I thought was an artistic person. I remember once I had a towel wrapped around my head like a turban. He came over to me and he said, "You know, you're really beautiful." I said, "What?" Nobody had ever said that to me before. He said, "You have an ancient-looking face. A face like an ancient Roman statue." . . . The way he said it, it was an internal thing, much deeper than superficial beauty. He educated me, he took me to museums and told me about art. . . . He encouraged me to go to New York. He was the one who said I could do it if I wanted to.*

---

* Denise Worrell, "Now: Madonna on Madonna," *Time*, May 27, 1985, http://www.time.com/time/magazine/article/0,9171,957025-1,00.html.

The renowned modern ballet dancer Pearl Lang performing onstage. When an 18-year-old Madonna learned that she could take a dance course in North Carolina with Lang, she jumped at the chance, despite her father's reluctance.

Madonna soon boarded a bus and headed south. A short time later, Madonna auditioned before Lang, who selected her as one of the 20 students for the project.

Just as she had found ways to stand out in her classes in Michigan, Madonna found ways to stand out in Lang's classes. On one occasion, Lang recalled Madonna showing up for class dressed in a torn leotard held together by a very large safety pin. Lang scolded Madonna, telling her that the pin was dangerous—it could come undone and injure one of the male dancers as he lifted her. Lang sent the young student back to the dressing room to change. "That was Madonna," Lang said, shrugging. "She was always doing something to catch your eye, to get attention."[12]

Madonna spent six weeks at Duke University. When the summer project ended, the young dance student approached Lang. Lang recalled:

> She . . . asked me if I might need anyone in my New York company. I told her that there was a possibility, but I knew she had no money. I pointed out that first she had to go back to Michigan before she could take off again for New York. I asked her how she was going to manage to get there, find a place to live, and have enough money to eat. Her answer was typically Madonna, when she told me not to worry about it, that she would work it out.[13]

Lang counseled Madonna to finish her classes at Michigan, and a few days later Madonna returned home. That fall, she started her sophomore year at Michigan.

QUEST FOR STARDOM

After returning to Ann Arbor and beginning the fall semester, Madonna found herself far less interested in her classes. She was still an excellent student, but after studying with Lang over the summer, she realized the limitations of what the dance professors at Michigan could teach her. Flynn also realized that Madonna could probably learn little from additional dance classes in Ann Arbor. He told her the place she needed to be was New York. "There can be something thrilling about academic dance, but it has its limits," Flynn said. "Madonna was just so much bigger than that. I could see it even if she couldn't. There were just so many more things for her to explore and they were all in New York."[14]

Madonna thought over Flynn's advice for a long time. Dropping out of Michigan meant forfeiting her scholarship and passing up the opportunity to earn a college degree. Before making her decision, Madonna spoke with other college professors at Michigan, who urged her to remain in school. "We all gave her the usual 'New York City will still be waiting for you when you have more maturity and more to offer artistically,' but some are driven to leave despite adult recommendations," said one of her dance professors, Gay Delanghe. "Madonna had a [mentor] in Flynn and he

PEARL LANG

Madonna had good reason for defying her parents and spending the summer studying dance in North Carolina: The teacher, Pearl Lang, was regarded as one of the world's foremost dance instructors and choreographers.

A choreographer designs the movements and steps followed by the dancers during the performance. Writing in the *New York Times*, dance critic Anna Kisselgoff said, "There is no movement without [emotion] in Pearl Lang's choreography."*

Born in 1921 in Chicago, Illinois, Lang choreographed her first dance performance at the age of 10. For an elementary school geography assignment, Lang's class wrote a poem about the Nile River. The teacher, Sadie Kalman, set the poem to music and asked for a volunteer to choreograph a dance to accompany the poem. Lang quickly volunteered and even made the costumes—she had been taught to sew by her father, a furrier, who needed her help to sew the linings of the fur coats he repaired. Lang credits Kalman with igniting her passion for dance. "We were taught that whatever you do, you do to the best of your ability," Lang said. "You don't settle for the surface of the idea. You dig deeper to see what more you can get out of it. For three years we looked at a motto on the wall in Miss Kalman's room: 'Build thee more stately mansions.' That, hopefully, had to become a part of what I have been doing."**

told her to follow her heart. . . . She was young, naïve and without good advice, [that] would be my view of it."[15]

Midway through her sophomore year at Michigan, Madonna stopped going out to the Ann Arbor clubs on nights and weekends. Instead, she found a job at a campus ice cream shop, where she worked every evening after

Lang soon moved on to classical dance. At the age of 16, she choreographed an entire ballet to the classical piece, *A Little Serenade*, by the eighteenth-century Austrian composer Wolfgang Amadeus Mozart. When Lang turned 20, she was accepted into a dance company headed by Martha Graham, the New York-based pioneer of modern dance. Lang soon emerged as one of the stars of Graham's productions, taking lead roles in many performances. Meanwhile, on the Broadway stage, she danced in such musicals as *Carousel, One Touch of Venus, Finian's Rainbow*, and *Allegro*.

In 1952, Lang left Graham's company to form her own dance company, the Pearl Lang Dance Theater, and to also work as a guest choreographer for the Dutch National Ballet, the Boston Ballet, and the Batsheva Dance Company of Israel. Later, she co-founded the American Dance Center with modern-dance pioneer Alvin Ailey. Among her students were Eliot Field and Bruce Marks, both of whom would go on to careers as successful dancers and choreographers. Lang died at the age of 87 in 2009.

---

* Jack Anderson, "Pearl Lang, Dancer and Choreographer, Dies At 87," *New York Times*, February 27, 2009, p. A21.
** Jennifer Dunning, "Still Paying Heed to Graham's Cry," *New York Times*, September 16, 2001, p. B18.

classes. She also took a weekend job as a waitress at an Ann Arbor tavern. She saved all the money she earned from these part-time jobs, knowing that in a few months she was likely to be on her own in a big city far away from home.

At the end of her sophomore year at Michigan, Madonna announced to her stunned parents that she planned to drop out of college and move to New York to pursue a career as a professional dancer. In July 1978, still only 19 years old, she bought a one-way airline ticket to New York City.

Flynn drove her to the airport in Detroit, where the teacher and pupil had a tearful farewell. After arriving in New York, Madonna instructed the taxi driver to drop her off in the center of town. A few minutes later, she stepped out of the cab and onto the sidewalk in Times Square. With all her possessions packed in a single suitcase and her waitressing money in her pocket, Madonna had no idea where she would sleep that night, but she had arrived in New York, ready to begin her quest for stardom.

Living on Popcorn and Yogurt

Lionel Bishop knew all about living the life of a young dancer in New York. Although New York is the home of the Broadway stage, many off-Broadway theaters, and numerous ballet and modern-dance companies, most young dancers constantly struggle to find work in the city. In order to support themselves, many have to take jobs in other industries while also finding time to audition and attend dance classes.

As a professional dancer, Bishop had lived that life for a number of years. On one summer day in 1978, Bishop found himself out of work. He had injured a leg while dancing and was hobbling through Times Square with the help of a cane. Suddenly, a young woman carrying a suitcase approached him. "She . . . asked if I knew where she could rent a cheap room and then plowed right ahead asking me a million questions about New York," Bishop recalls. "There was something about her. She was adorable."[1]

Madonna was fortunate to have encountered Bishop. Although a naïve young woman on her own among strangers could very easily have fallen prey to all manner of con artists, muggers, or others with even darker intentions, Bishop turned out to be a true friend who was empathetic toward her plight. He said:

> She piqued my curiosity, and I found myself asking her what she was doing in New York, where she came from, you know, all the questions that I usually could care less about knowing. Don't ask me why, but when she told me she had just arrived and wanted to be a dancer, I invited her to stay with me.[2]

Madonna lived in Bishop's apartment for two weeks, soon finding a job in a doughnut shop and a room of her own. Before leaving, Madonna promised to stay in touch with Bishop, but she never did look him up again. According to Bishop, the next time he saw her was on a television screen seven years later as she performed the song "Material Girl" in a music video.

POSING FOR ART STUDENTS

After arriving in New York, Madonna was simply another out-of-work dancer. Back in Ann Arbor she was one of the most talented dancers on campus, but here, in New York, Madonna found it very difficult to stand out from the crowd.

Over the next few months, Madonna worked in a variety of low-paying jobs while auditioning for dance companies and stage productions. Often without money, she lived on a diet of popcorn, yogurt, and doughnuts. She also had

Madonna laughs while leaning toward a mirror to apply lipstick in this 1979 photo. When she arrived in New York City, she knew no one and struggled to make it as a dancer. Within four years, she had recorded her first album, the self-titled *Madonna*.

a string of boyfriends, many of whom quickly learned that Madonna's interest in them seemed to have more to do with where they would take her to dinner than in developing a relationship.

Madonna found that she could earn extra money posing nude for art and photography students—in fact, she discovered that she could earn more money in an hour sitting motionless and unclothed than she could earn all day working as a waitress. The teachers who hired her were amazed that she seemed to have no inhibitions whatsoever and would often carry on ordinary conversations with the students while posing naked. "I basically spaced out, and thought about a million things other than I was stark naked while a bunch of people sketched me,"[3] she said.

Meanwhile, Madonna found few opportunities to earn paychecks as a dancer. Soon after arriving in New York, Madonna auditioned for Pearl Lang, who gave her a job in her dance company. It was hardly full-time work and the paychecks were not regular or substantial. Madonna danced in a half-dozen performances for Lang's company, the American Dance Center. Most were modern dance productions set to jazz music. Lang was very satisfied with Madonna's work but could not help but notice that the young dancer had grown rail-thin. Lang wondered how often Madonna was eating. Lang called a friend at the Russian Tea Room, an upscale New York restaurant, who agreed to hire Madonna to work at the coat-check counter. While working at the Russian Tea Room, Madonna was able to get a free meal every day in the restaurant kitchen. "I'm sorry to say, but I'm pretty sure that was the one decent meal she was getting,"[4] said Lang.

HEADING FOR PARIS

Whenever Madonna auditioned for dance roles in stage productions, most producers asked her to sing a few bars.

She had no formal training as a singer, but, clearly, she did have talent. "Most of the people auditioning were much more professional than I was—they brought sheet music and they'd give it to the piano player, and I would just wing it and sing songs I knew from the radio,"[5] she says.

In late 1978, Madonna auditioned for a job as a dancer for producers who were organizing an international tour for Patrick Hernandez, a French recording star. Hernandez had recorded the disco tune "Born to Be Alive," which hit the top of the charts. Hernandez's producers wanted to hire 20 dancers for the show. Over the course of four busy days, the producers auditioned more than 1,500 dancers with plans to whittle down the competition to 50 finalists, who would be asked to perform one final time. Of those finalists, they planned to hire the best 20 performers.

Most of the dancers auditioned in front of Hernandez, as well as a producer, Muriel Van Lieu, and a choreographer. Van Lieu remembers the moment Madonna took the stage:

> When my choreographer asked her to show us how she moved, I must admit, I was knocked out. She was fantastic, and to this day, I'm convinced that with all her videos and stage shows, she holds back, because I never saw anyone with a better dance technique. In fact, my choreographer was bothered. He came running down from the stage and whispered in my ear, "Listen, Muriel, excuse me, but I don't think I have to bother giving her a combination to follow because she is absolutely elastic, like rubber, and she has already shown us that she can do 10 times better than I would ask her at this audition."[6]

Van Lieu wanted to hear the young dancer sing, but, at first, Madonna refused. Madonna told Van Lieu that she did not have a trained voice and she was certain there were others auditioning who could out-sing her. Madonna said she did not want to lose her chance at a dancing job because her voice was weak. Van Lieu insisted, though, finally convincing Madonna to sing a few bars of "Happy Birthday." Satisfied that Madonna could carry a tune, Van Lieu agreed to make Madonna a finalist.

The next day, Muriel's husband, Jean, sat in on the auditions. As head producer for the show, Jean Van Lieu would be making the final decisions on which dancers to hire. When he saw Madonna perform, he was bowled over by her talent but decided she would not be right for the Hernandez tour. Instead, he had bigger plans—he wanted to bring her to Paris, France, and make her a star. "We told her," Muriel Van Lieu recalls, "that we were convinced that she could be a star in her own right."[7] In the spring of 1979, Madonna left New York for Paris.

MAKING A DEMO TAPE

The French producers provided Madonna with money to spend and a luxurious apartment in Paris—a lifestyle that was quite different for the girl from Michigan who had been forced to live for months on popcorn and yogurt. They even provided her with a tutor to give her French lessons. They talked to Madonna about their plans to book her at top European nightclubs. They also talked about a record deal.

After a few weeks, though, it became clear to Madonna that these plans were stalled; the French producers failed to send her out to a single nightclub audition and no record deal materialized. In fact, the only positive experience Madonna could find in the whole episode was her discovery of the Paris flea markets. She spent hours picking through the tables, buying cheap jewelry, colorful tops and skirts, assorted bangles, and other accessories that would soon define her style. Finally, after three months, she gave up on her French adventure and returned to New York.

Arriving back in the United States, Madonna found things no easier than when she had left. Convinced she would never make it as a dancer, Madonna changed her focus and joined a rock band as a singer. The band, known as Breakfast Club, was headed by an old boyfriend, Dan

IN HER OWN WORDS

Madonna wrote her first song, "Tell the Truth," in 1979, while singing for a rock band named Breakfast Club, which was led by her then boyfriend, Dan Gilroy. In an interview, she recalled:

> It was maybe four chords, but there were verses and a bridge and a chorus, and it was a religious experience. I had decided that if I was going to be a singer, I had to earn it. I had to learn how to play an instrument. We were living in an abandoned synagogue in Queens, and in return for music lessons I modeled for Dan, who was a painter. I was his muse, and he taught me how to play power chords.
>
> While they were off at their day jobs, I'd play drums. I learned by listening to Elvis Costello records. Then, one day, I wrote a song, and the words just came out of me. I was like, "Who's writing this?" When their drummer quit, I got to be the drummer, and one night . . . I begged them to let me sing a song and play guitar. That microphone position was looking more and more inviting.*

* Austin Scaggs, "Madonna Looks Back," *Rolling Stone*, October 29, 2009, pp. 48–50.

Gilroy, and his brother Ed. The Gilroys lived in a former synagogue in Queens, New York, which they had converted into a music studio. Madonna moved in with the Gilroys and soon started accompanying them on their gigs. Dan Gilroy taught her to play the guitar and drums. She also started writing her own songs.

Over the next two years, the band would undergo many personnel and name changes, but it was nevertheless getting a lot of gigs in New York's club scene. After a quarrel with Dan Gilroy, though, Madonna left the band and formed her own group with an old boyfriend from Michigan, Steve Bray. By now, Madonna had made it clear to Bray and the other band members that she was in charge and that the band's name would be "Madonna." Bray felt that Madonna was being self-centered. He asked her: "Is everything about you?"[8]

It was during this time that Madonna made a demo tape of some of the bouncy dance songs she had performed in the clubs. She took the demo around the city, bugging disc jockeys at dance clubs to play the her music. Most brushed her off—unknown singers and musicians were constantly handing them demo tapes, many of which were amateurish. At a club named Danceteria, though, Madonna convinced DJ Mark Kamins to listen to the tape. Kamins liked what he heard and agreed to play it during his set. "It's not like I had to take it home to listen to it first," Kamins said. "I love spontaneity. I believe it's the magic of life. Madonna had a cassette. I threw it on, and it worked."[9]

FIRST RECORDING CONTRACT

The reaction to Madonna's song by the dancers on the floor convinced Kamins that record company executives should hear the tape. Kamins sent the tape to Seymour Stein, an executive with Sire Records, a Warner Brothers label. Stein, who trusted Kamins's taste in music, listened to the tape while recuperating from surgery in a hospital. Stein was so impressed that he immediately offered Madonna a recording contract. The contract was modest, just $15,000 for two singles, and did not offer her a chance to record an album. Still, to a young woman living on popcorn and yogurt, $15,000 was an enormous amount of money. Madonna, absolutely ecstatic, did not even wait for Stein to leave the hospital to sign the deal: She showed up at his hospital room to put her name on the contract. "I think if I was lying in a coffin but had my hand out ready to sign, that would've suited her," Stein said later. "She was very anxious to get her career going. She believed in herself that much."[10]

In October 1982, Madonna's first single, the pulsating dance song "Everybody," received nationwide release. Madonna wrote the song with Bray; Kamins oversaw the studio recording session. The lyrics tell a simple story, inviting everybody to get up and dance. Reactions by music critics were mixed. "The rhythm of this track is especially stiff and the extended length merely emphasizes it," huffed music critic Rikky Rooksby. "At the very end, the drums are pulled out, leaving Madonna repeating the 'get up and do your thing' phrase."[11] But *Rolling Stone* critic Don Shewey found himself hooked on the song's electric beat as well as the quirky vocals by the singer. "Madonna . . . has a voice that takes some getting used to," Shewey wrote.

> At first, it doesn't sound like much at all. Then you notice its one distinguishing feature, a girlish hiccup that the singer uses over and over until it's irritating as hell. Finally, you get hooked, and you start looking forward to that silly little catch in her voice. It

> helps that she writes good tunes—catchy and bare to the bone.[12]

The critics may have been unsure of what to make of this new singer, but music fans soon embraced her. "Everybody" quickly shot to the top of the dance charts, peaking in third place on *Billboard*'s Hot 100 list. Following this positive reaction, Sire Records made plans for Madonna to record an album. Recalling those hectic, wild and exciting days in the New York dance scene and the emergence of a new star, Kamins said, "Music is like a horse race. Madonna had timing on her side, fashion on her side, and her get-up-and-go. She was on a mission. She never stopped."[13]

The Madonna Look

Madonna recalls the first time she realized she had made it as a recording star. It was 1982, and her single "Everybody" had just been released. "At about 7 o'clock at night I had the radio on in my bedroom, on [a New York radio station] WKTU, and I heard 'Everybody.' I said, 'Oh, my God, that's me coming out of that box.' It was an amazing feeling."[1]

"Everybody" wasn't just playing on WKTU—the song was playing on radio stations all over the country. Its success convinced Madonna's record company that it had a new star under contract. The label quickly made plans for Madonna to record an album. The disc, *Madonna*, was released in the summer of 1983. The album featured several fast-paced tracks, all intended to get its listeners on their feet and dancing. In addition, to "Everybody," the other hit singles included "Borderline," "Lucky Star," and "Holiday." *Madonna* was certified gold within a year of its release, meaning it sold more than 500,000 copies. Eventually, the album sold a million copies and was certified platinum—and then triple platinum.

To promote the album, Madonna appeared on *American Bandstand*. In the pre-MTV era, *American Bandstand*, hosted by Dick Clark, was the premier television venue for recording artists to introduce new material. Fans who tuned in that day saw a performance by a vibrant young woman: her ears, neck, arms and waist dripping with oversized costume jewelry; her navel exposed, hair tangled, clothes layered haphazardly, feet shod in clunky shoes. It appeared as though her outfits were assembled at thrift shops, which, of course, they were. "I get a lot of stuff in thrift shops," Madonna admitted at the time to a reporter.

> I have always sort of elaborated with my dance clothes. I used to live in my dance clothes, my tights and leotards, but I always personalized them. I'd rip them all up and make sure the runs got really big and had a pattern to them. I started wearing bows in my hair because one day when my hair was long, I couldn't find anything to tie it back. So I took an old pair of tights and wound them around my head, and I liked the way that looked.[2]

The cover photo for *Madonna* featured a close-up of the singer, dressed very much in the "punk-chic" style that would become the "Madonna look," copied by millions of teenage girls. The title for the album was also significant—the artist intended to be known only by her first name. For Madonna and her fans, for the remainder of her career, one name would say it all.

Madonna's early style, seen here, influenced fashion in the early to mid-1980s and inspired millions of teenager girls to imitate her. Throughout her career, she would change styles countless times.

THE MATERIAL GIRL

Although it is likely that Madonna's talent would eventually have been discovered, there is no question she hit the recording industry at just the right time. The pop music scene of the 1980s was in need of a new female superstar. There were some major male stars at the time, notably Prince and Michael Jackson, but the top female stars of the day—Cyndi Lauper, Deborah Harry, Olivia Newton-John, and the Pointer Sisters, among others—were not quite megastars. Clearly, the record industry was waiting for the next big trendsetter to arrive on the scene. That trendsetter would be Madonna. And if anybody doubted her potential, they need only check the sales for her second album, *Like a Virgin*.

As with *Madonna*, the singer's second album includes a selection of fast-paced dance tunes. *Like a Virgin* hit first place on the *Billboard* charts in December 1984. Its title track included some edgy lyrics about premarital sex that conservative groups denounced as unfit for teenage audiences. Their furor was further fueled by the image that appeared on the album cover: Madonna posing seductively, propped up on silk cushions, and dressed in a lacy corset.

Madonna helped stir the controversy when she performed the title song on the MTV Music Awards. Wearing a sheer costume with a slight resemblance to a wedding gown, as well as a belt buckle that spelled out the words "Boy Toy," Madonna brought the song to an end by writhing in ecstasy on the stage and exposing her underwear. Sitting at home that night, singer Melissa Etheridge watched the performance. She recalls, "I remember thinking, 'What is she doing? She's wearing a wedding dress. Oh, my God, she's rolling around on the floor! Oh, my God!' It was the most brave, blatant sexual thing I've ever seen on television."[3]

Although many parents, conservative leaders, and other critics focused on "Like a Virgin," there was another song on the album that had a lot to say about the materialistic mood of the country in the 1980s: "Material Girl." In the song, Madonna makes it clear that the boy for her is the boy who can provide her with expensive gifts. For the video, Madonna shed the punk-chic look and instead offered a

IN HER OWN WORDS

For the cover photo for *Like a Virgin*, Madonna shed her punk-chic style for a much sexier look. It would be the first of many style changes for Madonna. She credits photographer Steven Meisel, who shot the cover photo for the album, for helping her reinvent her image. On why she changed her style, Madonna recalled:

> I guess the music I started to write had a more seductive quality, and I unconsciously morphed into that. It also had to do with the fact that I was doing more photo shoots. I was being styled and dressed. Before that, I was doing everything myself. I had no makeup artist, I was taking dance tights and tying them around my head and throwing a few rosaries around my neck.
>
> After that, it was Steven Meisel and fashion people putting me in corsets. I think people put a lot of emphasis on the whole reinvention of my image, and it's always been a lot less calculated than people think. It's just evolution and what I'm interested in, the books I read or the clothes that I see. . . . I think it's boring to stay the same. A girl likes to change her look.*

---

* Austin Scaggs, "Madonna Looks Back," *Rolling Stone*, October 29, 2009. pp. 50–51.

tribute to legendary movie star Marilyn Monroe. Hair dyed blond, dressed in an expensive evening gown, Madonna was swept off her feet by adoring male dancers who showered her with jewels.

With *Like A Virgin*, Madonna had turned herself into something more than a pop singer—she was now a sex symbol. Teenage girls dressed like her, while teenage boys tacked pictures of her to their bedroom walls. Madonna said:

> My image to people, I think, is that I'm this brazen, aggressive young woman who has an OK voice with some pretty exciting songs, who wears what she wants to wear and says what she wants to say. . . . Sex symbol? . . . I guess I would be perceived as that because I have a typically voluptuous body and because the way I dress accents my femininity, and because a lot of what I am about is just expressing sexual desire and not really caring what people think about it. Maybe that would make you a sex symbol.[4]

Meanwhile, her albums were in high demand: At one point in 1985, American record stores were selling some 80,000 copies a day. To promote *Like a Virgin*, Warner Bros. arranged a national tour. The first show, scheduled for Radio City Music Hall in New York, sold out in 24 minutes.

Critics were not yet sold on Madonna. They found *Like a Virgin* full of light and puffy tunes. Writing in *Rolling Stone*, Debby Miller said, "On the hit title song, Madonna is all squeals. . . . She doesn't have the power or range of, say, Cyndi Lauper, but she knows what works on the dance floor."[5] Madonna found such reviews frustrating. "In the beginning, I was called everything from a Disco Dolly to

Madonna, as seen here in her "Material Girl" video from 1985, was inspired by Marilyn Monroe, the film actress of the 1950s and 1960s who remains an enduring cultural icon.

a One-Hit Wonder," Madonna fumed. "Everyone agreed that I was sexy, but no one would agree that I had any talent, which really irritated me."[6]

BIRTH OF A MOVIE STAR

Nevertheless, things were moving quickly now for Madonna. In 1985, she made the cover of *Time* under the headline: "Madonna: Why She's Hot." Inside, the magazine admonished its readers:

> Now then, parents, the important thing is to stay calm. You've seen Madonna wiggling on MTV—right, she's the pop-tart singer with the trashy outfits and the hi-there belly button. What is worse, your children have seen her. You tell your daughters to put on jeans and sweatshirts, like decent girls, and they look at you as if you've just blown in from the Planet of the Creeps. Twelve-year-old girls, headphones blocking out the voices of reason, are running around wearing T-shirts labeled VIRGIN, which would not have been necessary 30 years ago. The shirts offer no guarantees, moreover; they merely advertise Madonna's first, or virgin, rock tour, now thundering across the continent, and her bouncy, love-it-when-you-do-it song "Like a Virgin."[7]

The magazine interviewed a number of young female fans who felt empowered by Madonna's style and attitude. Her female fans said they wanted to be able to dress outrageously and tease their boyfriends. "I like the way she handles herself, sort of take it or leave it," 17-year-old Kim Thomson told the magazine. "She's sexy but she doesn't need men, really. She's kind of there by herself."[8] Teresa Hajdik, also 17, added, "She gives us ideas. It's really women's lib, not being afraid of what guys think."[9]

Until now, Madonna's style was being transmitted mostly through her music, but movie audiences would soon get to see what she was all about. A year before, when Madonna was still a star on the rise, director Susan Seidelman signed her to play a supporting role in the film *Desperately Seeking Susan*. Madonna was cast as Susan and asked to do little more than play herself—a free spirit surviving by her wits on the tough streets of New York.

For the role of Susan, Seidelman had auditioned a number of up-and-coming young actresses, including Ellen Barkin, Melanie Griffith, Kelly McGillis, and Jennifer Jason Leigh—all of whom would go on to major film careers—but was not satisfied with their performances. So she looked into the New York music scene and soon heard the name "Madonna" over and over again. In fact, at the time Madonna was living just around the corner from the director's apartment. For her first audition, Madonna showed up riding her bicycle. Seidelman recalls, "Although she wasn't an experienced actress, there was something about her attitude. She was so self-confident and right for the character. I thought, 'If we can bring this quality to the part that will be amazing.'"[10]

The film tells the story of a bored housewife, Roberta, played by Rosanna Arquette, who assumes Susan's identity after bumping her head and temporarily losing her memory. In Susan, movie fans saw the Madonna they had gotten to know from her album covers, TV appearances, and live performances: dressed in thrift shop clothes, her hair unkempt, her mouth working over a wad of bubble gum, her attitude brazen but charming. Seidelman said, "She really insisted on keeping her own style and we agreed."[11]

The film was released just as *Like a Virgin* was climbing the charts, and—mostly because of Madonna's popularity—turned out to be one of the unexpected hits of the year, particularly since the soundtrack included a song she recorded for the film, the bouncy dance tune "Into the Groove." Madonna received strong reviews from film critics for the raw energy she brought to the screen. *Chicago Sun-Times* film critic Roger Ebert wrote:

> What I liked in *Desperately Seeking Susan* was the cheerful way it bopped around New York, introducing us to unforgettable characters, played by good actors . . . it has its moments, and many of them involve the different kinds of special appeal that Arquette and Madonna are able to generate.[12]

MADONNA AND THE ABORTION DEBATE

In the song "Papa Don't Preach," Madonna sings about the plight of a teenage girl who discovers she is pregnant. In the song, the girl makes it clear to her father that she intends to have the baby.

The song caused a stir in the abortion debate, which has simmered since 1973, when the U.S. Supreme Court held in *Roe v. Wade* that a woman may abort her pregnancy for any reason, up until the fetus becomes viable. Groups opposing abortion rights said the song sends a strong message to teenage girls, proving they have alternatives to terminating their pregnancies. "Abortion is available on every street corner for young women," said Susan Carpenter-McMillan, president of the California chapter of Feminists for Life in America. "Now what Madonna is telling them is, hey, there's an alternative."*

Abortion-rights groups complained that the song does not address the complicated issues of teenage pregnancy; Madonna fails to examine how a young girl could expect to care for the baby or the likelihood that the girl and her child would be forced into poverty and living on public assistance. Said Alfred Moran, executive director of the New York chapter of Planned Parenthood, "The message is that getting pregnant is cool and having the baby is the right thing and a good thing and don't listen to your parents, the school, anybody who tells you otherwise—don't preach to me, Papa. The reality is that what

ANOTHER HIT ALBUM

With two hit albums in release and a movie earning good receipts at the box office, Madonna's label was anxious to get her back into the studio to record a third disc. That album, released in 1986, was titled *True Blue*. Critics believe *True Blue* is the album in which Madonna truly shows her

Madonna is suggesting to teenagers is a path to permanent poverty."** *Boston Globe* columnist Ellen Goodman added:

> Adolescents are fed the pop image of a love that is zipless and parenthood that comes without bills or diapers. But even Madonna, 27, and a lady in control of her life, knows better. . . . Does this sound like a sermon? The song says, "Papa, don't preach." Let's make a deal instead. Papa and Mama will call off the preaching, if pop stars call off the propaganda.***

For her part, Madonna was shocked at the uproar. She released a vague statement urging her fans to not draw the wrong conclusions about the meaning of the song and admonishing everyone to remember that the song's story was foremost. Otherwise, she refused to comment, leaving both sides wondering about which side she favored in the abortion debate. Said her publicist, Liz Rosenberg, "She's singing a song, not taking a stand. Her philosophy is people can think what they want to think."****

---

* Georgia Duella, "Madonna's New Beat is a Hit, But Song's Message Rankles," *New York Times*, September 18, 1986, p. B1.
** Ibid.
*** Ellen Goodman, "The Pied Piper of Pregnancy," *Boston Globe*, September 23, 1986, p. 19.
**** Duella, "Madonna's New Beat is a Hit, But Song's Message Rankles," p. B1.

talent as a singer. One of the tracks on the album, "Open Your Heart," was co-written by veteran songwriter Gardner Cole. The song's lyrics tell a simple story of a woman questioning why her boyfriend won't respond to her love. The music, though, was hardly simple. "It's a powerful song with a high range for her," Cole says. "She wasn't used to belting stuff out, and this opened up a whole new range for her. It's one of the first songs where she used a hard voice—most of the others were pretty light, but with 'Open Your Heart' she had to dig in. It's not easy to sing, it took her a long time to get it right."[13] Meanwhile, the song also helped solidify Madonna's reputation as a sexy performer guaranteed to shock parents. The video for "Open Your Heart" featured Madonna dancing in a skimpy outfit in a seedy nightclub; at the end of the song, she dances off with a young boy she befriends.

"Open Your Heart" shot to first place on the *Billboard* Hot 100 chart, but other songs from the album also scored well. Another track from the album that hit the top of the *Billboard* chart was "Papa Don't Preach," which relates the story of a teenage girl who tells her father about her pregnancy.

The album may have featured the vocal gymnastics of "Open Your Heart" and the heavy message in "Papa Don't Preach," but those tracks also made Madonna's fans still want to get up and dance. For the fans who were looking for a more mellow-sounding album, *True Blue* had something for them as well: Both the 1950s-style title track and the Latin-themed "La Isla Bonita" presented listeners with a variety of influences. As the executives at Warner Bros. expected, *True Blue* turned out to be a huge hit: The album was certified seven times platinum in the United States and went on to worldwide sales of some 24 million copies. Madonna was now a bonafide superstar.

Stormy Relationships

While Madonna was living on yogurt and popcorn and singing in crowded and smoky New York City nightclubs, another future star was having a much easier time of it. Sean Penn arrived in New York at roughly the same time as Madonna. The son of Leo Penn, a Hollywood TV director, Sean had been acting since childhood, featured mostly in supporting roles in numerous TV series.

At the age of 20, Penn arrived in New York, determined to hone his acting skills on the Broadway and off-Broadway stages. Because of his father's connections and his modest success as a TV actor, Penn found many doors open to him. Directors quickly recognized his natural talent and cast him in a number of productions. Soon, he was commuting back and forth between New York and California, where he

A 1986 photo of Madonna with her husband, the actor Sean Penn, who later became a two-time Academy Award winner for his roles in *Mystic River* (2003) and *Milk* (2008). Details of their tumultuous relationship filled tabloid pages throughout their brief marriage.

found himself in demand as a screen actor. In 1982, Penn won rave reviews for playing the goofy surfer Jeff Spicoli in the hit movie comedy *Fast Times at Ridgemont High*. Now regarded as a major star, Penn had his pick of roles.

Madonna met Penn on the set while filming the video for "Material Girl." The young actor had been invited to the studio by a friend to watch the video's production. She recalled:

> I was standing at the top of these steps, waiting while people were doing some lighting, and I looked

> down and noticed this guy in a leather jacket and sunglasses, sort of standing in the corner, looking at me. I came down the steps and walked right by and said, "Hi," but very cold, before I realized it was Sean Penn. Hours went by, and it had gotten dark, and I saw him poke his head around the corner again. I was like, "Are you still here?"[1]

Penn and Madonna chatted for a few minutes. Feeling sorry that she had earlier treated him coldly, Madonna hurried back to her dressing room, where she retrieved a rose, then gave it to Penn as a gift.

Their romance would become a hot item in the tabloids, as Penn and Madonna found themselves stalked by photographers and film crews. Penn reacted angrily to the attention; he often lashed out at the photographers, particularly after drinking. Despite these incidents, Madonna and Penn married in August 1985 during a lavish ceremony at a friend's Malibu mansion as news helicopters buzzed overhead. It would be the start of a brief and stormy relationship. The media labeled them the "Poison Penns."

UNEXPECTED PUBLICITY

Just before the wedding, Madonna found herself with some unexpected publicity: Some nude photographs taken during her struggling days in New York had found their way into the hands of the publishers of *Playboy* and *Penthouse* magazines, which soon published them.

Publication of the photographs became a big national story. Each magazine was reported to have paid fees as high as $100,000 to the photographers for the rights to print the pictures. Both magazines reported huge sales of the "Madonna nude" issues as members of the curious public scrambled to catch a glimpse of one of music's biggest stars in the revealing photos. It seemed the only person involved in the whole affair who was not making out financially was Madonna, who, years before, had signed away the rights to the pictures for the $25 modeling fees she had been paid.

Actually, Madonna was bemused by the attention given to the photos—after all, she had never denied working as a nude model and believed their publication only enhanced her reputation as an uninhibited performer. That summer, as the magazines hit the newsstands, Madonna performed during the Live Aid concert, a huge charity event staged at a stadium in Philadelphia to raise money for famine relief efforts in Africa. When she took the stage, the crowd of 90,000 erupted in wild applause. Madonna's manager, Freddy DeMann, was asked if he thought the publication of the pictures would ultimately hurt the star's career. DeMann laughed. "Don't you get it?" he replied. "What would it cost to get that kind of publicity? You can't buy that kind of promotion."[2]

BOX OFFICE BOMB

Madonna may have enjoyed the attention of the national press, but Penn was far less accommodating. Following their wedding, Madonna and Penn found themselves harassed by the tabloids while trying to forge their very active careers. Indeed, his attitude toward the tabloids became evident on their wedding day. Wealthy friends of Penn's parents made their California beachfront mansion available to the couple for the wedding party. During the party, as the news helicopters hovered overhead, Penn traipsed onto the beach and wrote an obscenity in the sand. He also talked about finding a gun and taking a few shots at the copters.

Meanwhile, Penn starred in *At Close Range*, a gritty crime drama, then made what would be an embarrassing career move by starring with his wife in the comedy-adventure *Shanghai Surprise*, a box office bomb derided by critics.

Set in 1930s, the film tells the story of two people caught up in a drug smuggling caper in China. For Penn, the thin plot and lighthearted action hardly tested his talents as a serious actor. For Madonna, it would be her first role after *Desperately Seeking Susan*, a film in which she had been asked to play a character much like herself. This film, however, required her to assume the role of Gloria Tatlock, a prim missionary shocked by the grim world of 1930s China. Of course, Madonna was hardly what anyone would regard as prim, and the role proved to be too demanding for her acting talents. Michael Janusonis, film critic for the *Providence Journal*, wrote:

> Putting her in high-buttoned black suits, sending her out among the Chinese masses and hoping that she could convince us that the spirit of the Lord hangs heavy on her breast must have been someone's idea of wishful thinking. She may sing like a bird, but her acting amounts to memorizing dialogue and then parroting it back to the camera with the forceful urgency of someone who has no conviction about what she's saying. Hence her Miss Tatlock never comes alive and there is precious little screen chemistry between her and Penn, her husband in real life.[3]

Even though *Shanghai Surprise* had been filmed in the Chinese city of Macau, there was no escaping the tabloid press. Much to Penn's anger, reporters and photographers seemed to follow the couple everywhere. It also became clear to Madonna that her husband had a serious drinking problem. Indeed, he once told a magazine interviewer, "I prefer the bar to the gym any day. I like to drink and I like to brawl."[4]

PERMANENT SPLIT

Madonna would be in for even more skewering by the movie critics when she starred in the screwball romantic comedy *Who's That Girl.* The film tells the story of a young woman, played by Madonna, who is framed on a murder charge and aims to prove her innocence. Again, the film suffered from a thin plot and Madonna's inability to give life to her role. "Madonna moves through most scenes with a jerky false walk that might have passed in a music video but here seems bizarre," huffed New York *Newsday* film critic Drew Fetherston. "[S]he has made a film that may disappoint even her most uncritical admirers."[5] There was some salvation, though, because the soundtrack album sold well, thanks mostly to Madonna, who contributed four singles.

In the summer of 1987, she launched the *Who's That Girl* Tour, which gave her an opportunity to get away from her husband for a time. His drinking had grown worse, and so had his tirades against the ever-present tabloid photographers. Soon, others were feeling his wrath. Friends could not help but notice that Madonna and Penn seemed to argue constantly. While visiting a Los Angeles nightclub, the couple encountered a friend, songwriter David Wolinski, who greeted Madonna with a kiss on the cheek. Suddenly, Penn kicked and beat him. Penn was arrested, charged with assault, and placed on probation by the court.

In fact, she went on the *Who's That Girl* Tour while Penn was in jail—he had been drinking heavily and, when confronted by the ever-present paparazzi, slugged a photographer. He was arrested on an assault charge and this time sentenced to 60 days in jail. After the tour ended, she rejoined Penn to find him still drinking, in addition to being angry and abusive. In December 1987, Madonna filed for divorce. After reconciling, Madonna and Penn spent

After her successful turn starring in *Desperately Seeking Susan* (1985), Madonna sought other film roles. Here she is seen in a car in a sequence for the film comedy *Who's That Girl* (1987), a box-office and critical disappointment.

another year together, but in late 1988, the police were called to the couple's home in California.

According to the police report, Madonna was "in a state of complete hysteria. Her clothes were torn. Her face was cut and bleeding, and she had bruise marks on her neck, arms, back, and legs."[6] Madonna filed a domestic violence report against Penn, who would have been prosecuted for the assault, but Madonna ultimately decided to drop the charges. Instead, she filed for divorce, and this time the split was permanent.

As for Penn, he would eventually straighten out his life. He gave up drinking, became much more selective in his film roles, and would go on to win two Academy Awards as Best Actor for his roles in *Mystic River*, a dark drama, and *Milk*, a biography of Harvey Milk, the first openly gay man to hold a major political office in the United States.

BEING BREATHLESS

With a bad marriage and a string of bad movies now behind her, Madonna got back to doing what she does best: making

TRUTH OR DARE—ANOTHER SIDE TO MADONNA

Fans who thought Madonna was little more than a party girl intent on shocking her audiences saw another side to the singer in the documentary *Truth or Dare*. The film, released in 1991, followed Madonna as she toured North America, Europe, and Japan in 1990 on her *Blond Ambition* Tour. The documentary takes its name from the game Truth or Dare, which Madonna plays late in the film with her dancers, as they reveal secrets about themselves.

Directed by rock video veteran Alek Keshishian, the documentary shows Madonna dancing suggestively and using an abundance of profanity, but fans also saw the singer acting as a mother hen around her dancers, soothing them in their times of distress and helping smooth over disputes among the cast members. She also recites poetry, leads the dancers in a prayer circle before each performance, and is filmed in a tearful visit to the cemetery near Detroit, Michigan, where her mother is buried. Madonna admits on camera that going home is not easy for her. Her boyfriend at the time, actor and director Warren Beatty, shows up from time to time during the film, although he is clearly uncomfortable with a movie crew peeking in on his relationship with the singer.

music. *Like a Prayer*, released in early 1989, featured some edgy songs. The video for the title track showed many provocative images—a murder prompted by racial hatred, Madonna posing seductively in a church, kissing a saint, then singing in front of burning Ku Klux Klan-style crosses. Religious groups protested, insisting that the images were in poor taste, and pressured MTV to stop showing the video, which the network agreed to do. As with "Papa Don't

Later in the film, when police in Toronto, Ontario, Canada, threaten to arrest Madonna because she performs a simulated sex act on stage during a concert, Madonna stands up to them. She refuses to change the performance, arguing that to do so would be a violation of her freedom of expression. Disgruntled, and clearly aware that arresting Madonna would draw international headlines, the police let the show go on.

Film critics gave the movie high marks for revealing a side of Madonna that the public does not normally see. *Newsday* critic Jack Matthews wrote:

> *Truth*, narrated by the icon herself, maintains an easy balance between the hyperkinetic concert scenes, the candid documentary footage and the interviews with Madonna's friends, colleagues and family. Keshishian's cameras, as many as 22 at some venues, captured the concerts from every possible angle, and with the other material adding context, her performances take on vastly greater dimension than we ever got watching her on HBO.*

* Jack Matthews, "It's True . . . It's Daring," *Newsday*, May 10, 1991, p. 82.

Preach," Madonna felt the message of the song and video had been blown out of proportion. "The 'Like a Prayer' video was about overcoming racism and overcoming the fear of telling the truth,"[7] Madonna explained.

While religious leaders and other critics argued over exactly what message Madonna was trying to convey, the album went quadruple platinum. A second single from the album, "Express Yourself," earned critical acclaim as a positive message to young girls to wear their feminism proudly. Music critic Rikky Rooksby wrote:

> A typical upbeat number with Madonna exhorting the women in her audience not to go for second-best, to express their feelings, and get their men to express theirs. . . . Here, Madonna dismisses the satin sheets and gold baubles of material success. If it doesn't work, then you're better off on your own.[8]

"Express Yourself" has remained one of Madonna's most popular songs, and she has included performances of the song in most of her tours.

Meanwhile, no longer married to Penn, Madonna enjoyed her freedom and soon found herself in many well-publicized relationships. Among her newfound boyfriends were John F. Kennedy Jr., the son of the former U.S. president, and movie star and director Warren Beatty, whom she met just before the filming of *Dick Tracy*. Madonna was cast by Beatty to play the film's *femme fatale*, the love-starved torch singer Breathless Mahoney.

Dick Tracy was the most ambitious film of Madonna's career. It featured huge stars; in addition to Beatty, other big-name actors in the movie included Al Pacino, Dustin Hoffman, and James Caan. The producers spent nearly $50 million on the lavish production, which was expended on 1930s-era sets, costumes, and cars. The movie was based on the exploits of comic strip detective Dick Tracy, a character created by the late cartoonist Chester Gould. Beatty directed the film and played the role of Tracy. The film featured original music, with Madonna performing most of the songs.

After a series of film flops, Madonna hoped *Dick Tracy* would revive her movie career. This time, the critics gave her high marks. In *USA Today*, Mike Clark wrote, “It’s tough to say whether *Tracy* will revive Madonna’s movie career . . . it does, for now, zap the stigma of *Shanghai Surprise* and *Who’s That Girl*. She emotes, she carries scenes.”[9] Alas, though, the movie had trouble connecting with audiences. It scored respectable receipts at the box office but was hardly the hit that the film’s producers expected it to be.

As for her relationship with Beatty, the two soon drifted apart. Beatty would go on to marry actress Annette Bening, while Madonna pursued numerous relationships, none of which seemed to have staying power.

Connecting With Evita

Soon after Madonna arrived in New York looking for work as a professional dancer, the musical *Evita* opened on Broadway. The production had been a smash hit on the London stage, and with actress and singer Patti LuPone in the title role, it was heading for similar success in America.

Madonna, working in a doughnut shop and living from paycheck to paycheck, could never have afforded a ticket to a Broadway musical. Nevertheless, she was in the audience soon after the show opened; a friend who worked at the theater had sneaked her in. Madonna watched the entire production from the rear of the theater, hiding behind a pillar. Standing in the dark, watching the story of Eva Perón unfold before her, Madonna was awestruck by the singing and dancing of the production as well as the personal saga of the former first lady of Argentina, to whom she felt an emotional attachment.

Years later, as she prepared to portray Eva Perón in the film version, Madonna woke up one morning in a Buenos Aires hotel room and felt as though the spirit of Evita had taken over her body. She said, "Last night I dreamed of Evita. I was not outside watching her. I was her. I felt her sadness and her restlessness. I felt hungry and unsatisfied and in a hurry. . . . She wanted her life to matter. She didn't have time for the bureaucracies of government. She needed results."[1]

PUSHING BOUNDARIES

After breaking up with Sean Penn and Warren Beatty, Madonna found herself more in the news for the failed relationships in her love life and less so for her latest albums and film roles. Soon after ending her relationship with Beatty, she briefly dated Tony Ward, who had danced in some of her videos. Other men who entered and left her life in quick succession were the rap star Vanilla Ice, professional basketball player Dennis Rodman, and Jim Albright, one of her bodyguards. And then, while jogging in New York's Central Park, she found herself irresistibly drawn to another jogger—a tall and lean personal trainer named Carlos Leon, who would soon become her constant companion.

Now in her mid-thirties, Madonna had long since dropped the punk-chic look and was dressing much more fashionably, favoring the styles of some of the major French and Italian designers. She was also an exercise fanatic; her once shapely body was now toned. And she needed to be in shape, as the early 1990s were turning out to be a particularly busy and productive period for her. She acted in a number of film roles and churned out several albums during this period. In most cases, Madonna worked hard at solidifying her image as a sexually liberated woman willing to test American society's notions about morality and good taste.

Indeed, in 1990, she released the single "Justify My Love," a song that was accompanied by a controversial music video, later banned from MTV. Also, in 1992, she produced a coffee table book titled *Sex* that featured photographs of the singer posed in various states of undress, cavorting with other celebrities in simulated sexual positions. To take the pictures, she enlisted photographer Steven Meisel, who had shot a number of her album covers.

Critics found the whole project in bad taste—from the book's $50 price tag, to its Mylar wrapping that discouraged gawkers from thumbing through it in bookstores, to the photography, which they regarded as low quality. "I don't much care what Madonna does so long as she does not do it in the streets and frighten the horses," wrote *New York Times* book critic Vicki Goldberg. "Madonna specializes in breaking taboos, but this time it struck me as ugly."[2] And *Newsday* book critic Francine Prose wrote, "*Sex* simply isn't a turn-on; it's boring and dull and unsexy."[3]

Madonna complained that the critics did not understand the purpose of the book: It was to make people more comfortable talking about sex and their bodies. She insisted that people who are afraid to talk about such matters harbor a number of unhealthy hang-ups. "In all my work, my thing has always been not to be ashamed—of who you are, your body, your physicality, your desires, your sexual fantasies," she said. "The reason there is bigotry, and sexism and racism and homophobia . . . is fear. People are afraid of their own feelings, afraid of the unknown . . . and I am saying, 'Don't be afraid.' "[4]

The book was released as Madonna's new album, *Erotica*, also hit the market. The CD went double platinum, but music critics suggested that only Madonna's most devoted fans would find anything of interest on the disc and even found her singing uninspired. "Madonna's infantile vocal and flat delivery are anything but assertive,"[5] complained *Rolling Stone* music critic Arion Berger.

A MOVIE ABOUT BASEBALL

Meanwhile, Madonna sought to build on the positive reviews she had received for her screen work in *Dick Tracy*. She first starred in the murder mystery *Body of Evidence*, a film so laden with sexual imagery that the producers had to chop several erotic scenes in order to avoid an NC-17 rating. The film was critically panned, with many film reviewers placing the movie on their annual "Worst Films of the Year" list.

On the other hand, Madonna played a role in the 1992 film *A League of Their Own*, which told the story of the

DID YOU KNOW?

Madonna starred in *A League of Their Own* alongside Tom Hanks, Geena Davis, and Rosie O'Donnell. The film tells about the all-female baseball leagues of the 1940s, which were organized while many major league players served in World War II. The movie—directed by Penny Marshall, who had gained fame in the 1970s as a star of the TV comedy *Laverne and Shirley*—includes a very famous line of dialogue. Hanks, who plays Jimmy Dugan, a washed-up major league player managing the all-female team, confronts a team member who is sobbing. Not believing what he sees and hears, Dugan shouts at the woman, "There's no crying in baseball!"*

---

* "Memorable Quotes From *A League of Their Own*," IMDB.com, http://www.imdb.com/title/tt0104694/quotes.

Madonna received critical acclaim for her role in *A League of Their Own*, a 1992 film costarring *(at left)* Tom Hanks and Rosie O'Donnell. In the movie, she played Mae Mordabito, a tough-talking ballplayer from New York.

all-female baseball teams that competed during World War II because most of the male major leaguers were serving in the military. Madonna played the role of plucky and free-spirited centerfielder Mae Mordabito. It was a supporting role, but Madonna received high praise for the energy she brought to the part. (Before filming began, she not only learned how to play baseball but also learned as much as she could about the all-female leagues.) *Hartford Courant* film critic Malcolm Johnson wrote, "The big bat of the female leads belongs to Madonna, whose Mae Mordabito carries the feistiness and grit of a '40s city-bred athlete. . . . Madonna gives *A League of Their Own* the edge and gameness it needs."[6]

Soon after *A League of Their Own*, Madonna went back to testing the limits of what society would allow her to do. Indeed, her 1993 tour, titled the *Girlie Show*, featured plenty of suggestive dancing and costumes that left little to the imagination. And in early 1994, Madonna shocked television audiences when she appeared on *The Late Show with David Letterman* and launched into a profanity-laden dialogue with the TV host. When it was all over, a visibly shaken Letterman—trying vainly to keep his sense of humor—told his guest, "I'm happy you could come by now and gross us all out."[7]

PORTRAYING EVA PERÓN

Madonna may have delighted in shocking her audiences, but there is no question that she badly wanted a film role that would elevate her to Hollywood's "A" list of actresses. Looking back on her cinematic failures—*Shanghai Surprise*, *Who's That Girl*, and *Body of Evidence*—Madonna realized she had not done a good job of selecting roles or finding competent filmmakers. "I really want to be recognized as an actress," she said.

> I've learned that if you surround yourself with great writers and great actors and a great director and a great costumer or whatever, it's pretty hard to go wrong. In the past, I've been in a big hurry to make movies and I haven't taken the time to make sure all those elements were in line and good enough. It's a waste of time to do something mediocre. Unless you absolutely believe in every aspect of it, then you shouldn't waste your time.[8]

In late 1994, Madonna learned that the producers of the film version of *Evita* were searching for a singer and actress to play the lead role of the late first lady of Argentina. The musical had premiered on Broadway in 1979, starting a run of nearly four years. Now, its authors, composer Andrew

(continues on page 66)

WHO WAS EVITA PERÓN?

Eva Duarte met Colonel Juan Perón during a time of great turmoil in Argentina. It was 1944. A military coup had just overthrown the government. Perón had been placed in charge of the Department of Labor and Social Welfare, a position that won him favor among the nation's workers. When an earthquake hit the town of San Juan, leaving thousands homeless, Perón enlisted some of Argentina's major entertainers to organize relief efforts.

At the time, Eva had been living in Buenos Aires for nearly a decade and had risen from dance-hall girl to a prominent role on a popular drama broadcast on Argentine radio. During a festival to raise money for the victims, Eva and the colonel began their romance.

A year later, Perón was appointed vice president during a shake-up of the government. But that fall, in another shake-up, Perón was arrested and imprisoned. Thousands of workers—known as the *descamisados*, or the "the shirtless ones"—took to the streets and demanded his release. Eva Duarte led the march through the streets of Buenos Aires, rallying support for the imprisoned colonel. Later, she wrote, "I flung myself into the streets searching for those friends who might still be of help to [Perón]. . . . As I descended from the neighborhoods of the proud and the rich to those of the poor and humble, doors were opened to me more generously and with more warmth."*

On the night of October 17, 1945, Argentine officials released Perón. The colonel appeared on the balcony of Casa Rosada and promised to hold free elections. Perón was elected president in 1946 and, a short time later, married Eva.

She became an enormously popular first lady of Argentina, leading drives to raise money and food for the impoverished. She helped women gain the right to vote in Argentine elections and mediated labor disputes between workers and their employers.

Eva Perón, the second wife of President Juan Perón of Argentina, served as first lady of Argentina from 1946 until her death in 1952 and was the inspiration for *Evita*, a musical production with music by Andrew Lloyd Webber and lyrics by Tim Rice.

The first lady also made many trips into the poorest neighborhoods of Buenos Aires and other cities to inspect living conditions; if she found people living in squalor, she organized efforts to bring them relief. In 1947, Evita traveled to Europe, visiting Spain, Italy, Portugal, France, Switzerland, and Monaco. It was a tour that was well covered by the newsreel cameras of the day, giving Argentines an enormous sense of pride to see their first lady accepted into the halls of European power.

In 1951, as Perón was preparing to run for president again, a movement swelled within the country to draft the first lady as the vice presidential candidate. She eventually declined but stood at her husband's side as he won reelection. Argentines would see her in public for the last time in 1952, at her husband's second inauguration. By then, she had been diagnosed with cancer. She died a short time later, at the age of 33. The whole nation mourned.

---

* John Barnes, *Evita, First Lady: A Biography of Eva Perón*. New York: Grove Press, 1978, p. 46.

(continued from page 63)

Lloyd Webber and lyricist Tim Rice, were trying to bring *Evita* to the screen. The film's director, Alan Parker, wanted Michelle Pfeiffer to play the role of Eva Perón, but Pfeiffer had just given birth to her first child and did not think she could maintain a grueling film schedule. Others under consideration included Meryl Streep and Glenn Close. Madonna believed she would be a natural fit for the role; she wrote a four-page letter to Parker, telling him why she believed she would be perfect for the lead and how she identified with the former street waif who rose from poverty to marry the most powerful man in Argentina.

Parker and Webber were skeptical, but Rice championed her cause and convinced the others to award the title role to Madonna. "When I was chosen to make *Evita*, I knew I wasn't Andrew Lloyd Webber's first choice," Madonna said later. "I don't think he was particularly thrilled with my singing abilities. I knew I was going in with odds against me. That's an awkward position to be in. You feel everyone's waiting for you to stumble."[9]

And yet, even Webber could not deny that Madonna seemed to be a natural fit for the role. Evita Perón and Madonna had both arrived in a big city virtually penniless, seeking stardom. Both were brunettes who dyed their hair blond. Both were strong-willed women who aimed to get what they wanted. Both women were not afraid to show their emotions.

Madonna immersed herself in the role, studying the life of the woman she would play. She also took tango lessons, because Evita had danced in one of Buenos Aires' gloomy tango parlors, and also took singing lessons to give her voice a more operatic quality. Indeed, *Evita* may have been performed on the Broadway stage but it included no spoken dialogue; it was presented more as an opera than as the typical American musical, such as *The Music Man* or *West Side Story*.

RECOGNIZED AS AN ACTRESS

The film co-stars Spanish actor Antonio Banderas as Ché Guevara, the narrator who tells the story of Evita's life, and British film star Jonathan Pryce as Juan Perón, the colonel who seized power in 1940s Argentina. The story follows young Eva Duarte as she runs away from her rural village, makes her way to Buenos Aires, and forges a career as an actress, finally meeting and marrying Perón. In addition to the play's signature ballad, "Don't Cry for Me Argentina," the production also includes a number of stirring songs, including the robust "New Argentina," in which Evita and Juan promise to transform their backward country into a modern and free society. Webber and Parker also added songs for the film version, including the ballad "You Must Love Me," which was sung by Madonna.

The film opened on Christmas Day in 1996 to enthusiastic reviews by critics—particularly for its female lead. Jay Carr wrote in the *Boston Globe*:

> In throwing herself at the role with a nonstop single-mindedness, Madonna does more than just merge with the icon of Evita. More than casually familiar with reinvention herself, she goes back to the Hollywood movie star models they both admired, learned from, identified with. It's no secret that Madonna was really rolling the dice here, trying for the big-screen credibility that has so far eluded her. And she brings it off triumphantly, not so much overwhelming us as winning us with the nakedness of her ambition, with which she animates that of Eva Duarte from the sticks.
>
> Her way with the music will surprise her fans. There's much more finish to her singing here, more softness, more of an effort to reach into the music than she has shown before. In short, there's more

> vulnerability than brass, more introspection than we've ever heard from Madonna. The new song she got Lloyd Webber and Rice to write for her, "You Must Love Me," is a cry for validation, the cry of an actress addicted to the adoration of the multitudes. Amazingly, she makes Evita's signature song, "Don't Cry for Me Argentina," tingle with freshness as she croons it to the teary masses on the balcony of the actual Casa Rosada, where the actual Eva stood.[10]

The film turned out to be a commercial success as well, earning some $140 million at the box office. "You Must Love Me" won the Academy Award for Best Song; the film was also nominated for four additional Academy Awards. As for Madonna, she earned the recognition she had long sought when she won a Golden Globe Award for best actress. Presented by the Hollywood Foreign Press Association, the Golden Globes are not the biggest award for acting given in Hollywood—that is, of course, the Oscar—but, they are highly coveted within the entertainment community. In January 1998, when her name was called at the awards ceremony and she accepted the trophy, Madonna said: "I have been so incredibly blessed in this past year."[11]

In London

Just before filming for *Evita* concluded, Madonna learned she was pregnant. Carlos Leon was the father. It was an unexpected turn of events during a hectic time in her life; she was, after all, still filming a major Hollywood production. "You could have knocked me down with a feather," she said later.

> I certainly wasn't planning for it to happen when it did. I had more than enough things to worry about, just getting through the movie. I didn't want to do anything to sabotage the film. On top of all that, to take on board the reality of motherhood . . . it was like, "Oh, God, this is the last thing I need."[1]

Madonna told Alan Parker, the film's director, who promised to accommodate his star by giving her time to rest between takes. They also decided to keep her pregnancy a secret until after filming wrapped up to avoid the barrage of reporters and photographers they knew would descend on the star as she worked to finish the production. A few months after filming ended, Madonna let a friendly tabloid columnist leak the news of her pregnancy.

Although Madonna felt a great deal of affection for her boyfriend, she did not envision him as a husband and elected not to marry Leon. In October 1996, her daughter, Lourdes Maria Ciccone Leon, was born. Madonna has remained on good terms with Leon, who is very much a part of his daughter's life.

To Madonna, the arrival of Lourdes—her mother calls her Lola—was a godsend. She had long wanted a child of her own and was delighted by the arrival of a girl. Now, Madonna could give her daughter the type of relationship she was denied when her mother died. As images of Lourdes have started popping up in the press, the girl—now a teenager—bears a striking resemblance to her mother.

GIFT FROM A GODDESS

Pregnancy and childbirth slowed Madonna down a bit, but by 1997, she was recording and performing again. Her album, the dance-oriented *Ray of Light*, won a Grammy Award—remarkably, Madonna's first. Music critics saw the album as a turning point in her career: The lyrics on the album tracks reflected a deep introspection, as though Madonna were trying to figure out the course of her life. The title track told about the overwhelming speed of life on Earth. Another single from the album, "Frozen," was a soulful plea to people to care about others. "Drowned World (My Substitute for Love)" questioned whether the

Madonna and her daughter, Lourdes Leon, arrive at "A Night to Benefit Raising Malawi and UNICEF" hosted at the United Nations in New York City on February 6, 2007.

price of fame is too high. In "Mer Girl," Madonna relived the sadness she felt over her mother's death.

Musically, the album put a heavy emphasis on electronic beats. "My intention was to make a record that I'd enjoy listening to," Madonna said. "This album is reflective of where I am in my life right now—in terms of my musical interests and in terms of my personal beliefs. I feel like I've been enlightened, and that it's my responsibility to share what I've learned so far with the world."[2] One critic wrote in *Newsweek*, "*Ray of Light* shows a woman in transition being unusually candid about her own insecurities. . . . What a thrill it is to watch the premier diva of the '80s fight to grow up and stay relevant in her own way."[3]

Following *Ray of Light*, Madonna recorded another dance album, *Music*, which shot to the top of the charts, eventually going triple platinum. As with *Ray of Light*, *Music* featured a heavy emphasis on pulsating, electronic sounds. One of the tracks included on the album was Madonna's version of "American Pie." Originally recorded in 1971 by folk singer Don McLean, "American Pie" tells the story of the rise of rock 'n' roll music and the loss the singer felt at the death of rock pioneer Buddy Holly, who died in an airplane crash in 1959. Critics questioned whether a pop diva, even one of Madonna's stature, should be toying with a musical classic, but McLean said he felt honored that Madonna had chosen to perform a cover of his song. "I have heard her version and I think it is sensual and mystical," McLean told reporters. "I hope it will cause people to ask what's happening to music in America. I have received many gifts from God but this is the first time I have ever received a gift from a goddess."[4]

Musically, it had been a productive, creative, and rewarding time for Madonna—winning a Grammy and receiving critical praise for her albums and words of encouragement from McLean, a certified music legend. In the movies, though, it was the same old story. She starred in the comedy *The Next Best Thing* (2000), but the movie—and Madonna's acting—were roundly panned by the critics, and the film flopped.

MOVING TO LONDON

By now, Madonna had collected a new boyfriend, British actor and writer Andy Bird. He was a friend of Alek Keshishian, the director of the documentary about Madonna, *Truth or Dare*. In 1998, Madonna and Bird moved into a

IN HER OWN WORDS

Acting in the movies sounds like a glamorous job, but Madonna has found out otherwise. During the filming of *Evita*, she kept a diary that was later published in *Vanity Fair*. She wrote at one point:

> My wig feels like a vise grip on my head. I have decided that acting in movies is a very humiliating job. People sit around all day scrutinizing you, turning you from left to right, whispering behind the camera, cutting your nose hairs, plucking stray eyebrow hairs, and patting down your sweat while they fill in the lines on your face with spackle.
>
> When they are setting up the next shot, you are told to go and wait in your trailer like a doggy and that is where you have ample time to be hypercritical of yourself. You wonder if you're pretty enough or good enough or thin enough or attractive enough and you inevitably feel like a slab of beef.*

---

* Madonna, "Madonna's Private Diaries," *Vanity Fair*, November 1996, p. 224.

fashionable London house together. For Madonna, it was a difficult relationship to maintain. Her many recording, touring, and acting projects often took her away from London. And when the couple did find time to be together, they often found themselves fighting. In 1999, they parted company.

Madonna decided to remain in London. She had found two very good friends—fashion designer Stella McCartney, the daughter of former Beatle Paul McCartney, and Trudie Styler, the wife of the singer Sting. Prince Charles was another acquaintance; the heir to the British throne invited Madonna to his country home for dinner. Madonna had fallen in love with England and planned to make the country her permanent residence.

Shortly before breaking up with Bird, Madonna attended a party given by Sting and his wife; at the party she met an on-the-rise film director named Guy Ritchie. The pair soon developed a close relationship. He was unlike any man she had known. He seemed almost aloof about her celebrity—hardly impressed, it seemed, that he was dating the biggest star in pop music. Moreover, Ritchie liked nothing more than dropping into a British pub, sipping a pint of ale and joshing with his mates. Madonna had never enjoyed alcohol and was hardly the type to sit in the booth of a smoky bar, enjoying chitchat with Ritchie's chums, but she was so smitten with her new boyfriend that she endured his habits and went along.

Of course, when a star of Madonna's magnitude drops into an English pub for a pint, she is likely to draw attention. It did not take long for the British tabloid press to start following the couple around London. Soon, the British tabloids came up with a nickname for Madonna: Madge. To this day, Madonna says she is stumped by its meaning; some have told her it is short for "Your Majesty," while others say it is a common English term for "housewife." Whatever the meaning of the nickname, the tabloids found the word fit neatly into their headlines.

DANGER IN LOS ANGELES, WEDDING IN SCOTLAND

In 2000, Madonna learned that she was pregnant again, this time with Ritchie's baby. The couple flew to Los Angeles to await the birth. The baby arrived early on the morning of August 11. Home alone the night before the birth, Madonna started bleeding. She called her doctor, who suspected a condition known as a detached placenta. The placenta is the bag of tissue and fluid that holds the fetus in the mother's womb during pregnancy; if it becomes detached from the womb, the baby might not receive its life-sustaining nutrients from the mother. The doctor sent an ambulance for Madonna. Next she called Ritchie, who was spending the evening with friends.

By the time the paramedics arrived, Madonna was bleeding severely. The ambulance rushed her to a nearby hospital, with Ritchie racing behind in his car. Once at the hospital, the diagnosis of a detached placenta was confirmed. Her doctors made the decision to deliver the baby immediately by cesarean section. It meant the doctors would make a surgical cut into Madonna's lower abdomen to withdraw the baby. Two teams worked on the pop star—one to deliver the baby, the other to stop Madonna's bleeding. As the doctors worked, Madonna whispered, "Save my baby, just save my baby."[5]

For a few brief moments, the lives of both Madonna and her baby were in danger, but the quick response by paramedics as well as her doctors brought the situation under control. Madonna's baby boy was born at 12:54 A.M. The couple named the child Rocco.

Madonna and her husband, the film director Guy Ritchie, with their son, Rocco, born on August 11, 2000. They are photographed outside Dornoch Cathedral in Scotland after Rocco's christening. The couple divorced in 2008.

On December 22, 2000, Madonna and Ritchie married in an expensive and elaborate ceremony at a Scottish castle known as Skibo. Stella McCartney designed Madonna's $30,000 wedding gown.

Recalling Sean Penn's reaction when he saw the news helicopters buzzing above her last wedding party, Madonna went to great lengths to keep her second marriage ceremony a secret from the press. Madonna and Ritchie hired a security staff to patrol the 7,500-acre (3,035-hectare) grounds surrounding the castle and gave the guards instructions to keep all members of the media, as well as any other uninvited guests, far away from the castle.

As for the invited guests, they included Stella McCartney; movie star Gwyneth Paltrow; Sting and Trudie Styler; British actor Rupert Everett, who co-starred with Madonna in *The Next Best Thing*; and Matthew Vaughn, the son of American actor Robert Vaughn and the producer of Ritchie's movies.

Wearing the strapless ivory gown designed by McCartney as well as a diamond necklace and diamond tiara, Madonna strode down a winding staircase into Skibo's Great Hall, preceded by her 4-year-old daughter, Lourdes, the flower girl who sprinkled petals in her mother's path. Ritchie was dressed in a Scottish kilt. Later, Madonna and Ritchie sliced pieces from a wedding cake that was three feet (nearly one meter) high. After the ceremony, when Madonna tossed her bouquet into the crowd, it was caught by Lourdes.

ON TOUR AGAIN

At the age of 43, Madonna was now a wife and mother of two young children. Still, she was hardly ready to put her career on hold for domestic life. She launched the *Drowned World* Tour, featuring just as many revealing costumes and suggestive dances as any of her previous tours. In fact, she often performed in a black T-shirt that read "Mother" on the front and a familiar profanity on the back.

Madonna also intended the *Drowned World* Tour to be the most elaborate of her career. In addition to a large cast of dancers as well as a live band, Madonna made plans to feature all manner of visual effects, some of which required lasers, strobe lights, smoke machines, trapeze wires, and huge TV screens. One dance required the use of a mechanical bull—the type ridden by barroom cowboys. The stage covered nearly 5,000 square feet (465 square meters) and had to be taken apart and reassembled in each venue. In all, more than 100 tons (90.7 metric tons) of equipment had to be hauled from city to city.

Although the costs as well as the logistical problems of moving so much equipment started to add up, Madonna had no plans to change anything. "I don't see the point of doing a show unless you offer something that is going to mind-boggle the senses," she said. "It's not enough to get on stage and sing a song. It's all about theater and drama and suspense."[6]

Despite all the problems and enormous cost of producing the show, the tour turned out to be a tremendous success. Some 750,000 people bought tickets as the tour played venues across North America and Europe. "Nothing holds back Madonna," wrote *New York Times* music critic Jon Pareles after attending a concert. "Not love, not pop expectations, not tastefulness, not religion, not the laws of physics. Her *Drowned World* tour . . . is a 105-minute pop spectacle as performance art, devoted to the idea that Madonna can do what she wants."[7]

ANOTHER BOX OFFICE FAILURE

After finishing the tour, Madonna and Ritchie headed for the Mediterranean Sea islands of Malta and Sardinia to film *Swept Away*, a remake of the 1974 film of the same name by avant-garde filmmaker Lena Wertmüller. The film tells the story of a working-class sailor and a rich and snobby woman who survive a shipwreck and are marooned on a deserted island. The wealthy woman soon comes under the sailor's control, as she has no idea how to survive without him. The film says a lot about the enormous gulf that exists between the working and privileged classes and how circumstances can result in a reversal of roles. The remake was directed by Ritchie and starred Madonna in the role of the wealthy socialite. In a creative bit of casting, Adriano Giannini—whose father, Giancarlo Giannini, played the sailor in the original—was cast in the role of the sailor.

The remake was a disaster, universally panned by critics who rated it as one of the worst films of the year. Moreover, Madonna received a cruel skewering by the critics, who found her acting laughable. In *People*, Leah Rozen wrote:

> Madonna's latest film confirms that when it comes to having a movie career, the Material Girl has yet to find the right material. I'm betting she never will. To be blunt, Madonna simply isn't a movie star, even with real-life husband Guy Ritchie directing her. Up there, bigger than life, she seems ill at ease and tentative, confident only of the fact that her body is better toned than those of any of her costars.[8]

Since making her first movie, Madonna could look at her film work and find few roles that were critically acclaimed—Susan in *Desperately Seeking Susan*, Mae in *A League of Their Own*, Breathless in *Dick Tracy*, and Eva Perón in *Evita*. Indeed, as Susan, Mae, and Breathless, she was simply being asked to play versions of herself, while in the role of Argentina's first lady, she had recreated the life of a woman with whom she felt an emotional attachment. Virtually all her other movies were flops. Following the release of *Swept Away*, Madonna would occasionally make cameo appearances in films, but she would never again agree to play a lead role.

A Search for Spiritual Guidance

After achieving enormous measures of fame and wealth, many celebrities often turn to spiritual leaders or institutions to help guide their lives. They find themselves confused by the adoration heaped on them and search for the meaning of life.

Some celebrities turn to mainstream religious practices: Actor Richard Gere is a devotee of Buddhism, while singer Cat Stevens changed his name and turned to Islam. Other celebrities have sought out leaders and groups that are regarded as out of the mainstream of modern religious thought. In the 1960s, for example, The Beatles sought spiritual guidance in transcendental meditation (TM) taught by an Indian mystic, the Maharishi Mahesh Yogi. TM largely includes techniques that help the participant clear his or her mind of troubling and distracting thoughts. In more recent times, actor Tom Cruise has embraced the Church of Scientology, which preaches that the immortal soul, known as the "thetan," has been passed from individual to individual over the course of trillions of years.

In Madonna's case, she discovered Kabbalah. Kabbalah, a Hebrew word that means "receiving," is a form of ancient Jewish mysticism that seeks to answer complex questions about the nature of physical and spiritual life and the roles individuals play in God's plan for the universe. Kabbalists believe the movement of the planets can affect their lives; moreover, they believe they have the power to affect the movement of the planets. They also strive to understand the meaning of numbers, believing numbers hold the key to understanding the Bible as well as other aspects of life.

And Kabbalists believe Hebrew words have hidden meanings. For example, they believe the name *Adam* is derived from the Hebrew words *adama*, which means "earth," and *dam*, which means "blood"; Eve is derived from the Hebrew word *hava*, which means "life."

Madonna discovered Kabbalah in 1996 while she was pregnant with Lourdes and living in Los Angeles. She soon became a devotee; she has adopted a Kabbalah name, Esther, and has traveled through Israel, visiting holy Jewish shrines. She has also contributed $20 million to finance a school for Kabbalah education in Los Angeles.

Many Jewish leaders have rejected Kabbalah, insisting that it does not reflect mainstream Jewish thought. "She's misrepresenting Judaism," says Peter Anik, a spokesman for the Jewish Community Federation of Louisville, Kentucky. "It's a real watered-down distortion [of Judaism]; a trendy, new-agey magic thing."[1] Sara Reguer, chairwoman of the department of Jewish Studies at Brooklyn College in New York, notes, "What Madonna is doing is sacrilegious. She's not Jewish, so she has no idea. [Kabbalah] has got nothing to do with Judaism."[2]

CHILDREN'S BOOK AUTHOR

By now, Madonna and Ritchie had settled into life at Ashcombe, a seventeenth-century estate on 1,000 acres (405 hectares) near Britain's famous Stonehenge monument. As part of Britain's gentrified class, Madonna picked up an English accent and took up horseback riding—an activity that caused her to break three ribs, her collarbone, and her hand in a fall. "It was the most painful thing that ever happened in my life,"[3] she said.

While raising Lourdes and Rocco, she gained something of an insight into a child's world and authored several books for children. Partially inspired by what she learned during her Kabbalah training, the books address such traits as jealousy, envy, and selfishness. The first book, released in 2003, is titled *The English Roses*. The 48-page book tells the story of rivalry and friendship among four 11-year-old girls growing up in London. The four friends—Nicole, Amy, Charlotte, and Grace—find themselves jealous of a new girl in the neighborhood, Binah, who is blessed with radiant beauty. The story then turns magical: A fairy takes the girls on a journey, during which they learn that Binah leads a troubled life. In learning the truth about Binah, the four friends develop feelings of compassion and a desire to help the new girl overcome her troubles.

Madonna said the story is semiautobiographical. "As a child, I experienced jealousy and envy toward other girls for any number of reasons: I was jealous they had mothers, jealous they were prettier and richer," she said. "It isn't until you grow up that you realize what a waste of time those feelings are."[4]

The English Roses proved to be an enormous success, selling more than a half-million copies. Writing in the *Hartford Courant*, Carole Goldberg said:

Madonna reads her best-selling children's book *The English Roses* to children at the Barnes & Noble store in Rockefeller Center in New York City on September 29, 2003.

It's a sweet little tale with a tart-tongued, pumpernickel-loving fairy godmother who teaches a valuable lesson about envy and friendship. . . . In it, four little girls—the English roses of the title—learn with the help of a dream and some fairy dust, that Binah,

MADONNA AND FRIDA KAHLO

Madonna is one of the world's foremost collectors of the art of Frida Kahlo, a Mexican artist who painted from the 1930s until her death in 1954. Kahlo was a surrealist, meaning her work blended images of the real world with the make-believe. (The word is taken from the term "super realism," which was used to first describe the surrealist movement.)

Kahlo produced 143 paintings during her lifetime, about a third of which are self-portraits. Most of her self-portraits depict the artist amid supernatural images. In *The Little Deer,* for example, Kahlo has painted her head on the body of a stag that has been shot by nine arrows. Critics have suggested that Kahlo painted the image to show her deep personal suffering.

Born in 1907, Kahlo was afflicted with polio as a young girl and grew up among the turmoil and bloodshed of the Mexican Revolution. She aspired to become a doctor but had to drop out of medical school after she was injured in a bus accident. Kahlo then turned to painting.

In 1929, Kahlo married Mexican artist Diego Rivera and, with him, later provided a haven for Russian communist leader Leon Trotsky, who had been chased out of the Soviet Union by his rival, dictator Joseph Stalin. Soon after Trotsky

the beautiful but motherless girl they have been shunning, had a sadder life than they imagined.[5]

The book spent several weeks atop the *New York Times*' children's book bestseller list. Later, Madonna wrote 10

moved out of the couple's home, Stalin dispatched assassins to Mexico and had Trotsky murdered.

During their marriage, Kahlo and Rivera maintained a stormy relationship, trading charges of infidelity. Madonna has studied Kahlo's life and has compared the artist's marriage to Rivera to her marriages to Sean Penn and Guy Ritchie.

> I mean, she was crippled physically and emotionally in ways that I'm not. But she was also married to a very powerful and passionate man and was tormented by him. Although he loved her and was supportive of her as an artist, there was a lot of competition between them. There weren't that many female artists at the time, and the Latin community is a very macho environment. It was very hard for her to survive that and have her own identity. And I can identify to a certain extent with having that awareness of the male point of view of what a woman's role is in a relationship. It's tough to fight it. She was very courageous, which I admire and can relate to.*

* Barbara Victor, *Goddess: Inside Madonna*. New York: Harper Entertainment, 2001, pp. 329–330.

sequels to *The English Roses* featuring the same characters and also published several other titles, including *Mr. Peabody's Apples*, *Yakov and the Seven Thieves*, *The Adventures of Abdi* and *Lotsa De Casha*.

COURTING CONTROVERSY

Madonna may have been spending her spare time studying Jewish mysticism and writing children's books, but she still aimed to maintain her influence over the pop music world. Professionally, she did not want to disappoint her fans and served notice that, even at the age of 45, she could still cause an earthquake in the entertainment world.

In 2003, Madonna joined Britney Spears and Christina Aguilera onstage at the MTV Music Video Awards. Spears and Aguilera started the performance by singing a duet of "Like a Virgin," each dressed in versions of the faux-wedding gown that Madonna had worn nearly two decades before (complete with "Boy Toy" belt buckles).

At first, it appeared as though the two pop stars were performing a tribute to Madonna, but then Madonna, dressed in a costume resembling a man's tuxedo, joined them onstage, singing her new release, "Hollywood." Near the end of the song, as the three singers came close together, Madonna suddenly kissed Spears and Aguilera in turn on the mouth. The audience erupted in cheers.

Although Madonna's kisses for the two younger singers may have seemed spontaneous, the scene had been rehearsed beforehand. In fact, Aguilera told reporters afterward, she was enthusiastic about the idea—knowing it would shock the audience and cause a national stir—but Spears balked at kissing Madonna during rehearsals and had to be talked into it. "I had no problem in kissing her every time," Aguilera said. "Britney was a little shy at first. Madonna kept having to go, 'Britney, kiss me, kiss me.' "[6]

Some critics suggested the stunt had been concocted by Madonna to boost sales of her new album, *American Life*, which featured the single "Hollywood." Sales of the album had been lagging, they suggested, and Madonna's sudden and "unexpected" kisses planted on the lips of Spears and Aguilera were performed for shock value to boost sales. "So she kissed Britney and Christina Aguilera during an MTV awards show," complained *Buffalo News* columnist Libby Meader. "Was this art, as she would claim? Or desperate mouth-to-mouth resuscitation for her pop-icon status?"[7]

Indeed, before the MTV awards show, "Hollywood" had failed to crack most of the top-40 lists. But now, with the whole country talking about "the kiss," sales soon picked up and, eventually, *American Life* was certified platinum. Critics also pointed out that Spears had not recorded a hit since 2001, and the publicity could not have hurt her, either.

Despite Madonna's antics with Spears and Aguilera in front of a national TV audience, Madonna still considered herself a serious music maker. *American Life* was the ninth studio album of her career. The black-and-white photo on the album cover featured Madonna striking a pose reminiscent of a famous portrait of Ché Guevara, the Argentine revolutionary who helped lead the Cuban Revolution that installed communist leader Fidel Castro in power. Critics suggested that Madonna intended the photo to represent an antiwar message: As the album was released, the United States was preparing to invade Iraq.

Critics found the songs in the album a bit darker than what fans had come to expect from Madonna. No longer was Madonna singing about being showered with material possessions or the thrills of finding new love. In the title track, the one-time Material Girl now questioned whether her material possessions—her automobiles and soy lattes as well as her stylists, trainers, managers, and butlers—truly define success in America. Writing in *Rolling Stone*, Ben Ratlif said, "Madonna Ciccone has done it again: The . . . guitar player from London via Detroit has taken the pulse of the nation. . . . Madonna is ready to apply what she's learned to the outside world. Specifically: Materialism isn't good for us."[8]

DIVORCE

In 2004, Madonna toured again and also released a documentary, *I'm Going to Tell You a Secret*. As with *Truth or Dare*, the documentary shows Madonna rehearsing for concerts and auditioning dancers, and it features some scenes from her home life. The documentary depicts Ritchie as a supportive husband who is able to handle his wife's celebrity with a nonchalant attitude, but, in truth, there were some serious problems brewing at home. "Obviously, they've been struggling for a while,"[9] Madonna's friend, Trudie Styler, told an American TV interviewer.

Soon, the friction found its way into the tabloid press—a circumstance that could certainly be expected when a marriage involving an internationally famous pop music diva and a movie director begins to fall apart. The tabloids were full of rumors. One British newspaper, the London *Daily Mail*, reported that Ritchie barked at his wife, who was 10 years his senior: "[You] look like a granny."[10] Another paper reported that when Madonna was injured in her horseback riding accident, Ritchie was thousands of miles away, busy on a movie set. The paper reported that Madonna was angry that Ritchie refused to shut down production and hurry home to see her. The London *Observer* reported that Ritchie had infuriated his wife by failing to develop an interest in Kabbalah. Ritchie told the newspaper, "I have sympathies with many philosophies. . . . It'd be a mistake [for me] to be a follower of anything, really."[11]

The truth was probably far less sensational than those rumors would suggest. Quite simply, as Madonna and Ritchie pursued their separate careers, they had grown apart. Each traveled extensively, finding they were spending little time together. Madonna told a German newspaper, "We no longer have the idealistic expectation of a relationship. I gave up the dream that he is the perfect husband. He gave up the expectation that I am the perfect wife."[12]

In November 2008, Madonna and Guy Ritchie were granted a divorce by a judge in London. Their marriage had lasted not quite eight years.

Enduring Icon

Now in her 50s, Madonna continues to be a force in popular music. She released a new album in 2008, *Hard Candy*, and promoted it on the *Sticky & Sweet* Tour, which sold more than $400 million in tickets worldwide. In writing and recording the songs for *Hard Candy*, Madonna left the dour messages of *American Life* and got back to doing what she always did better than anyone else—getting people on their feet and dancing. Composed mostly of electric dance tracks, the album cover shows Madonna's lighter side: Dressed like a professional boxer, wearing a championship belt around her waist, Madonna is seen taping her wrists, as a boxer would before he puts on his boxing gloves. The message was clear: Madonna was getting back in the ring.

Madonna enlisted several collaborators for the album, including singer Justin Timberlake, who co-wrote five of the songs and provided backup vocals on four of the album's tracks. Record producer Pharrell Williams assisted in the production of the disc. "I didn't have any idea what kind of music I wanted to make," said Madonna.

> I just knew I wanted to collaborate with Pharrell and Justin. I needed to be inspired and thought, "Well, who's making records I like?" So I went, "I like that guy and I like that guy." It's not like we hit it off right away. Writing is very intimate. You have to be vulnerable and it's hard to do that with strangers. I had ups and downs before everybody got comfortable, but I grew very fond of Pharrell and Justin.[1]

Critics praised the album. Writing in *People*, Chuck Arnold said, "Rocking a blinged-out boxing belt emblazoned with a big M, Madonna strikes a prizefighter's pose on the cover of her new disk. And *Hard Candy*—the early frontrunner for party album of the year—shows that, at . . . 50, she's still the undisputed champion of diva pop."[2]

The album quickly hit the top of the charts and was soon certified platinum. A single from the album, "4 Minutes," peaked in third place on *Billboard*'s Hot 100 chart. It was the thirty-seventh time in her career that Madonna had scored a Top Ten hit, breaking a record held by Elvis Presley.

Since beginning her music career in 1982, Madonna has sold more than 200 million albums. Moreover, her estimated personal worth of more than $500 million makes her one of the richest women in the world. She has even been featured on the cover of *Forbes*, a business magazine, which wrote about her business and financial savvy.

ANOTHER KISS

Part of that savvy includes making sure her music and tours remain as controversial as ever. For her 2006 *Confessions on a Dance Floor* Tour, she sought to deliver an antiwar message. During the performance, Madonna wore a crown of thorns while strapped to a cross. Behind her, images of world leaders flashed on a screen. The images included contemporary figures but also photographs of past dictators like Adolf Hitler and Joseph Stalin. As the tour traveled from country to country, local officials denounced the scene and threatened to close down the show if she did not cut out the act on the cross. Madonna refused and, in the end, local officials respected her right to free speech. In America, though, the NBC television network planned to air a documentary on the tour but, after receiving complaints from a number of American religious leaders, deleted the scene from the final cut of the show.

In 2009, NBC did, however, air a humorous skit featuring Madonna on *Saturday Night Live*. The skit started out with Madonna singing a duet with new pop star Lady Gaga. Soon, the singers start bickering, and then a nasty catfight breaks out, with the two divas wrestling, pulling each other's hair, and hurtling insults. "Hey, guess what Madonna?" Lady Gaga says during the scuffle. "I'm totally hotter than you."[3] Finally, they calm down and nearly kiss (comedian Kenan Thompson, who had been mediating the melee, jumped into the middle of the smooch at the last second).

In taking part in the skit, Madonna was spoofing the scene at the MTV awards six years earlier when she planted serious kisses on Britney Spears and Christina Aguilera. This time, the critics accepted the scene for what it was—a joke. "Sorry Britney and Christina, Madonna has found herself a new blond pop star to smooch,"[4] wrote *New York Daily News* TV critic Christina Everett.

In August 2008, Madonna performs during her highly anticipated *Sticky & Sweet* Tour to promote her number-one album *Hard Candy* at the Millennium Stadium in Cardiff, Wales.

Later, Madonna said she enjoyed appearing with Lady Gaga and has great respect for her music. "I can see myself in Lady Gaga," Madonna says. "In the early part of my career, for sure. When I saw her, she didn't have a lot of money for her production, she's got holes in her fishnets, and there's mistakes everywhere. It was kind of a mess, but I can see that she's got that 'it' factor. It's nice to see that at a raw stage."[5]

Madonna may be enjoying herself more than ever, but her more than 50-year-old body has taught her a lot about pain. After a show, she admits to aching all over—particularly in the knees and shoulders—and must sit in a tub of ice for several minutes. She attributes some of the

DID YOU KNOW?

After her divorce from Guy Ritchie, Madonna moved back to New York City, where she bought a home on the city's opulent Upper East Side. Her new mansion is far different from the rented rooms, basements, and tiny apartments she lived in as a struggling dancer and singer in New York in the 1970s and 1980s.

For starters, the home is 57 feet (17.4 meters) wide—about three times as wide as the typical New York townhouse. (A previous owner bought three townhouses on the block, knocked out the interior walls, and converted them into one huge mansion.) It includes 26 rooms, 13 of which are bedrooms. It has a 38-foot-wide (11.6-meters-wide) living room as well as nine fireplaces. Out back, Madonna and her children can enjoy a 3,000-square-foot (279-sq.-m.) garden. Said the *New York Times,* "With a two-car garage on the premises, the new owner could whisk her children to the park by limousine in about as much time as it would take to go by elevator from a Fifth Avenue penthouse to the lobby."*

---

* Josh Barbanel, "Madge in the Back of Beyond," *New York Times*, June 26, 2009, p. RE2.

pain to the injuries she sustained in her fall from the horse. During the *Sticky & Sweet* Tour, she reprised an old song, "Into the Groove," but performed it while jumping rope—a maneuver that took its toll on Madonna's joints. "I come home and sit in an ice bath for 10 minutes," Madonna explained.

> It's really painful when you get in, but it feels so good afterward. I'm an athlete. My ankles get taped before the shows, and I have treatments and physical therapists. It's from years and years of abuse, dancing in high heels, which is not great on your knees. All dancers have injuries, but we just deal with them. We get acupuncture and therapy, and just keep going.[6]

FIGHTING FOR MALAWI'S CHILDREN

After her divorce from Ritchie, Madonna moved back to New York City, buying a $40 million townhouse on East 81st Street. Socially, she was rumored to be dating Alex Rodriguez of the New York Yankees, but according to Rodriguez, the two are just friends. In 2009, the tabloids reported that Madonna had become romantically involved with Jesus Luz, a 22-year-old Brazilian model. Later that year, she was reported to have ended her relationship with Luz to date Marc Schimmel, a millionaire businessman.

Even if she does not marry again, Madonna has taken steps to enlarge her family. In 2006, she learned about the plight of orphans in the African nation of Malawi, one of the poorest countries on the planet. It is estimated that between 1 million to 2 million Malawian children are orphans or have otherwise been abandoned by their parents. Many are growing up in crowded orphanages, while others must fend for themselves on the streets. Many have been born infected with HIV, the virus that causes AIDS.

Madonna met an activist from Malawi, Victoria Keelan, who begged her to get involved. Keelan told Madonna, "Look, if you are in the business of helping children, we have over a million orphans here in Malawi and the problem is insane. It's an emergency. They need your help."[7] Keelan challenged Madonna to use her money and influence to bring positive change to the children of Malawi.

Madonna decided to see for herself. Still married to Guy Ritchie at the time, they flew to Malawi, where Madonna toured some of the orphanages and was appalled at what she found. "It's difficult to watch people suffer, but it's so hard to watch children suffer," she said. "To see children lying on the ground in a daze, in a pool of urine with flies buzzing around their heads. It's unfathomable."[8]

On one trip to a Malawi orphanage, Madonna encountered a young child who caught her eye. He was an 18-month-old boy whose 14-year-old mother died shortly after giving birth. Following the mother's death, the father abandoned the child, leaving him in the care of the squalid orphanage. Struck by the child's story, Madonna and Ritchie decided to adopt the boy, whom they planned to name David.

To win custody of the child, it took quite a bit of legal wrangling. Under the law in Malawi, adoptive parents must reside in the country for at least 18 months before they can take possession of a child. Moreover, once the story hit the news that a wealthy pop star wanted to adopt the child, the boy's father, Yohane Banda, suddenly stepped forward and balked at releasing custody of the boy to Madonna and her husband. Finally, the Malawi courts agreed to bend the rules in Madonna's favor, finding that she had the means to take the child out of poverty and raise him in luxury. Indeed, the Malawian judge suggested that, when David grows up, he might find it in his heart to return to Malawi and assist his people in ways he could never do had he grown up an orphan. David's biological father also relented and allowed the adoption to proceed.

Madonna is seen with her Malawian son, David, in April 2007. In May 2008, after a long ordeal, Madonna won final approval from the high court in Malawi to permanently adopt the toddler from one of Africa's poorest countries. The ruling brought to an end to a saga that Madonna has described as more painful than giving birth.

"The government people told me it would be a good thing for the country," Banda shrugged. "They said he would come back educated and be able to help us."[9]

MADONNA AS A DIRECTOR

After appearing in a number of cinematic flops, Madonna may have finally found her place in the movies—as a director. In 2008, Madonna directed the comedy *Filth and Wisdom*, about three down-and-out roommates sharing an apartment in London. The characters include A.K., a rock musician; Holly, a would-be ballerina forced to work as an exotic dancer; and Juliette, a pharmacist's assistant who also happens to be addicted to drugs.

To play the roles, Madonna drafted unknown actors, although, for the role of A.K., she cast Eugene Hütz, leader of the punk band Gogol Bordello. Madonna co-wrote the script with Dan Cadan, who had worked as an assistant to Madonna's former husband, director Guy Ritchie. The title is drawn from A.K.'s observation that "filth and wisdom are two sides of the same coin"*—in other words, one cannot experience wisdom until one has emerged from filth.

Madonna says her decision to direct *Filth and Wisdom* marks a definite change in her career. She said:

> I've been inspired by films since I started dancing . . . and I think it was one of my secret desires, but I was afraid to just say, "I want to be a director." But then one day I said, "OK, stop dreaming and do it." But I didn't want to do it the Hollywood way, and talk through agents. I decided it all had to be generated by me, so I wrote it.**

The film received mixed reviews. Many critics praised the acting but found Madonna's directing uneven. *Boston Globe* movie

Madonna has done more, though, than change the life of one young child. She has donated $15 million to construct a school, the Raising Malawi School for Girls. Madonna said:

critic Ty Burr sniped, "Now that Madonna and Guy Ritchie have called it quits, all that remains is the issue of custody. Madonna should get the children. . . . Based on her directorial debut, Ritchie should get the filmmaking career."*** But *New York Times* movie critic Manohla Dargis was more encouraging:

> *Filth and Wisdom* is a ridiculously easy target, but it also creaks and strains with more ambition than most mainstream throwaways that just recycle the usual guns and poses. Not that Madonna has gone in for originality, which isn't really her thing: rather, instead of repurposing a genre, she has riffled through the art-house catalog for inspiration, as evidenced by the film's intentionally grubby visual texture, jumpy editing, direct-address commentary, freeze frames and other tricks. Although the somewhat rough visual style doesn't feel especially organic or natural for a director who has built a slick international brand with mind-blowing calculation, it does keep you interested from scene to scene.****

---

* Leslie Felperin, "*Filth and Wisdom*," *Variety*, February 14, 2008, http://www.variety.com/story.asp?l=story&r=VE1117936209&c=-1.
** Rich Cohen, "Madonnarama!" *Vanity Fair*, May 2008, p. 210.
*** Ty Burr, "Madonna Runs Out of Steam," *Boston Globe*, October 24, 2008, p. G9.
**** Manohla Dargis, "Stripping and Other Noble Pursuits," *New York Times*, October 17, 2008, p. C10.

> Growing up in a privileged life, I took education for granted, but coming to Malawi has taught me a lot of things. I realized how much [children] deserve to be educated and so, for me, the best thing I could do was to build a school, a unique school that will create future female leaders, scientists, lawyers and doctors, and if this school is successful it will be used as a model to replicate in other countries.[10]

In late 2009, Madonna, accompanied by her children—Lourdes, Rocco, and David— returned to Malawi to participate in the groundbreaking ceremony for the school.

Madonna has also produced a documentary about the children of Malawi, *I Am Because We Are*. The title is based on a phrase from African folklore that says people can only survive as a community. Madonna, who has made the documentary available for free viewing on www.youtube.com, appears in the film and also narrates the story of Malawi's orphans. In the film, she notes:

> People always ask me why I chose Malawi. And I tell them, "I didn't, it chose me." I got a phone call from a woman named Victoria Keelan. She was born and raised in Malawi. She told me that there were over 1 million children orphaned by AIDS. She said there weren't enough orphanages. And that the children were everywhere. Living on the streets. Sleeping under bridges. Hiding in abandoned buildings. Being abducted, kidnapped, raped. She said it was a state of emergency. She sounded exhausted and on the verge of tears. I asked her, how . . . how could I help? She said, "You're a person of resources. People pay attention to what you say and do." I felt embarrassed. I told her I didn't know where Malawi was. She told me

> to look it up on a map, and then she hung up on me. I decided to investigate, and I ended up finding out much more than I bargained for, about Malawi, about myself, about humanity.[11]

In 2009, Madonna adopted a second child from Malawi, four-year-old Chifundo James. Madonna has renamed the girl Mercy.

NEVER OUT OF STYLE

As Madonna tours and continues to make music, she has noticed the wide range of ages in her audience. Teenagers wearing her old punk-chic look are flocking to her shows, but their mothers are also in the audience: Longtime Madonna fans, they have dressed in punk-chic as well—bangles, oversized earrings and other floppy costume jewelry, layered tops, fingerless gloves, lacy corsets worn on top, torn fishnet stockings held together by safety pins, leggings cut off at the ankles, mismatched socks, clunky shoes, tangled hair. The Madonna look may be coming back. Or, perhaps, the look, as with all things about Madonna, has just never gone out of style.

CHRONOLOGY

1958 Madonna Louise Veronica Ciccone born in Bay City, Michigan, on August 16.

1976 She graduates from Adams High School in Rochester, Michigan, and enrolls at the University of Michigan as a dance student.

1977 Madonna spends the summer in Durham, North Carolina, as a student of world-famous choreographer Pearl Lang.

1978 She drops out of the University of Michigan and moves to New York City to pursue a career as a professional dancer.

1982 Madonna works as a singer for a rock band and cuts a demo tape that is heard by record company executive Seymour Stein, who signs her to a contract, In October, she releases her first single, "Everybody."

1983 Her first album, *Madonna*, is released; the album is eventually certified triple platinum.

1984 Her second album, *Like a Virgin*, is released; the disc climbs to the top of the *Billboard* charts.

1985 Madonna's first film, *Desperately Seeking Susan*, is released to strong reviews and box office sales; she marries actor Sean Penn.

1986 She releases third album, *True Blue*, featuring the controversial song "Papa Don't Preach." She appears in the film *Shanghai Surprise*, her first in what would be a long series of acting flops.

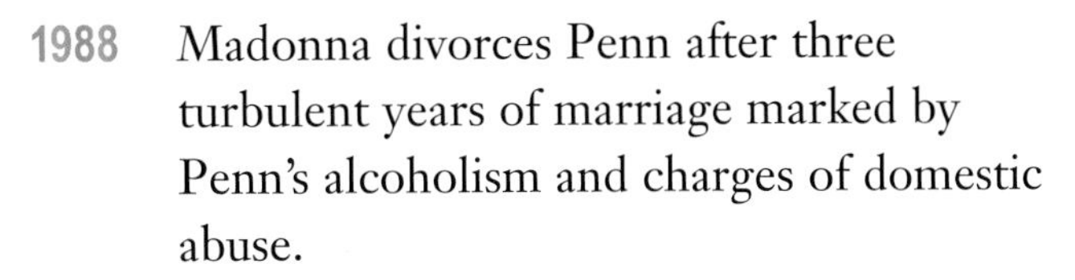

1988 Madonna divorces Penn after three turbulent years of marriage marked by Penn's alcoholism and charges of domestic abuse.

1989 She releases her fourth album, *Like A Prayer*; the title track prompts complaints from religious leaders, while another track, "Express Yourself," is regarded as a positive message about feminism.

1990 Madonna receives positive reviews for her portrayal of Breathless Mahoney in the film *Dick Tracy*.

1991 *Truth or Dare*, the documentary of Madonna's *Blond Ambition* Tour, is released to positive reviews.

1992 Madonna poses nude for the coffee table photography book *Sex*; she plays the role of Mae Mordabito in the film *A League of Their Own*.

1994 She shocks a national TV audience by uttering numerous profanities while appearing as a guest on *The Late Show with David Letterman*.

1995 Madonna is cast as Eva Perón in the film version of *Evita*.

1996 After Argentine President Carlos Menem balks at her selection for the role of Eva Perón, she flies to Buenos Aires and convinces Menem of her sincerity and devotion to the role; she gives birth to daughter Lourdes.

1998 Madonna wins the Golden Globe Award for her portrayal of Eva Perón.

2000 She gives birth to a son, Rocco, by English film director Guy Ritchie and marries Ritchie in Scotland.

2003 Madonna authors her first children's book, *The English Roses*; she shocks a national MTV audience when she kisses Britney Spears and Christina Aguilera on camera.

2006 She becomes an activist for the plight of Malawi orphans and adopts a Malawian child named David.

2008 Madonna divorces Ritchie; releases her eleventh studio album, *Hard Candy*; and promotes the album on the *Sticky & Sweet* Tour.

2009 She spoofs her kisses with Spears and Aguilera by getting into a mock catfight and nearly kissing Lady Gaga on *Saturday Night Live*; she adopts a second child from Malawi, whom she names Mercy.

2010 Madonna releases *Sticky & Sweet Tour*, her third live album. She announces her plans to direct *W.E.*, a film based on a script she wrote with Alek Keshishian.

NOTES

CHAPTER 1

1. Madonna, "Madonna's Private Diaries," *Vanity Fair*. November 1996: p. 176.
2. Barbara Victor, *Goddess: Inside Madonna*. New York: Harper Entertainment, 2001, p. 22.
3. Ibid.
4. Madonna, "Madonna's Private Diaries," p. 176.
5. Victor, *Goddess: Inside Madonna*, pp. 28–29.
6. Ibid., p. 45.
7. Ibid., p. 46.
8. Ibid., p. 47.

CHAPTER 2

1. Andrew Morton, *Madonna*. New York: St. Martin's Press, 2001, p. 49.
2. Ibid., p. 56.
3. J. Randy Taraborrelli, *Madonna: An Intimate Biography*. New York: Simon & Schuster, 2001, p. 9.
4. Ibid., p. 10.
5. Ibid., p. 11.
6. Larry King, "Interview With Madonna." CNN.com, October 19, 2002: http://transcripts.cnn.com/TRANSCRIPTS/0210/19/lklw.00.html.
7. Austin Scaggs, "Madonna Looks Back," *Rolling Stone*. October 29, 2009: p. 48.
8. Taraborrelli, *Madonna: An Intimate Biography*, p. 23.
9. Lucy O'Brien, *Madonna: Like an Icon*. New York: Harper Entertainment, 2007, p. 26.
10. Taraborrelli, *Madonna: An Intimate Biography*, p. 32.
11. Ibid., p. 30.
12. Victor, *Goddess: Inside Madonna*, p. 188.
13. Ibid., pp. 188–189.
14. Morton, *Madonna*, p. 64.
15. Ibid.

CHAPTER 3

1. Victor, *Goddess: Inside Madonna*, p. 52.
2. Ibid., pp. 52–53.
3. Ibid., pp. 207–208.
4. O'Brien, *Madonna: Like an Icon*, p. 36.
5. Scaggs, "Madonna Looks Back," p. 48.
6. Victor, *Goddess: Inside Madonna*, p. 229.
7. Ibid., p. 231.
8. O'Brien, *Madonna: Like an Icon*, p. 42.
9. Ibid., p. 57.
10. Ibid.
11. Rikky Rooksby, *Madonna: The Complete Guide to Her Music*. New York: Omnibus, 2004, p. 28.
12. Don Shewey, "Madonna," *Rolling Stone*. September 29, 1983: http://www.rollingstone.com/artists/madonna/albums/album/213974/review/6068215/madonna.
13. O'Brien, *Madonna: Like an Icon*, p. 59.

CHAPTER 4

1. Scaggs, "Madonna Looks Back," p. 50.
2. Denise Worrell, "Now: Madonna on Madonna," *Time*. May 27, 1985. http://www.time.com/time/magazine/article/0,9171,957025-1,00.html.
3. Taraborrelli, *Madonna: An Intimate Biography*, p. 88.
4. Worrell, "Now: Madonna on Madonna."
5. Debby Miller, "Like a Virgin," *Rolling Stone*. January 17, 1985: http://www.rollingstone.com/reviews/album/246700/review/6210108?utm_source=Rhapsody&utm_medium=CDreview.
6. Taraborrelli, *Madonna: An Intimate Biography*, p. 90.
7. John Skow, "Show Business: Madonna Rocks the Land," *Time*. May 27, 1985: http://www.time.com/time/magazine/article/0,9171,957012,00.html.

8. Ibid.
9. Ibid.
10. O'Brien, *Madonna: Like an Icon*, p. 86.
11. Ibid., p. 87.
12. Roger Ebert, "*Desperately Seeking Susan*," *Chicago Sun-Times*. March 29, 1985: http://rogerebert.suntimes.com/apps/pbcs.dll/article?AID=/19850329/REVIEWS/503290301/1023.
13. O'Brien, *Madonna: Like an Icon*, p. 102.

CHAPTER 5

1. Victor, *Goddess: Inside Madonna*, p. 282.
2. Morton, *Madonna*, p. 135.
3. Michael Janusoni, "Madonna's New Movie is a Mission of Mediocrity," *Providence Journal*. August 30, 1986, p. A10.
4. Victor, *Goddess: Inside Madonna*, p. 308.
5. Drew Fetherston, "Madonna in '*Who's That Girl*,'" *Newsday*. August 8, 1987, p. 7.
6. Victor, *Goddess: Inside Madonna*, p. 330.
7. O'Brien, *Madonna: Like an Icon*, p. 134.
8. Rooksby, *Madonna: The Complete Guide to Her Music*, p. 32.
9. Mike Clark, "An Arresting '*Tracy*'; Beatty Cops a Stylish Cartoon Coup," *USA Today*. June 14, 1990, p. D1.

CHAPTER 6

1. Madonna, "Madonna's Private Diaries," p. 188.
2. Vicki Goldberg, "Madonna's Book: Sex, and Not Like a Virgin," *New York Times*. October 25, 1992, p. A33.
3. Francine Prose, "A Naked Madonna's Raunchy Inspirations," *Newsday*. October 27, 1992, p. 42.
4. O'Brien, *Madonna: Like an Icon*, p. 163.

5. Arion Berger, "Madonna: *Erotica*," *Rolling Stone*. November 26, 1992: http://www.rollingstone.com/reviews/album/130835/review/6067636/erotica.
6. Malcolm Johnson, "In Film About Women, Tom Hanks is the Big Hit," *Hartford Courant*. July 1, 1992, p. F1.
7. O'Brien, *Madonna: Like an Icon*, p. 199.
8. Taraborrelli, *Madonna: An Intimate Biography*, pp. 243–244.
9. Ibid., p. 245.
10. Jay Carr, "*Evita*: More Powerful Than Ever; Both the Musical and Madonna are Transformed on Screen," *Boston Globe*. January 1, 1997, p. C1.
11. Bob Thomas, Associated Press, "Madonna, Cruise Take Globes for Acting; *Evita* Wins as Film," *Buffalo News*. January 20, 1997, p. A10.

CHAPTER 7

1. Victor, *Goddess: Inside Madonna*, p. 350.
2. Larry Flick, "WB Expects Madonna to 'Light Up' International Markets," *Billboard*. February 21, 1998: p. 1.
3. Karen Schoemer and Yahlin Chang, "A Kinder, Gentler Diva," *Newsweek*. March 2, 1998: p. 77.
4. "McLean Delighted By New Slice of 'Pie,'" *Albany Times Union*. February 16, 2000, p. A2.
5. Victor, *Goddess: Inside Madonna*, p. 388.
6. O'Brien, *Madonna: Like an Icon*, p. 253.
7. Jon Pareles, "Sea of Self-Love, But Who's Drowning?" *New York Times*. July 27, 2001, p. E21.
8. Leah Rozen, "*Swept Away*," *People*. October 21, 2002: p. 44.

CHAPTER 8

1. Tamara Ikenberg, "Kabbalah Chameleon: Real Doctrine is More than Madonna's Latest Reinvention," *Louisville Courier-Journal*. August 25, 2004.
2. Ibid.
3. Neil Strauss, "How Madonna Got Her Groove Back." *Rolling Stone*. December 1, 2005: p. 70.
4. "The Global Release of Madonna's First Children's Book Makes Publishing History," Calloway Arts & Entertainment news release, September 15, 2003: http://www.callaway.com/news_091503.htm.
5. Carole Goldberg, "Mama Madonna: Her First Kid's Book," *Hartford Courant*. September 16, 2003, p. D1.
6. Tracy Connor, "Divas Shooting from the Lip," *New York Daily News*. August 30, 2002, p. 2.
7. Libby Meader, "There Are No Limits Anymore," *Buffalo News*. September 15, 2003, p. C5.
8. Ben Ratliff, "*American Life*," *Rolling Stone*. April 22, 2003: http://www.rollingstone.com/reviews/album/273997/review/6067443?utm_source=Rhapsody&utm_medium=CDreview.
9. Joey Bartolomeo and Rennie Dyball, "Madonna and Guy Ritchie: How It Fell Apart," *People*. November 3, 2008: p. 54.
10. Ibid.
11. Ibid.
12. Ibid.

CHAPTER 9

1. Rich Cohen, "Madonnarama!" *Vanity Fair*. May 2008: p. 210.
2. Chuck Arnold, "*Hard Candy*," *People*. May 5, 2008: p. 45.

3. "Lady Gaga Fights Madonna, Debuts 'Bad Romance' on *Saturday Night Live*," *Rolling Stone*. October 5, 2009: http://www.rollingstone.com/rockdaily/index.php/2009/10/05/lady-gaga-fights-madonna-debuts-bad-romance-on-saturday-night-live.
4. Christina Everett, "Battle of the Blond Divas! Madonna and Lady Gaga Face Off in Catfight in *Saturday Night Live* Skit," *New York Daily News*. October 4, 2009: http://www.nydailynews.com/gossip/2009/10/04/2009-10-04_madonna_and_lady_gaga_face_off_in_catfight_in_saturday_night_live_skit.html.
5. Skaggs, "Madonna Looks Back," p. 52.
6. Ibid.
7. Jim Yong Kim, "Saving Malawi's Children," *Vanity Fair*. June 2007: http://www.vanityfair.com/politics/features/2007/07/kim200707.
8. Kim, "Saving Malawi's Children."
9. Joseph Kayira and Scott Baldauf, "In Malawi, Uproar Over Madonna and Child," *Christian Science Monitor*. October 19, 2006.
10. "Madonna Gets to Work on Multimillion-Dollar Girls' School in Malawi," *Times* (London). October 27, 2009: http://www.timesonline.co.uk/tol/world/africa/article6891224.ece.
11. Cohen, "Madonnarama!" p. 210.

BIBLIOGRAPHY

Anderson, Jack. "Pearl Lang, Dancer and Choreographer, Dies At 87." *New York Times*, February 27, 2009: p. A21.

Arnold, Chuck. "*Hard Candy*." *People*. Vol. 69, No. 17. (May 5, 2008): p. 45.

Barbanel, Josh. "Madge in the Back of Beyond." *New York Times*, June 26, 2009: p. RE2.

Barnes, John. *Evita, First Lady: A Biography of Eva Perón*. New York: Grove Press, 1978.

Bartolomeo, Joey, and Rennie Dyball. "Madonna and Guy Ritchie: How It Fell Apart." *People*. Vol. 70, No. 18. (November 3, 2008): p. 54.

Berger, Arion. "Madonna: *Erotica*." *Rolling Stone*, November 26, 1992. Available online. URL: http://www.rollingstone.com/reviews/album/130835/review/6067636/erotica.

Burr, Ty. "Madonna Runs Out of Steam." *Boston Globe*, October 24, 2008: p. G9.

Carr, Jay. "*Evita*: More Powerful Than Ever; Both the Musical and Madonna are Transformed on Screen." *Boston Globe*, January 1, 1997: p. C1.

Clark, Mike. "An Arresting '*Tracy*'; Beatty Cops a Stylish Cartoon Coup." *USA Today*, June 14, 1990: p. D1.

Cohen, Rich. "Madonnarama!" *Vanity Fair*. Vol. 50, No. 5. (May 2008): p. 210.

Connor, Tracy. "Divas Shooting from the Lip." *New York Daily News*, August 30, 2002: p. 2.

Dargis, Manohla. "Stripping and Other Noble Pursuits." *New York Times*, October 17, 2008: p. C10.

Duella, Georgia. "Madonna's New Beat is a Hit, But Song's Message Rankles." *New York Times*, September 18, 1986: p. B1.

Dunning, Jennifer. "Still Paying Heed to Graham's Cry." *New York Times*, September 16, 2001: p. B18.

Ebert, Roger. "*Desperately Seeking Susan*." *Chicago Sun-Times*, March 29, 1985. Available online. URL: http://rogerebert.suntimes.com/apps/pbcs.dll/article?AID=/19850329/REVIEWS/503290301/1023.

Everett, Christina. "Battle of the Blond Divas! Madonna and Lady Gaga Face Off in Catfight in *Saturday Night Live* Skit." *New York Daily News*, October 4, 2009. Available online. URL: http://www.nydailynews.com/gossip/2009/10/04/2009-10-04_madonna_and_lady_gaga_face_off_in_catfight_in_saturday_night_live_skit.html.

Felperin, Leslie. "*Filth and Wisdom*." *Variety*, February 14, 2008. Available online. URL: http://www.variety.com/story.asp?l=story&r=VE1117936209&c=-1.

Fetherston, Drew. "Madonna in '*Who's That Girl*,'" *Newsday*, August 8, 1987: p. 7.

Flick, Larry. "WB Expects Madonna to 'Light Up' International Markets. *Billboard*. Vol. 110, No. 8. (February 21, 1998): p. 1.

"The Global Release of Madonna's First Children's Book Makes Publishing History." Calloway Arts & Entertainment news release, September 15, 2003. Available online. URL: http://www.callaway.com/news_091503.htm.

Goldberg, Carole. "Mama Madonna: Her First Kid's Book." *Hartford Courant*, September 16, 2003: p. D1.

Goldberg, Vicki. "Madonna's Book: Sex, and Not Like a Virgin." *New York Times*, October 25, 1992: p. A33.

Goodman, Ellen. "The Pied Piper of Pregnancy." *Boston Globe*, September 23, 1986: p. 19.

Ikenberg, Tamara. "Kabbalah Chameleon: Real Doctrine is More than Madonna's Latest Reinvention." *Louisville Courier-Journal*, August 25, 2004.

Janusoni, Michael. "Madonna's New Movie is a Mission of Mediocrity." *Providence Journal*, August 30, 1986: p. A10.

Johnson, Malcolm. "In Film About Women, Tom Hanks is the Big Hit." *Hartford Courant*, July 1, 1992: p. F1.

Kayira, Joseph, and Scott Baldauf. "In Malawi, Uproar Over Madonna and Child." *Christian Science Monitor*, October 19, 2006.

Kim, Jim Young. "Saving Malawi's Children," *Vanity Fair*, June 2007. Available online. URL: http://www.vanityfair.com/politics/features/2007/07/kim200707.

King, Larry. "Interview With Madonna." CNN.com. October 19, 2002. Available online. URL: http://transcripts.cnn.com/TRANSCRIPTS/0210/19/lklw.00.html.

"Lady Gaga Fights Madonna, Debuts 'Bad Romance' on *Saturday Night Live*." *Rolling Stone*, October 5, 2009. Available online. URL: http://www.rollingstone.com/rockdaily/index.php/2009/10/05/lady-gaga-fights-madonna-debuts-bad-romance-on-saturday-night-live.

Madonna. "Madonna's Private Diaries." *Vanity Fair*. No. 435. (November 1996): p. 176.

"Madonna Gets to Work on Multimillion-Dollar Girls' School in Malawi." *Times of London*, October 27, 2009. Available online. URL: http://www.timesonline.co.uk/tol/world/africa/article6891224.ece.

Matthews, Jack. "It's True . . . It's Daring." *Newsday*, May 10, 1991: p. 82.

"McLean Delighted By New Slice of 'Pie.'" *Albany Times Union*, February 16, 2000: p. A2.

Meader, Libby. "There Are No Limits Anymore." *Buffalo News*, September 15, 2003: p. C5.

"Memorable Quotes From *A League of Their Own*." IMDB.com. Available online. URL: http://www.imdb.com/title/tt0104694/quotes.

Miller, Debby. "*Like a Virgin*." *Rolling Stone*. January 17, 1985. Available online. URL: http://www.rollingstone.com/reviews/album/246700/review/6210108?utm_source=Rhapsody&utm_medium=CDreview.

Morton, Andrew. *Madonna*. New York: St. Martin's Press, 2001.

O'Brien, Lucy, *Madonna: Like an Icon*. New York: Harper Entertainment, 2007.

Pareles, Jon. "Sea of Self-Love, But Who's Drowning?" *New York Times*, July 27, 2001: p. E21.

Prose, Francine. "A Naked Madonna's Raunchy Inspirations." *Newsday*, October 27, 1992: p. 42.

Ratliff, Ben. "*American Life*." *Rolling Stone*, April 22, 2003. Available online. URL: http://www.rollingstone.com/reviews/album/273997/review/6067443?utm_source=Rhapsody&utm_medium=CDreview.

Rooksby, Rikky. *Madonna: The Complete Guide to Her Music*. New York: Omnibus, 2004.

Rozen, Leah. "*Swept Away*." *People*. Vol. 58, No. 17. (October 21, 2002): p. 44.

Scaggs, Austin, "Madonna Looks Back." *Rolling Stone*. (October 29, 2009): p. 47.

Schoemer, Karen, and Yahlin Chang. "A Kinder, Gentler Diva. *Newsweek*. Vol. 131, No. 9. (March 2, 1998): p. 77.

Shewey, Don. "*Madonna.*" *Rolling Stone*. September 29, 1983. Available online. URL: http://www.rollingstone.com/artists/madonna/albums/album/213974/review/6068215/madonna.

Skow, John. "Show Business: Madonna Rocks the Land." *Time*. May 27, 1985. Available online. URL: http://www.time.com/time/magazine/article/0,9171,957012,00.html.

Strauss, Neil. "How Madonna Got Her Groove Back." *Rolling Stone*. No. 988 (December 1, 2005): p. 70.

Taraborrelli, J. Randy. *Madonna: An Intimate Biography*. New York: Simon & Schuster, 2001.

Thomas, Bob. Associated Press, "Madonna, Cruise Take Globes for Acting; *Evita* Wins as Film." *Buffalo News*, January 20, 1997: p. A10.

Victor, Barbara. *Goddess: Inside Madonna*. New York: Harper Entertainment, 2001.

Worrell, Denise. "Now: Madonna on Madonna." *Time*. May 27, 1985. Available online. URL: http://www.time.com/time/magazine/article/0,9171,957025-1,00.html.

FURTHER RESOURCES

BOOKS

Cross, Mary. *Madonna: A Biography*. Westport, Conn.: Greenwood, 2007.

Fearns, Les, and Daisy Fearns. *Argentina*. New York: Chelsea House, 2005.

Fidler, Merrie A. *The Origins and History of the All-American Girls Professional Baseball League*. Jefferson, N.C.: McFarland, 2006.

Morrison, John. *Frida Kahlo*. New York: Chelsea House, 2003.

O'Connell, Jean Gould. *Chester Gould: A Daughter's Biography of the Creator of Dick Tracy*. Jefferson, N.C.: McFarland, 2007.

Perón, Eva, Joseph A. Page, and Laura Dail. *Evita: In My Own Words*. New York: New Press, 1996.

WEB SITES

All-American Girls Professional Baseball League
http://www.aagpbl.org

Evita Perón Historical Research Foundation
http://www.evitaperon.org

Kabbalah Centre, Los Angeles
http://www.kabbalah.com

Madonna's Official Web Site
http://www.madonna.com

U.S. State Department Background Note: Malawi
http://www.state.gov/r/pa/ei/bgn/7231.htm

PICTURE CREDITS

Page

9: AFP PHOTOS/SERGIO GOYA/AFP/Getty Images
16: Newscom
20: Ray Fisher/Time Life Pictures/Getty Images
27: Michael McDonnell/Hulton Archive/Getty Images
37: Richard E. Aaron/Redferns/Getty Images
41: Alamy
48: Getty
53: Newscom
62: Picture Desk
65: AFP PHOTO/Getty Images
71: Rabbani & Solimene/WireImage/Getty Images
76: © THE SCOTSMAN/CORBIS SYGMA
83: Frank Micelotta/Getty Images
93: Frank Micelotta/Getty Images
97: AFP PHOTO/STRINGER/Newscom

INDEX

Y

ABOUT THE AUTHOR

HAL MARCOVITZ is a former newspaper reporter who makes his home in Chalfont, Pennsylvania, with his wife, Gail, and daughter, Ashley. He has written more than 150 books for young readers, including biographies of civil rights leaders Al Sharpton and Eleanor Holmes Norton, farm labor organizer César Chávez, and film director Ron Howard. In 2005, his Chelsea House biography of U.S. House Speaker Nancy Pelosi was named to *Booklist*'s list of recommended feminist books for young readers.

PRINCIPLES OF DANCE AND MOVEMENT NOTATION

Other books by Rudolf Laban

MODERN EDUCATIONAL DANCE
EFFORT *(with F. C. Lawrence, M.C.)*
THE MASTERY OF MOVEMENT
CHOREUTICS

LABAN'S PRINCIPLES OF DANCE AND MOVEMENT NOTATION

by
RUDOLF LABAN

SECOND EDITION
Annotated and edited by
RODERYK LANGE

WITH 114 BASIC MOVEMENT GRAPHS
AND THEIR EXPLANATION

ART WORK BY DIANA BADDELEY

Publishers PLAYS, INC. *Boston*

American edition published by Plays, Inc.
1975

Library of Congress Cataloging in Publication Data

Laban, Rudolf von, 1879–1958.
Laban's principles of dance and movement notation. *Second edition, revised and annotated by Roderyk Lange*. 1st London ed. (Macdonald & Evans) published in 1956 under title: Principles of dance and movement notation.
Includes indexes.
1. Dance notation. 2. Movement notation. I. Title. II. Title: Principles of dance and movement notation.

GV1587.L26 1975 793.3'2 75–11503
ISBN 0–8238–0187–X

Filmset by Northampton Phototypesetters Ltd.
Printed in Great Britain by
J. W. Arrowsmith Ltd.
Bristol

FOREWORD

For many years Macdonald and Evans have devoted themselves to promoting the work of Rudolf Laban. This second edition of *Principles of Dance and Movement Notation*, prepared with their usual care and understanding, reaffirms the enduring worth of Laban's work in the field of kinetography.

Roderyk Lange's task, as revisor, has been to bring the text into line with the many changes that have occurred and are constantly occurring in the interpretation and application of kinetography, while remaining true to the spirit of the original work.

It gives me great pleasure to congratulate Mr. Lange, on behalf of Laban's successors and all enthusiasts of kinetography, upon the high quality of his work. We hope that this book, in its new form, will find the widest possible circulation wherever Laban's kinetography is used.

Roland Laban

Semriach, Austria,
November 1974

CONTENTS

PREFACE TO THE FIRST EDITION

OUR movement and dance notation makes use of the principles on which Beauchamp's and Feuillet's choreography was built up some 300 years ago.*

In a sharp contrast to the fascinating mantic-mystical movement symbolism of thousands of years, Beauchamp and Feuillet created a notation system based on the rational observation of dance movement. The graphic principles which have been kept intact in our notation are the following:

(*a*) The central line separating movements of the right side of the body from those of the left.

(*b*) The partitioning of this middle line by bar-strokes indicating a metrical division of time.

(*c*) The use of directional signs and shape symbols guiding the dancer or moving person in space.

(*d*) The indication of basic body actions, such as gliding, hitting, etc. by special stress signs.

Feuillet's dances were written along a floor pattern line. We have abandoned this and written the movement sequences along a straight line.

While the old notation was restricted mainly to steps and movements of the legs, we have developed a richer vocabulary which includes the movements of the upper parts of the body and the arms, in accordance with the demands of our contemporary free dance forms and the use of notation in other fields, such as industry. A new analysis of the shapes of the movements which the body follows in space and a special stylisation of the directional signs became necessary.†

In the First Part I have acknowledged the work done by the younger generation of dance notators in the practical development of our dance script after it found its final form.

* Beauchamp's rights as inventor of his dance-notation were recognised by an act of the French parliament in 1666. Feuillet published dances written in this notation around 1700.

† The essential parts of this analysis and the struggle to establish the new directional signs are described in my book *Choreographie, i.e.* first volume, published by Diederichs, Jena, 1926.

The final graphic solution was laid down in my book *Schrifttanz* published by Universal Editions, (Vienna 1928).

In this Preface, I wish to acknowledge the great help given to me by pupils and assistants who worked with me at the time of my early experiments, and to other people in various occupations who have taken an interest in my work.

I am thinking especially of the sensitive and inspiring advice received from an excellent dancer, my late friend and colleague, Dussia Bereska. In the earlier part of this century she was the first and only supporter of my work in this field and she predicted the present development and success of notation with acute foresight.

With her fine sense of the flow of movement, Dussia Bereska had a deciding influence on the rhythmical partitioning of Feuillet's metrical bar line intervals. Her suggestion that the symbols might be written in different lengths to indicate the relative duration of each movement was an innovation which is still an outstanding feature of our notation today. I was at that period inclined to condense simultaneous bodily actions around a nucleus having the form of a cross. It is perhaps interesting to mention that this cross sign became later the basic symbol of my effort notation developed for the recording of body actions in industrial operations connected with the notation of psychosomatic states and inner attitudes. I was most encouraged and stimulated by the advice and suggestion of the first script enthusiasts. I will mention here Kurt Jooss, who, after finishing his studies as a pupil of Bereska and myself, surprised us one day with the proposal to duplicate Feuillet's right-left division of the movement sequences. We proceeded then to record the movements of trunk and arms in separate columns instead of inserting them in the upper part of the cross mentioned beforehand. This again has become, with some adaptations, a specific feature of our notation.

How much I am indebted, not so much for technical advice as for the inspiration and insight into choreographic matters given to me by many dancers and dance producers, can be only briefly touched upon here. When I mention a few of these people, it is because I have discussed with them not only the problems of dance script but also of script dance, the interpretation of written dances. Diaghilev and Fokine, and other prominent members of the Russian ballet and other ballet groups, encouraged me in the attempt to create a library of written dances. This is, after all, one of the main uses which the notation has to serve.

I remember also a great number of prominent musicians with whom I had fruitful discussions on this matter. I had the great fortune of having my choreographic creations accompanied by orchestras conducted by Toscanini, Furtwängler, Bruno Walter, Erich Kleiber and other famous

musicians, with whom I was able to try out practically the combination of written dance and written music.

My late friend, Siegfried Wagner, the son of Richard Wagner, opened the archives of his father to me, and I discovered to my great surprise the minute care with which this genius composed and notated the movements of all the characters of his casts.

I had the opportunity of reviving his notated movement creations, not only in dance scenes, such as the Tannhäuser Bacchanal, but also in singing parts, for the performances in Bayreuth of several of his music dramas.

When, finally, I express my indebtedness to the scientists, educationists, doctors and industrialists whom I have been able to help with my script in their studies of movement and in its practical application in schools, factories and hospitals, I can do so here in general terms only. My work in all these fields, besides strengthening my conviction of the great practicality and necessity of movement notation, has given me many technical hints which have been incorporated in the final formulation of the script.

Noverre, who in his "ballets d'action" created a free form of stage movement 200 years ago, was an enemy of dance notation because it was mainly used for the description of steps and leg movements. Beauchamp's and Feuillet's initiative has, however, opened much wider horizons than Noverre suspected. We now live to see that the adaptation of dance script to movement in general, as it is attempted in our notation, brings us more friends than enemies.

I am grateful not only to all our friends, but also to our enemies, who have involuntarily helped to overcome the initial weaknesses of the great vision of a literature of movement and dance, with its own language and its own symbolic representation of an important manifestation of the human spirit.

RUDOLF LABAN

Studio Lodge,
Addlestone,
Surrey.
April 1955.

PREFACE TO THE SECOND EDITION

LABAN'S initial ideas on a dance script are contained in his book *Choreographie* (Jena, 1926). An already completed outline of his notation system is presented in his publication *Schrifttanz* (Vienna, 1928). This was followed by a span of 28 years of further developments in his kinetography. Over that period Laban's notation system has been applied practically in many fields (education, ergonomic studies, rehabilitation, anthropology, theatre). Yet it was 1956 before Laban decided to publish the outlines of kinetography to document his invention. The result is the present book, which he entitled *Principles of Dance and Movement Notation.*

Of course, the system was constantly developing over the years involving contributions from many people. Textbooks of kinetography written by Laban's followers have appeared: *Labanotation* by Ann Hutchinson, New Directions Books, New York, 1954; *Abriss der Kinetographie Laban* by Albrecht Knust, Das Tanzarchiv, Hamburg, 1956, English translation *ibid* 1958; *Practical Kinetography Laban* by Valerie Preston-Dunlop, Macdonald & Evans Ltd., London 1969 being the main ones. The system has been widened; many analytical problems have been solved following the expansion of kinetography into different specialised areas.

Albrecht Knust has added to the system a big, new chapter on the notation of group movements. His *Encyclopaedia of Kinetography* written mainly in 1946–50 contains a wealth of evidence material (8 volumes, 2400 pages and 20,000 examples) supporting the foundation and rules of kinetography. This work has unfortunately not yet been published.

Shortly before and during World War II some differences arose because of the isolation between the different centres. The unification action carried on after the war by the International Council of Kinetography Laban has now nearly eliminated vital differences existing between the European "Kinetography" and the American "Labanotation." Even if small differences exist between different centres or even individual authors of kinetographic scores, the differing versions can still be read.

What is so remarkable is that the basic principles and the basic signs as invented by Laban have not been changed. They proved to be right and Laban could justifiably state in his book:

> ". . . throughout the whole of this period the fundamental signs that I invented have remained unaltered, which proves that the

underlying principles of the system as first devised by me are sound and practical " (p. 1)

In publishing this book Laban was first of all concerned with presenting the functional aspect of his notation system. During successive developments, many new areas and possibilities have been explored but sometimes one became, possibly, too remote from the intended compactness of the system itself. In this situation, it is surely appropriate that we should be reminded of the underlying principles of the system. It is this which makes the book even more relevant today. Developments are necessary, but they have, of course, to follow consequently and logically the rules of movement analysis. What is noteworthy is that Laban has had in mind the general principles underlying any kind of movement notation (p. 17). He states:

> "Our movement notation is based on the elementary motor principles of the human body " (p.11).

Kinetography is a *movement script* which secures the recording of movement progression. It has to represent the dynamic content inherent in movement not merely to provide an external picture (p. 4). This point is actually the asset of Laban's kinetography in comparison with many of the existing notation systems.

To be able to analyse movement properly one has to think in terms of movement. Movement is logically structured according to the functions of the human body in space and time and this has to be understood. Laban says in conjunction with this:

> "Very often it is not necessary to notate all the effects of movement contributing to a final effect " (p. 18).

Many details evolve out of a certain movement context and it is up to the notator to understand these connections when analysing movement. Therefore kinetography is devised in a way that if one thing is happening the other is automatically excluded (for example if both legs are gesturing one cannot put the bodyweight on them. Therefore no signs will be written in the support columns). This mirrors the functions of the body in space and time.

Of course, detailed description will be introduced according to the purpose of the recording. Laban also strongly stresses the necessity of understanding the signs of the script as having actual counterparts in real movement possibilities of the human body:

> "The motion characters of the script are compounded according to simple orthographical considerations which we have learned to appreciate in the long exercise of our experimental notation

activity " (p. 13).

The signs are symbols of a completed logical system and they respond to strict ranges of ideas. Any thoughtless mixing of symbol categories will cause a chain-reaction of inconsistencies. Therefore utmost care should be taken in developing and incorporating new signs:

> "A script can become universal only if its basic principles are clearly defined and its essence kept free from contamination " (p. 12).

In preparing the second edition of this book, we have decided to leave Laban's text unchanged, removing or adjusting a few points only which have been outdated or correcting evident mistakes which crept in on a few occasions (*e.g.* "four steps" instead of "five" as indicated by the kinetogram etc.).

The text of the First Part may appear a little old-fashioned and "central European" in style. Also, Laban uses metaphors and anecdotes to colour his discourse (*e.g.* the story of the stars' motion to be notated), but this does not affect the presentation of the principles of his system, which was his concern. For this reason all these digressions have been left as Laban wished them to appear. It gives a personal, and already a period touch to it.

The original text of the whole Second Part has been changed as little as possible. Instead annotations have been provided concurrently with Laban's text. Any differences which have been introduced since Laban's book first appeared have been dealt with. Any of the existing differences between the American (LAB) and European (KIN) schools have been pointed out.

Equipped in this way, the book is more accessible to all practitioners of Laban's system.

RODERYK LANGE

Les Bois,
St. Peter,
Jersey.
November 1974.

First Part

Movement notation and the fields of its application

My dance and movement notation has now been before the public since the 1930s, and I am proud of three facts. The first is that throughout the whole of this period the fundamental signs that I invented have remained unaltered, which proves that the underlying principles of the system as first devised by me are sound and practical. The second is that quite a large number of people have specialised in the work of notating dances, exercises and movements of artistic, educational, industrial and therapeutic nature, and by the practice of this new profession have added a useful store of knowledge and experience to my first experiments. The third fact, for which I am even more grateful than I am justly proud, is that I have lived to see several excellent dance creations of our time preserved for coming generations by being written down in my notation. In the many fields where this script is used, improvements have been effected in movement processes and techniques, together with clarifications of their practical and spiritual content, and both these desirable improvements have been secured because it has been possible to study and compare the written scores of recorded movement.

Fully a quarter of a century before the first publication of my system, I began to experiment with the idea of writing down movements as one writes words or music. Initially I had nothing more in mind than to record for my personal use, by a few meaningful scribbles, the steps or gestures I had invented, mainly for my large orchestral dance compositions.

Later, this embryo notation was made to serve my personal needs on a much larger scale. Besides scoring numerous opera ballets, my colleagues and I transcribed into this notation several large communal dance-plays which were then produced directly from it. In conjunction with my friend Knust, I wrote the movement score of a festival play for a thousand performers, and sent the notation to sixty towns from which the performers at the festival meeting were drawn. As our scores had been studied by the sixty local groups, the whole thousand people were able to dance together at the first rehearsal, performing not only the main motifs, but the whole rather elaborate choreography, lasting two hours, with very few mistakes or interruptions.

A few years later, notations were made of all the job-movements used by the employees of a big estate in their various activities. We surveyed and notated agricultural operations as well as those used in forestry, the mills, and the workshops connected with the estate. The subsequent analysis was used to improve work methods, to train apprentices, and to select operators as well as managers. How is this possible? For the simple reason that movement, when looked at by a trained observer and notator, reveals far more than a purely physical action.

The general public knows next to nothing of the principles of dance notation, or the large-scale applications of this important activity. Except to a few professional practitioners of movement, such as expert dancers, dance teachers, time and motion study engineers, physiotherapists and so on, the idea of a dance notation still appears to the mass of people as strange now as it did to me at the beginning of this century. I feel therefore that I must add an explanatory introduction to this brief exposition of the basic movement notation signs. Let me, then, start from the simplest premises.

Few people, when watching a dancer, will trouble to think much about what is actually happening in their own, or in the dancer's mind. Here, for example, is a child capering about more or less rhythmically, perhaps humming a tune while she does so. One would be inclined, according to temper and circumstances, either to be annoyed at the exhibition or to smile indulgently at the child's antics, and even derive a certain pleasure from them. One might perhaps comment mentally, "How clumsy!" or "How graceful!" A similar reaction might occur if one unexpectedly came upon a crowd of adults amusing themselves by performing their national dances. One might be neither annoyed nor bored, but actually enjoy the sight. Reflecting vaguely on the general mood which the dancers suggest, they might seem to the observer to be gay, or sad, or expressive of more mixed emotions. The dancers might sing while they dance, and it would be understood that they enjoy repeating some simple story of lyrical or dramatic worth. If we are very observant, we go beyond thinking, "How clumsy!" or "How graceful!" and begin to appreciate the appropriateness of the movement invention underlying the idea of the dance. Some performers may indulge in fiercely aggressive steps and body attitudes, while the movements of others may suggest modesty and gentleness. The story may be mimed, but not in a straightforward way as in dumb acting; instead, the moods and events are translated into the language of dance, in which all manner of leaps, twists, turns and other bodily movements occur that no one would use

in everyday life.

To observe people dancing for their own enjoyment is a different experience from that derived from attending a ballet executed by professional dancers. First of all, we have paid for our ticket in order to get entertainment, and maybe also some elation, from the show. The spectator of a theatrical dance performance is also more consciously receptive and critical than the casual observer of an impromptu dance. He will still react to clumsiness or grace of movement, and will also appreciate the appropriateness or otherwise of the movement invention to the theme of the dance. But besides this he will expect to be uplifted or enraptured by what he sees. If his desire is not gratified, he leaves the theatre dissatisfied, or at least with the empty feeling of having wasted the evening. Rapture and exultation may of course result from watching amateurs, but not necessarily. The amateurs dance for their own pleasure, and are under no obligation to please anyone but themselves. We see, therefore, that dancing involves invention, execution, and spiritually vitalising effects. Of these three requisites, the first, invention, interests us most at this point. This part of the content of the dance is most subject to human control. Weak and imperfect invention make a good execution, and the resulting exaltation, more difficult for the dancer than does a strong, well-devised composition. The same is true of drama and music. They must be well-invented and clearly composed in order to give the performing artist a suitable basis for his rendering of the work. Up to now dance compositions, unlike poetical and musical compositions, have rarely been written down in an intelligible form. This does not mean that dances have not been well composed. Ballets of extraordinary beauty and vital power have been invented, but, after relatively few performances, have passed into oblivion. When the original inventors and performers had disappeared, the dances could not be reproduced as dramatic and musical works could be from the libretto or the musical score. Put briefly, there is no real literature of dance, although a whole lot of books have been published about dancing in general, and the personalities involved. No faultless descriptions of valuable dances and ballets exist, although the necessity for notated editions of them is obvious to every dancer of distinction.

The several attempts that have been made to write down sequences of steps and gestures in graphical signs have remained relatively unfruitful. Their crudity reminds us of the early stages of script before our present alphabet had been evolved. Rough pictures of objects and hieroglyphs were used to describe the essential events, but to express

thought in its subtler nuances requires the phonetic notation of the sounds of speech. We would not know anything about Homer's epics, and other great works of the ancient poets, had they not been written down in phonetic signs; and the same is true of music. Indeed, we do not know anything about the music of the ancients, because no generally acknowledged musical notation of any value existed in antiquity. The invention of the conventional musical signs in which the works of composers have been recorded in the last few centuries, has made it possible for us moderns to perform the works of the great musicians of past ages, which otherwise would long ago have been forgotten. Lacking any system of musical notation, Bach and Beethoven would be no more than silent names to us. Yet nobody knows about the exact movement forms of ballets even of recent origin, though fame proclaims the names of the choreographers, and the appreciation with which their ballets were received in their time.

A new and generally acceptable dance notation comparable with the phonetic alphabet had to be built up. Pictures or diagrams of the external shapes of bodily positions and movements will not serve the ultimate purpose of notating the spiritual content of dances. It is true that one has to show in a notated dance which part of the body has been moved and its position after it has moved. It is also true that the precise time taken for each movement has to be recorded. But all this must be done in such a way that the essential feature of a dance, namely its flow of movement, is described in all its details.

The basic material of dance notation is the motion characters from which it is built up. An example will make clear the dependence of the new dance script on the motion structure. Take the conventional gesture of nodding to express assent; this could be described as "a bending of the head and neck forwards, followed by a relifting of the head into its normal position." One could easily find a graphic sign to depict the external form of this movement, and by adding to it a short or long musical note one could also express the relative speed of the nod. However, in the context of the whole flow of the movement, this nodding might acquire many differing shades of significance. It need not always remain an acquiescent sign of assent. It might express submission, shame, dejection, concentration, misgiving, hostility, and many other feelings. Such significations become clearer if the movements of other parts of the body are marked simultaneously. If, for instance, one or several steps in any direction are indicated at the same time as the nodding, and perhaps other movements as well, such as bending, turning or stretching the

arms, hands or trunk, the movement acquires a specific inner significance. When there is a combination of two or more of these movements, the whole chord of several movements will mean something entirely different each time. In most of these cases, the nodding will be divested of its conventional significance, *i.e.* assent, and will become part of a movement expression which cannot be translated immediately into simple words. For the language of movement consists only to a very small extent of conventional signs, replacing, as it were, words and phrases. The main bulk of movement and dance expression consists of motor elements, which can be freely combined to reveal something about the inner state of the moving person. Whether a person uses the language of movement for self-expression, liberation or enjoyment, or for the purpose of communicating with other people, is irrelevant to the present argument.

A generally acknowledged and readable notation of movement, based on the combination of motion characters, is needed today, not only for ballet but for all forms of dancing, and also for dramatic and practical movement studies.

The necessity for an adequate script is more urgent now even than it was because movement study has come to be recognised as a most important feature in industry, education and therapy. In all three fields a rich tradition of movement knowledge is running to waste, since many bodily actions and exercises cannot be preserved. We cannot rely solely on people's memory of movements; nor can the choreographer rely upon his memory, for he might have excellent ideas which he cannot use at the moment, and when the opportunity eventually comes when he can use them, he may find that the ideas have entirely escaped his mind.

Why is it that dancing has not found an adequate and generally accepted form of notation, as have music and poetry? One reason is, doubtless, the lack of a universal movement terminology. Such a terminology, together with a universal notation form, would enable everybody interested in movement to write down, not only occasional ideas for gestures and steps, but also whole ballets. Dance ideas fixed in script could be transmitted to other interested people at any distance in space or time. People in distant countries, as well as future generations, could have the benefit of reading movement ideas and become judges of their artistic or general value. By exchanging movement ideas, tastes and opinions on dance would be clarified, and an apparatus of criticism built up.

The introduction of a dance notation system would mean a revolution

in production and performance. Dancers would no longer be restricted to studying and performing their own inventions, or to relying on the imagination of a ballet master who happened to be at hand. Dancers could take their choice from the works of many gifted dance-authors, of whom they had no personal knowledge. Those who invent movement works which they are unable to or do not want to perform themselves could write them down and submit them to the judgment of the entire dancing world.

The two professions, namely the dance-author and the dancer, would probably become separated. It is easy to see that such a separation would provide good solutions to many of the problems of the modern dance stage. The dance public would be much enriched if they were able to see compositions of famous choreographers interpreted by specially talented performers. Anyone who reads press criticisms will agree that any criticism of a theatrical work, no matter whether it is drama, poetry or music, is enormously enhanced in value by consulting the book or score. But the ballet critic is not able to study the composition thoroughly from its score and compare it with the interpretation, at least not yet. He has to concentrate on the performance, and therefore often stresses mere technicalities without appreciating the theme and content of the work. The dance-author, the actual writer of a dance work, would be able to view his work more objectively when it was on paper, and had not as yet been interpreted by an unfortunate dancer who had perhaps spent much hard work staging an invention which might prove unsuitable. A written score would provide greater opportunity for comparing the various parts of a ballet with one another, and for polishing the composition in detail by excising the weaker parts, and by adding necessary variations.

After all, dance as an art cannot be based on spontaneous improvisations only. Movement compositions, as well as poetry and music, have to be carefully constructed and built up according to the general rules of artistic composition. The profound mistake of considering the charming movements of a handsome body as an indication of the artistic value of a dance creation is entirely obsolete today. The development of a movement idea through different logical stages is nowadays the only true criterion of the worth of a dance. Intelligent and tasteful presentation is a factor to be clearly distinguished from creative invention.

A notation based on the combination of motion characters makes it possible to write down all styles of dance, including classical ballet. Ballets of every style use movements built up from the same motor

elements. The variety of movement which can be built up from them is almost infinite, and any style with a limited number of variations, whether self-imposed or traditional, must of necessity build its movement forms out of these basic constituents of movement. Just as poetry, in every language, can be written down phonetically, so every stylised movement can be written down "motorically." The motor movement notation is the equivalent of the alphabet. It is, however, only a new principle of notation, not of dance expression or stylisation.

The most widely known product of the art of movement is the ballet. It arose out of the interplay of two distinct desires for showing movement, one leading to dance and the other to mime. Expressed in other words, pure movement as an expression of man's ineffable spirit is here contrasted with movement as a mirror of man's behaviour and actions in life as lived. Movement notation can serve both dance and mime. Historically, dance was probably the first form of movement expression, mime developing later. In rituals and tribal folklore, people tried to realise their higher selves by dramatising what they thought were their chief values and virtues, passing from strength, courage and optimism, to the ideals rooted in enthusiasm, love and sacrifice, and even to religious trance. All the unfathomable impulses and efforts of man became the content of dances. We still see today, in the relics of national dances, the embodiment of tribal ideals, exultation and pride, loveliness, gaiety or langour, cherished differently by each race according to its physical and psychical make-up. Man aspires to be something greater than he is, and knows that he can acquire the greatness that he covets, if only during the imaginative moments when he is lifted above himself in dance. Whether the sincere repetition of such dances produces deeper effects than this, and whether man's spirit is really strengthened by the decision to become his own better self, is an open question. I think we may learn more about this over the years, if we accustom ourselves to notating and pondering the structure of human movements.

At a later stage, dancers tried to represent heroes, gods and kings, and enact the story of their adventures. This enchantment of the personality, as it were by proxy, is without doubt an inner process different from that in pure or personal dancing. When mime became more refined, it dissolved dance movements into conventional gestures, thus disguising man's deeper wish for enhancement. Some two hundred years ago, a revolution against the artificial gesture-language, which had been fostered in the court ballets of the period, led to a fashion for passionate and over-emphatic behaviour on the stage. The names of the

great ballet choreographers, Noverre, Vigano, Angolini and others are associated with this revolt. But they could not, or would not, abolish the mime form, and tried to compete with the great tragedy and comedy of the dramatic theatre. Probably plenty of movement still remained in these "ballets d'action," but nothing of it has come down to us because of the lack of an adequate dance notation.

The dance theatre then retired into the sweet coolness of the romantic fairy-tale, in which it still sometimes indulges. Today, there are signs that the struggle for the enhancement of the personality in pure dancing may be revived, but we cannot follow up the actual history of dance styles and dance contents, because we have inherited no real "motor picture" of them. The inaccessible and valuable content of movement and dance, which cannot be explained in words, needs some form of description, and this can only be based on the motor facts of bodily action.

The dancer who wishes to express an inner state of mind or mood has to use the motor elements in definite order. Dance, like music, has its harmony, which does not consist only of soft, sweet expressions, but embraces all motor elements, including dissonant elements. It is a matter of personal taste whether a modern dance author breaks down sweetness into discord, or liberates grotesqueness by leading it into well-shaped harmony. Most modern choreographers use every facet of human experience, with the obvious intention of awakening in the spectator a heightened sense of the tension in life. This enlivening of the spectator by the free use of the innumerable shades and variations of life tension is perhaps the most valuable aspect of pure dancing on the stage at the present day. Yet whatever content of dance the composer may choose, and whatever style of presentation he may favour, he cannot really succeed in transmitting it to future generations if he does not build it with the bricks of the elementary motor faculties of the human body which remain unchanged throughout all ages. The procedure of the dance composer must be similar to that of the poet, who, no matter what his native tongue or subject of discourse may be, must build his words on the simplest phonetic faculties of the human voice. Although it is obvious that the words and phrases of the language of movement (for so the shapes and rhythms of dance may be called) have no determinable verbal meaning, they are nevertheless subject to an ordered principle, namely the balanced flow and harmony of movement. The structure and function of the body limits the number of movements which the human being can perform. We are not able to fly like birds, nor do we normally jump about on our heads as some clowns may do in the circus, and we

suffer many other limitations because of the structure and function of our bodies and minds; but we have the instinct of self-preservation, and therefore prefer movements which are conducive to physical and mental safety rather than those which would endanger body and soul. We are proud of our erect carriage, which both symbolises and guarantees our supremacy over the beasts; we like to keep a balance, and to use our "tentacles," the arms and hands, to satisfy our needs and desires. We attract, and are attracted by, that which we love, and repulse, and are repulsed by, anything hostile. In sleep, we close our eyes and relax our muscles, while we are full of interest and activity when awake. Our facial expression and bodily carriage can indicate morosity or cheerfulness according to our inner mood, but we can also feign moods, and hide our thoughts behind our movements, just as we can feign the loss of our normal balance in miming a drunkard's gait. We can be sincere or false in movement, and, curiously enough, it is by our movements that people are often made aware of our insincerity.

All this a good observer is able to write down in motor symbols. Movement events in our inner and outer life have a spiritual significance, and can be rendered in movement notation with more exactitude than when they are described in words. A skilled reader of movement notation can not only understand what the body of the dancer does, but he can shudder or smile on deciphering the mental and emotional contents of the symbols. Just as a skilled musician is able to hear with the inner ear the melody as he scans it in a musical score, so a skilled dancer can see with his inner eye the movements of the human body while reading the dance notation.

The striking thing is that the notation consists solely of a few signs, representing the elementary motor faculties of man, combined in various ways. The two score letters of the alphabet, with punctuation marks, are sufficient in most languages to write down all our thoughts. Barely two score signs are needed to depict all our movements, and to create permanent records of the whole content of ballets and dances. It must be stressed that we see not signs of shapes only, but also signs of rhythms. The latter are often considered solely as audible phenomena, an assumption which is certainly not true in dancing. By looking at any poetry of movement other than European ballet, the folk-lore of remote races, for example, one becomes intensely aware of the importance of rhythm in dance expression. It is true that this rhythm is usually made audible by the accompanying drumming or music, or, rather, that audible and visible rhythms become a unity in dance. The legend that the Indian

God Shiva danced the "Tandava" (Dance of Creation) to the rhythm of "The Sacred Drum" clearly reveals the part which rhythm plays in the movement content. The sacred drum is the symbol of that eternal vibration which has been thought to be the creative power ruling the world. The shapes of dance movements are visual patterns, which have in their flux and flow a visible rhythm. The spectator recognises the counterplay of definite mental states of balance and harmony as he watches the external shapes and rhythms of the dancer's body.

Javanese dancing originated from the shadow-plays, in which the contours of mobile marionettes are projected on a screen. In the drama, the puppets do not represent people but are symbols of human qualities and moral capacities. It is perhaps of interest to remark that dance and drama performed by living beings was introduced in Java as a spectacle as recently as two hundred years ago. It was a long time before the Javanese acquired a taste for watching living performances, and many of them still prefer the shadow-plays of their puppets. Is it because these shadows show purer movement than the living performer? The Javanese did, however, dance by themselves before they became reconciled to dance as a spectacle. If one dances alone one cannot see one's own movements, but one feels the motor action stimulating rhythmic vibration, and, added to it, the sense of the shape and pattern which the body draws in the air.

The sense of activity which one gets from dancing by oneself is essentially different from the relatively passive receptivity of the spectator of dancing. This explains why dance was for a long time in human history—or rather in human pre-history—a paramount means of education and therapy. In order to take advantage of the beneficial vibrations experienced in the shapes and rhythms of dance, the dance teacher or practitioner has to know more about the vibrations of movements and the basic motor rules which they obey.

Knowledge of this kind is in my opinion the best introduction to creating and understanding movement notation. As a basic motor script, movement notation can have various purposes. Some time ago, time and motion study used in industry to regulate working movement had to be amended as a result of investigations then being made into human effort. For this purpose dance notation proved to be a most appropriate aid. In assessing the physical and mental capacities of a person for a specific task, his habitual movement forms can give clear indications of his ability or otherwise to perform it, and, with other tests, build up a complete picture of his personality; and from the analysis of the movement notation

he can easily be placed into a suitable job.

Our movement notation is based on the elementary motor principles of the human body, and can be applied to a larger range of activities, which in turn has assisted its rapid dissemination. I have in justice to speak of *our* notation, for though I discovered the principles and invented the basic symbols, I could never have established it unaided, and successfully developed the final version. The struggle for the recognition of the pressing necessity for a basic dance notation serving all movement purposes is centred round a few people who are best called movement notators. The present notation form has been built up and tried out mainly in Europe and America. There are professional notators and interested persons all over the world, but they are all working in connection with one of three main groups.

The senior notator is Albrecht Knust, who has recorded the results of his extensive investigations into the motor rules of human body functions in a standard work of eight volumes, which still awaits publication. I have to acknowledge here Knust's generosity in allowing me to use his rich collection of basic notation examples in preparing this book. Knust has transcribed in our notation a number of ballets and many choral dance works besides a host of folk dances, some of them of exotic origin, from many countries.

Ann Hutchinson, and her staff of the Dance Notation Bureau in New York, have the great advantage of witnessing in that cauldron of all races a large number of dances in every style. The most active American stage dancers have taken up our notation as an instrument urgently needed in the profession, and this is largely due to the work of Ann Hutchinson. It may be mentioned here that the American group calls our system "Labanotation."

In England, Lisa Ullmann, and Sigurd Leeder in Switzerland, together with an appreciable circle of fellow movement notators, are spreading the use of the script in general and theatrical education. They emphasise the value of notating movement exercises and educational dance studies. All active notators are used to stressing the importance of notation as a means of keeping choreographic invention free from distortion by busy imitators. Besides the practical issues connected with the copyright of dance works, the use of notation has the effect of preserving the integrity of original works.

It is in this sphere of aesthetic property rights that the notators' fight has been fiercest, with the result that today our notation is officially recognised as a means of obtaining copyright for works on the art of

movement.

A script can become universal only if its basic principles are clearly defined and its essence kept free from contamination. It is inevitable that some small differences should have appeared in the way of writing. The two main centres, the Dance Notation Bureau in New York and the Kinetographisches Institut in Essen, have developed the notation according to their particular needs, and since means of communication were lacking during the war years, it is only comparatively recently that the opportunity has arisen to discuss these divergencies and to try to resolve them. This process of integration is now well under way, but the student should be aware of the slight variations so that he experiences no difficulty when reading a script whatever its source.

There are one or two minor variations which occur only when the movement is very stylised, or when it is necessary to write in minute detail. One is worth mentioning by way of example: the sign descriptive of a very light movement. All the variations are still based fundamentally on the original sign which I proposed twenty-five years ago, namely a comma, but in Europe it has been developed into an angular comma, while in America it has been rounded. Such small differences exist even in the ordinary spelling of words in the two continents. However, everybody is still able to read both versions.

One of the second generation of movement notators, Valerie Preston-Dunlop, to whom I am indebted for her help in arranging the examples in this book, has undertaken the meritorious task of acting as a communication officer between the various Notation Centres.

The special application which movement notation has found in industry has developed from the fact that dancers frequently handle objects and tools, *i.e.* stage properties, when on the stage. The close connection between the movements made when handling stage properties and those used in industrial operations is obvious. It was therefore not difficult to describe the workmen's task-movements in our notation, notwithstanding the differences between the stage and the industrial scripts. An essential point here is that the rhythmic-dynamic signs of my script had to be dovetailed into a more elaborate form for the special industrial purpose, where scientific analysis of the movement is the first and last consideration. The rhythmic-dynamic signs in stage script, whose aim is to describe rather than to investigate, could be kept more simple than the same sort of signs in industry, where they are used for analysing and notating the efforts of workers performing specific tasks, or undergoing movement tests, the tests being made to determine the

competence of the worker to perform a specific job.

Since the late 1940s, Frederic Charles Lawrence, the eminent business consultant, co-author with myself of the book *Effort* (MacDonald & Evans Ltd., London, 1947, 2nd ed. 1974), has introduced our specialist notation form into industry as a tool of the effort-assessor.

The psychological factors involved in movement notation, whether dealing with artistic work on the stage or with training in trade schools, technical institutes and factories, have made it possible to extend the use of the script to psycho-therapeutic investigation.

These fascinating sidelines branching off from dance notation have to be mentioned here in order to assign all the various applications to their right places. A person once asked me whether my notation might soon not be used for recording the movements of the stars in the sky. I was glad to assure him that no such invasion into the astronomer's domain was contemplated, for the simple reason that our movement notation could be used only to describe and analyse human movement. Still, the continuous emergence of brilliant new stage stars might for all I know offer the movement notator of the future a welcome subject for a fascinating whole-time study.

The motion characters of the script are compounded according to simple orthographical considerations which we have learned to appreciate in the long exercise of our experimental notation activity. Knust has collected in his great standard work some 20,000 basic movement graphs. This should not frighten anyone, for a modern dictionary contains some 40,000 to 50,000 words with explanations.

Such graphs represent something like the sound combinations of language which constitute words. In the examples given in this book I can give less than a hundredth part of Knust's collection, but I hope that despite its fragmentariness it will provide an introductory vocabulary of use to the ever-increasing number of friends of our notation, both those who are professionally connected with the art of the dance and also the ever-growing number of dance lovers and those interested in this new field of aesthetics and harmony.

Second Part

Introducing the necessity for thinking in terms of movement and the explanations of the graphs

MOVEMENT notation is a guide to the performance of definite movements depicted in a series of graphic symbols. The writing and reading of notation necessitates an exact knowledge of the signs by which the details of the flow of movement in the body are indicated.

Movement notation gives therefore more than a description in words could offer. Verbal explanation is bound to be much too long-winded for the stimulation of immediate performance. The reading of the notation graphs involves a certain amount of spelling of the successive details, but this spelling has to become fairly automatic, so that the whole complex of a motif is almost instantaneously absorbed and translated into action. The feel of movement preceding the performance is a mental act.

It is perhaps useful to stress the complexity of trying to explain a movement in words. Even with very simple motions, and even if they are described in a kind of telegram-style, it is very difficult to express the essentials of a movement precisely. Take, for instance, a "step." We have to ask immediately which leg is stepping, and arrive perhaps at the statement that it is a "right step." Considering next the direction of space into which the step is done, we might expand this to a "right step forward." We have to state now whether it is a large or a small step, and decide finally that it is a "right step forward of normal size"—which means that it is neither excessively long nor particularly short. Now comes the duration of the step. It is possible to perambulate in a slow dignified manner or to hurry hastily along, almost running. But this is not all; time-durations are relative to one another, and we have to know whether the step in question is quicker or slower than the other steps preceding or following it. If we know that it is quicker, we also want to know how much quicker it is. Our verbal description will then have to be expanded in the following way: "right step forward of normal size, twice as quick (or slow) as the preceding (or following) steps." We are not yet at the end of our enquiry, because it has still to be said whether the step ends in a standing position on a bent or a normally stretched leg, or whether the leg is elevated on the ball of the foot or on the toe. When this information is added to our description, it will in the chosen case run

as follows: "Right step forward of normal size and half the duration of the previous one, landing on the ball of the foot with stretched knee."

When we consider that all this can be expressed in a notation graph by *one single sign* or motion character, we will understand that the eye and the mind can absorb this picture not only much more quickly, but also as a single incentive to perform the movement without that mental reflection which is detrimental to spontaneous action.

One step is, of course, only a tiny part of a movement motif, in which several steps of different character might occur, accompanied perhaps by simultaneous arm gestures and expressive positions of the head and the hands. It is quite impossible to express in words the subtle co-ordination and relationships of several movements otherwise than in a very long-winded sentence. Nobody would be able to condense what he has read into a sudden and clear perception of the movement, inaugurating its immediate performance.

A motif, that is, a sequence of motions, is depicted in notation on a graph, condensed on the paper into a relatively small space which can be seen in one glimpse; and after a short training of the eye, such a graph can be simultaneously absorbed and interpreted.

The essential requirement for this is to learn to think in terms of movement. If it is desired to give a short survey of the principles of dance and movement notation, it is necessary to awaken this sort of thinking in the reader's mind. In my experience, the simple tabulation of the symbols, that is, the mere presentation of an alphabet of the letters of the language of movement, cannot serve this purpose adequately.

The presentation of the principal symbols of notation attempted in the following sections of this booklet might make uninspiring reading as far as the text is concerned. It is impossible to give such an explanation any literary charm. The strange world of the logic of movement has to be elucidated in its own terms and without even using the professional jargon of the dancer or the industrialist.

The essential text of the second part of this book consists, therefore, of the graphs of movements and motifs, while the verbal description of a few fundamental movement ideas and their symbols has to remain rather accidental.

There exist detailed orthographic conventions of writing used in the theatre, the factory, the school and in remedial work. Different movement motifs stand in the foreground of interest in each one of these professional applications of the script. It is true that aesthetic harmony, economy of effort or psychological significance can be found in any application of

the notation to a special purpose, but the stress on one or another of the characteristics of movement will change with the different final aims of the various occupations for which the recording is used.

We do not deal here with these specialised orthographies, but with the general principles underlying any kind of movement notation.

Before turning to the explanations of the movement graphs, some of these general principles will be briefly mentioned.

The flow of movement is felt in the body as a minor or major motion of the muscles of one or several parts of the body, and sometimes of the whole body.

This flow is seen by an observer in its result or effect as a slight or large displacement in space of one or several parts of the body, and sometimes of the whole body. What is first noticed by the observer and felt by the moving person is the slight movement in the spine, the legs and the arms. It is not at once realised where to or in what direction the movement leads. We are soon interested in the *duration* of the movement, which is represented in notation by a duration line. Duration lines of equal length signify an equal time duration.

Time units can be marked on a central staff line, and in reading the notation, it can be estimated how each movement of a part of the body lasts one or several time units. When the duration line ends the movement finishes also. It may re-start at a later moment.

Sometimes the movements of several parts of the body overlap, and several movements then have certain time units or counts in common.

In notation we have also to consider the effects of an initial impulse, which will be briefly characterised here.

We can discern:

The *fundamental movement* of a definite part or parts of the body.

The *tactile effect*, if the end of a moving part touches an object, *e.g.* if the foot (end-articulation of the leg) touches the ground, or if the hand (end-articulation of the arm) touches an object or person.

The *support effect*, when a foot, hand or any other part or parts of the body carries the weight.

The *prehensile effect* or grasp, *e.g.* when the hand grips an object. The prehensile effect can be combined with the support effect, *e.g.* in grasping the branch of a tree or a rung of a ladder and hanging on to it by the hands and arms.

Several subsequent support effects of any kind combine into the *ambulatory effect*, *e.g.* when two or more steps are taken, or several ladder rungs are hung on to, one after another. In any ambulatory effect

each progress from one support to the next has its own tactile or prehensile sub-section.

The *saltatory effect* arises from the flinging of the body from one place to the other, whereby the body is thrown into the air and remains for a short time without support, *e.g.* in a leap or jump or in acrobatic turns in the air. Every saltatory effect ends in a landing, *i.e.* in the regaining of a support. Producing the saltatory effect or fling involves an elastic rebounce.

The *rebounce effect* is also noticeable, in contrast to the touch (tactile effect), as a thrusting or pushing away of an object or a person.

The *swinging or pendulum effect* arises from the passive hanging down of one or several limbs, or of the whole body hanging on hands or feet, etc. In this case a wave of movements above the passively hanging part sets the latter into a swinging motion.

Very often it is not necessary to notate all the effects of movements contributing to a final effect.

This is, for instance, the case in ordinary stepping and walking, where the preparatory lifting and shifting of the stepping leg is omitted and only the final effect of the transference of the weight support is recorded.

In the more elaborate steps of dancing, which gain their expressive quality from the varying combination of various preparatory and intermediate effects, all these details must of course be notated.

There is here an important difference between movement notation and dance notation. This applies also, of course, to the detailed notation of the various movement effects in arm gestures, which are quite different in working actions and in dance movements.

SECTION A

The notation of the flow of movement in the body and the duration of movement*

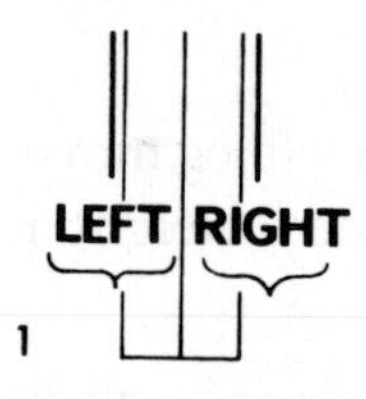

1

1. THE symbols of movement notation are inscribed in a system of three parallel lines, the staves. It is useful to position the staves vertically in writing the script, because an essential feature of the script thus remains constantly before the eye. This feature is that the central staff line divides the writing space into two halves; in the left half are notated the movements of the left side of the body, while the right half is reserved for movements of the right side of the body†.

Exceptions to this are the movements of the trunk and its main carrier the spine, which are written on both sides, immediately adjacent to and outside the two outer staff lines‡.

Movement impulses for the lower and upper extremities issue from the spine. Nerve tracks issuing from the left side of the spine convey the movement impulses to the left side extremities, and likewise where the right leg and arm are concerned.

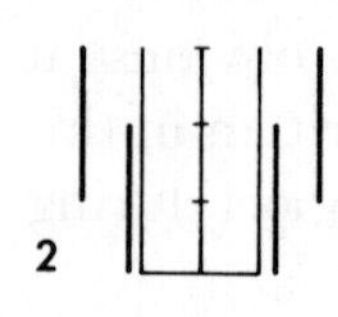

2

2. Spine and trunk movements often precede leg and arm movements. In graph 2 a spine and trunk movement initiates a simultaneous movement of both arms. Leg movements (*see* graphs 3, 4, 5) are inserted within the staves, while arm movements are written outside the staves (*see* graph 4), farther away from them than the spine-trunk movements.

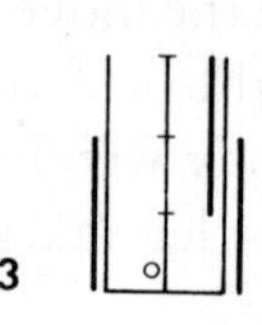

3

3. A spine-trunk movement (written on both sides of the staves) precedes a right leg movement. The left leg, supporting the weight of the body, is immobile. A nought is inserted adjacent to the central staff line to signalise a pausing of the flow of movement in the left leg§.

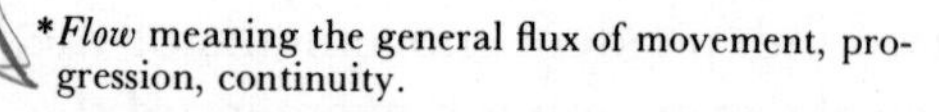

**Flow* meaning the general flux of movement, progression, continuity.

†General note. Now a double bar line is always needed to indicate the start of action. (KIN at the beginning of each column)

‡The two columns immediately to the right and left of the stave are now reserved for the movements of the *upper part of the body*. This technical term includes movements around and/or in the spine involving the shoulder girdle, or part of it, but excluding the hip joints. They are written with direction signs on both sides of the stave. Movements involving the whole trunk include the hip joint and are written with on one side of the stave only. This applies also to parts of the trunk.

§The nought indicating the pausing is called a *pause* or *retention sign*.

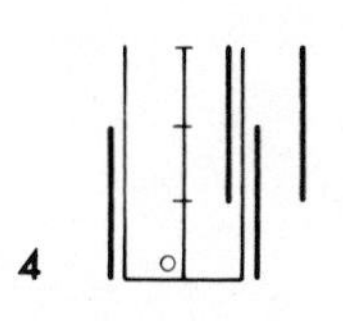
4

4. This graph shows a movement of the spine followed by simultaneous right leg and arm movements, which are again each of a duration of two time units. The movements of the trunk and the extremities overlap in time and move together for one time unit. The body weight is carried by the immobile left leg.

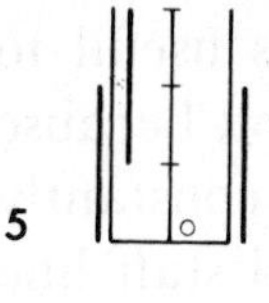
5

5. Shows the same movement as in (4), but a left leg movement follows the spine movement. The body weight is carried by the immobile right leg.

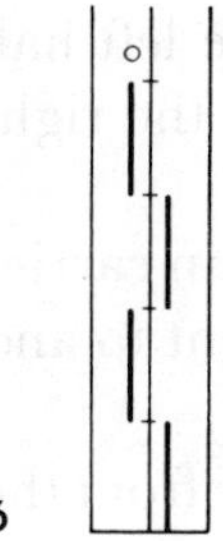
6

6. No spine movement precedes the independent right step, *i.e.* a taking over of the weight of the body from the left leg, which has initially carried the body weight after a transitory right leg gesture. In this graph the transference of the weight from the left to the right leg has the same duration of one time unit as the succeeding left step, and so on.

The stepping movement is written in the support column adjacent to the central staff line.

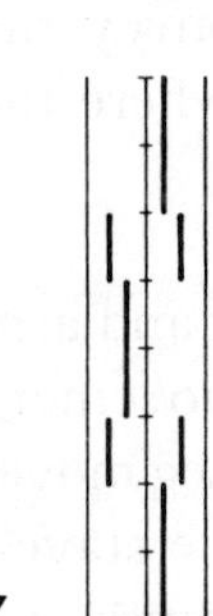
7

7. Gaps between steps—here of one time unit—signify a jump or leap. This becomes still more obvious if simultaneous right and left leg gestures are written in this gap, so that the body is evidently without support during this time unit.

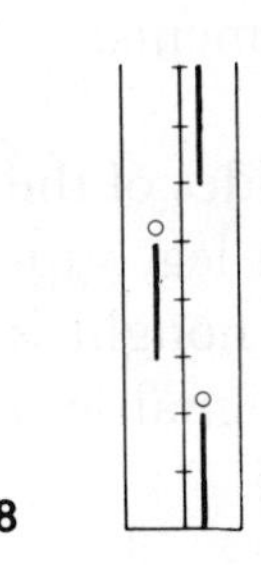
8

8. Here are shown the same gaps between subsequent supports as in the previous graph 7. The pause in the movement of the stepping leg is indicated by a nought or zero after the step. It prolongs the support of the body weight by the stepping leg in immobility until the other leg takes the weight over. No jump, of course, is made.

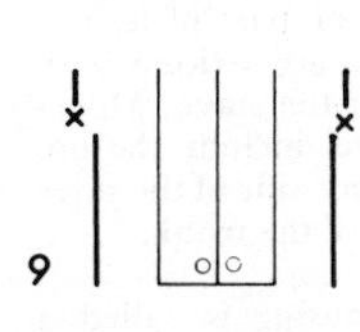
9

9. At the end of the two independent movements of the arms a sign for a prehensile or grasping movement of the hands (x) is added. Movements of the hand are notated a further small distance away from the staves, and have their own duration line, which is in the present example much shorter than the main arm movement. No touch of an

object is indicated, so that the contraction of the hand and fingers is an expressive movement and not connected with an objective action.

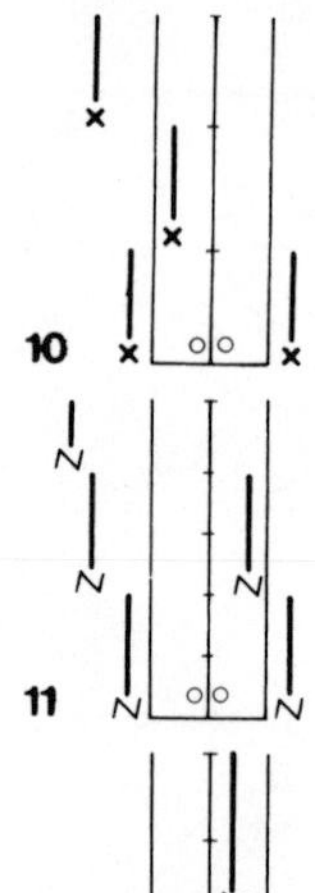

10. By the same contraction sign, bendings or contractions of the spine, of the legs or the arms can also be indicated.

11. The stretching or widening of a movement is indicated by an N-like sign. This sign is also used when the fingers of the hand are widely spread. See the last spreading movement of the left hand.

The sign is now written

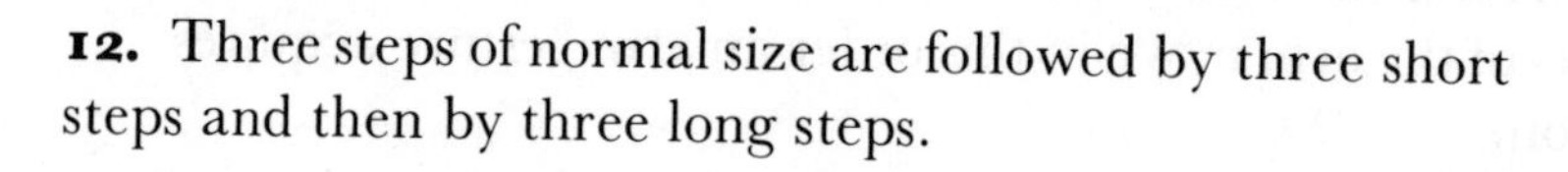

12. Three steps of normal size are followed by three short steps and then by three long steps.

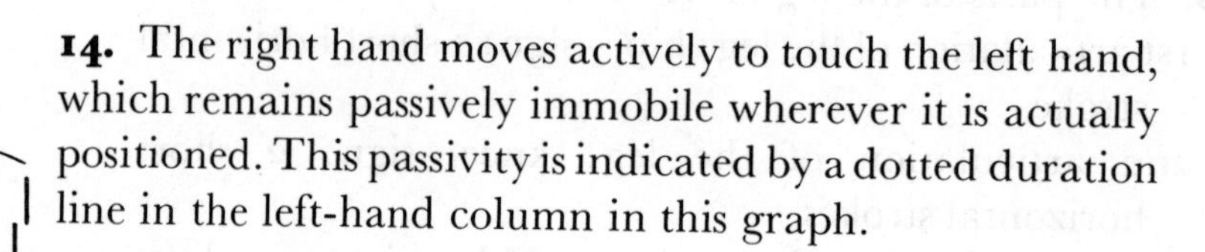

13. A horizontal bow connecting two parts of the body indicates touch. Here the hands touch one another, both in active movement.

14. The right hand moves actively to touch the left hand, which remains passively immobile wherever it is actually positioned. This passivity is indicated by a dotted duration line in the left-hand column in this graph.

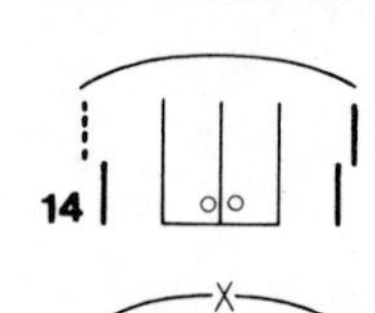

15. Both hands grip one another, both with active movement. The grip or grasp sign is the narrow sign (x) within the bow of touch.

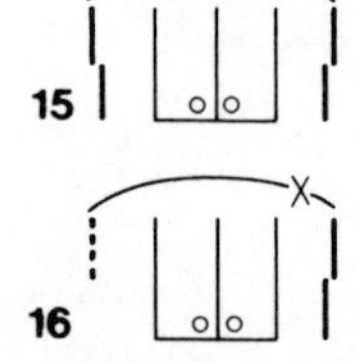

16. The right hand touches and grips the left hand in active movement. The left hand remains passive, immobile.

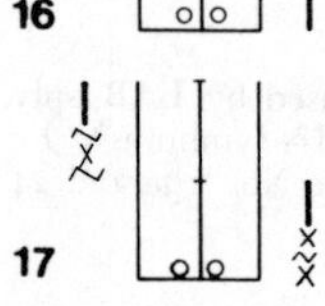

17. Rebouncing movements of the arms. The right bounces from narrow to wide and back to narrow, the left from wide to narrow and back to wide. Both movements are very quick.

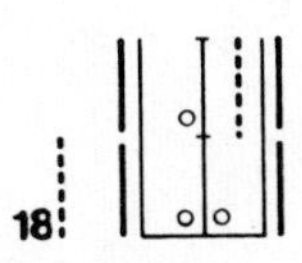

18. With an active movement of the spine both arms swing out passively. In the second half the passive right leg is set swinging by a trunk impulse.

19. The parts of the arm move successively:—

1st articulation of arm: shoulder—sign: 1 short inclined stroke

2nd articulation of arm: elbow—sign: 2 short inclined strokes

3rd articulation of arm: wrist—sign: 3 short inclined strokes

4th articulation of arm: hand—sign: 4 short inclined strokes

19

All affixed to short duration lines.

When the parts of the arm move in this order an arm gesture acquires a fluent expression.

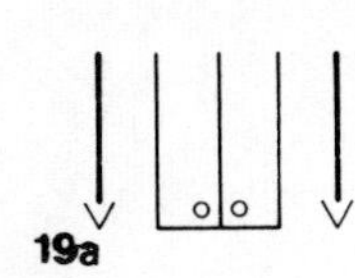

19a. The succession of the movements of the parts of the arm in the above order can be expressed in notation by a V-like *succession sign* inserted before the arm-gesture duration strokes.

20. The parts of the leg move successively:

1st articulation of the leg: hip—sign: 1 short horizontal stroke

2nd articulation of the leg: knee—sign: 2 short horizontal strokes

3rd articulation of the leg: ankle—sign: 3 short horizontal strokes

4th articulation of the leg: foot—sign: 4 short horizontal strokes

20

All crossing short duration lines.

When the parts of the leg are moved in this order, the leg gesture acquires a fluent expression.

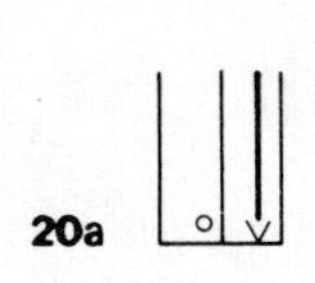

20a. The succession of the movements of the parts of the leg in the above order can be expressed in notation by a V-like *succession sign* inserted before the leg-gesture duration stroke.

now used by LAB only, the KIN symbol is V) *See* also Nos. 19a and 24.

Note that the signs for the sub-sections of the legs are the same for the right and left sides. For the arms, they are different for the right and left sides.

21

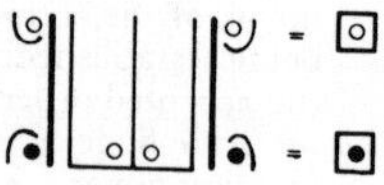

21. The parts of the spine move successively.

Order: Movement of the lower part of the spine (pelvis area), indicated by the centre of weight or gravity sign, a bow or square with a black disc in it; followed by movement of the upper part of the spine (chest area), indicated by a bow or square with a white disc in it.

The new centre of gravity sign is ●

pelvis sign

chest sign

both symbols are written in the first column outside the stave (on one side only).

21a

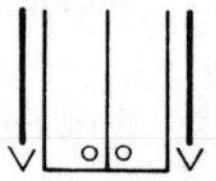

21a. The above order in the succession of the movements of the parts of the spine can be expressed in notation by the V-like succession sign.

22

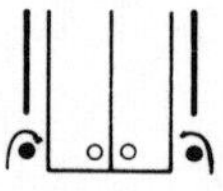

22. The sub-sections of the spine—and with them the parts of the trunk—can move separately. Here the lower (pelvis) area moves alone.

22a

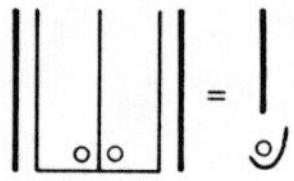

22a. The chest area of the spine and tunk moves alone.

23

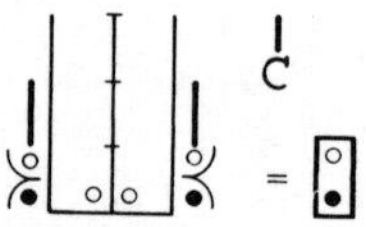

23. The whole torso moves as a whole without articulation, followed by an independent head movement. Sign for the head, a capital "C" (from *Caput* = "head" in Latin).

Note: To graphs 21 and 23 alternative signs used in dance notation for pelvis, chest and torso are added.

only now used.

24

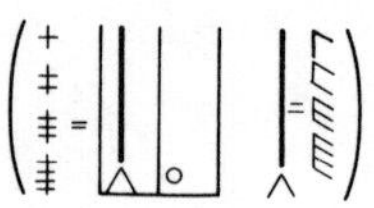

24. The parts of the arms and legs move less frequently in the reversed order of succession, which is then notated by an inverted succession sign (Λ).

The vertical bow joining the articulation of successively performed body movements indicates smooth transitions (*see* graphs 19, 24, 25).

25

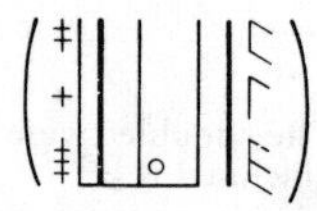

25. Any other order of independently moving parts of arms and legs is of course possible. For example, in graph 25, the order of the motions in the parts of the arms is wrist, shoulder, elbow, while the order of the motions of the parts of the left leg is ankle, hip, knee.

Note: No succession sign can be written for irregular movement sequences of parts of the extremities.

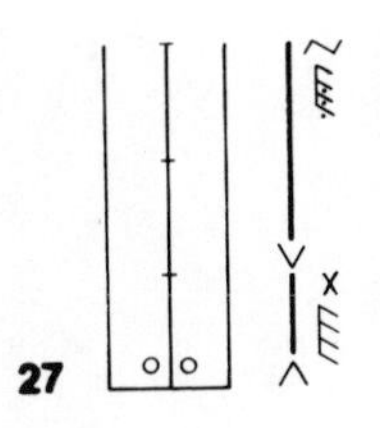

26. Shows the notation of fingers by dots inserted into the sign of the 4th arm articulation, the hand.

(*a*) = thumb.
(*b*) = index finger.
(*c*) = middle finger.
(*d*) = ring finger.
(*e*) = little finger.

This order results from Laban's dance style in the period when the rudiments of the script were being established. Now the accepted order is:
(*a*) little finger
(*b*) ring finger
(*c*) middle finger
(*d*) index finger
(*e*) thumb
LAB way of writing is

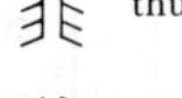

little finger, etc.

27

27. This graph shows, in the first motion, a shorter arm gesture with inverted succession of parts, in which the hand is narrowed in a grip-like fashion (all fingers bent); in the second motion, a longer arm gesture with everted succession of parts, in which three fingers of the hand, *i.e.* thumb, index finger and middle finger are widened (stretched).

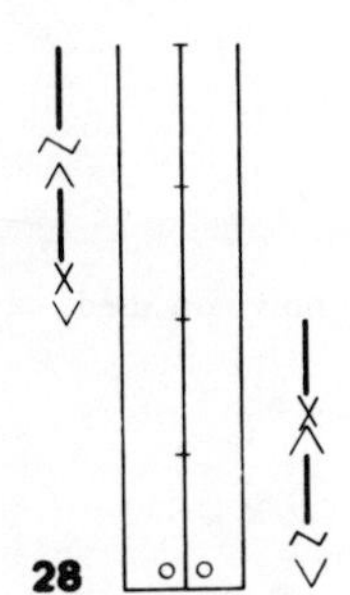

28. In the first motion everted succession of arm articulations is combined with a stretching or widening of the right arm.

In the second motion inverted succession of arm articulations is combined with bending or narrowing of the right arm.

In the third motion everted arm articulation is combined with bending or narrowing of the left arm.

In the fourth motion inverted arm articulation is combined with stretching or widening of the left arm.

Note: The same combination of everted and inverted articulation successions with either narrowing or widening is also possible for the legs.

The fundamental bodily actions of scooping, gathering (in contrast to strewing), and scattering (or pushing away) are based on such combinations of narrow and wide extensions of the limbs with definite orders of succession of the articulations.

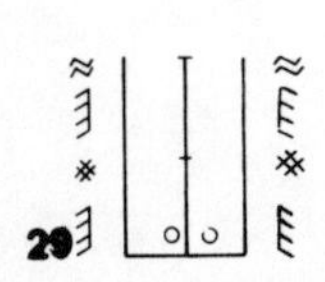

29. The graph shows both hands making a fist in the first motion, and spreading hands and fingers very wide in the second motion.

Note: This strong concentration and extension is indicated by a double narrow sign and a double wide sign.

The double wide sign now used is

30

30. The head can also be held either very low (narrowly) by bending and pressing the chin to the chest or very high (widely), as in the colloquial expression "with the nose in the air."

Duration strokes can be added if these actions, written in 29 and 30, are performed very slowly.

Following the consideration that the head cannot really become *narrower* or *wider* as a body part, a new way of writing has been established for these movements:

The double narrow and double wide signs are also used as prefixes to any kind of movement, as for instance for the indication of very short or very long steps.

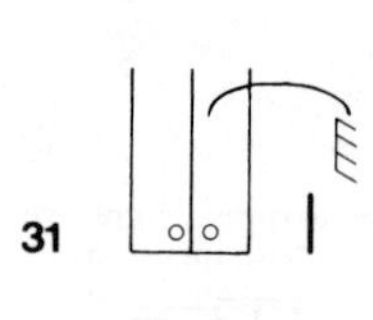

31

31. The touch sign—a horizontal bow—is also used to indicate the touching of the ground. In graph 31 an arm gesture is seen, in which the hand touches the ground; this is shown by the touching bow leading from the hand to the support column. No weight is transferred to the hand or arm in this case, nor in the following graph 32.

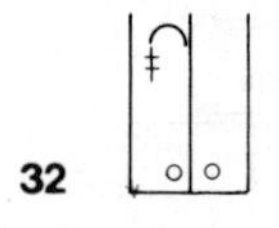

32

32. The left knee touches the ground, but without really kneeling on it.

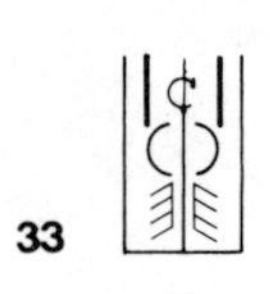

33

33. Here the weight of the body is transferred to both hands and the head.

This is now written as

Note: the small vertical bow connecting the hand-stand with the head-stand shows that both happen simultaneously. The legs move, that is, leave the ground, during the combined head- and hand-stand.

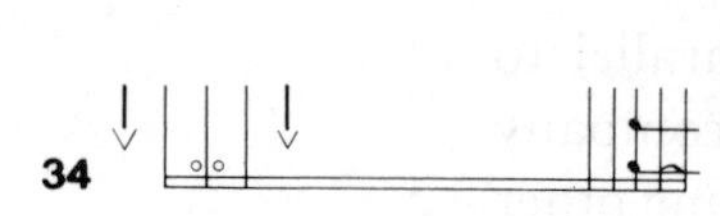

34

34. The weight reposes on both feet, while the arms perform gestures consisting of an everted succession of their articulations.

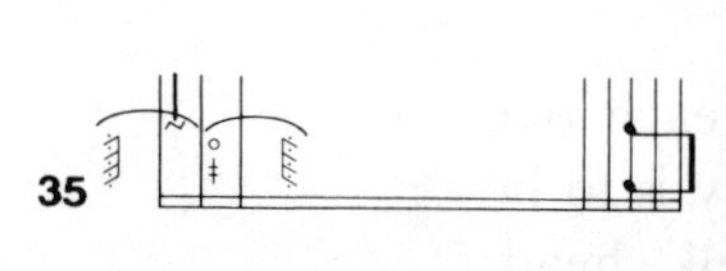

35

35. Kneeling on the right knee, while the fingers of both hands touch the ground, without, however, carrying weight. The left leg moves away in a wide movement.

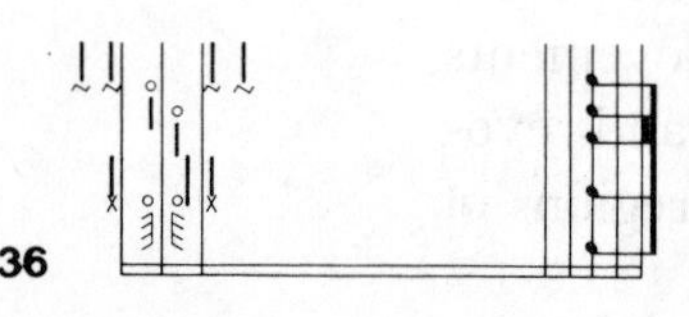

36

36. Hand-stand on both hands. A right-leg gesture connected with a contraction of the trunk leads to a standing on the right foot and then on both feet. While the feet take

over the weight, the trunk and both arms stretch widely.

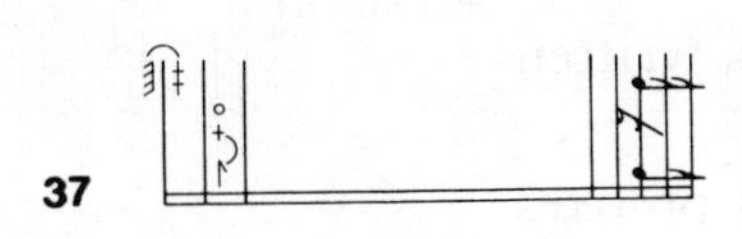
37

37. The body lies on the right shoulder and hip, *i.e.* on the right side. Note the connecting bow as a sign of simultaneity. The left hand touches the left knee.

This is now written as (*See* also 102)

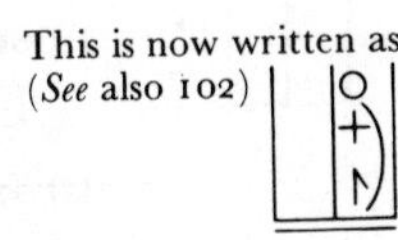

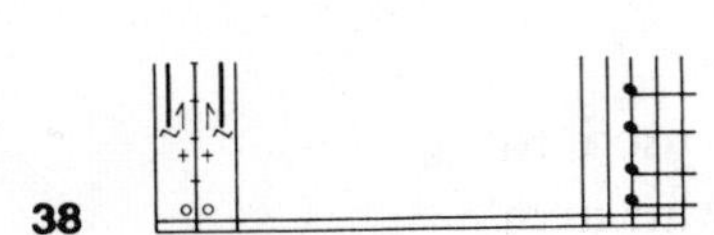
38

38. Standing on both feet, followed by sitting, and then by lying down on the whole torso (hip-shoulders, *see* graph 23); in the lying position both legs are stretched far out.

39. Note the repetition sign for the movement sequence, which consists of two equal (=) signs, one on the left at the bottom and the other on the right at the top of the movement notation.

The new repeat signs are (*See* also Nos. 98, 99, 100)

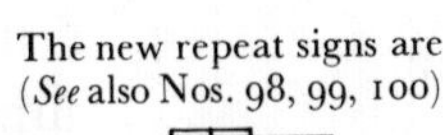

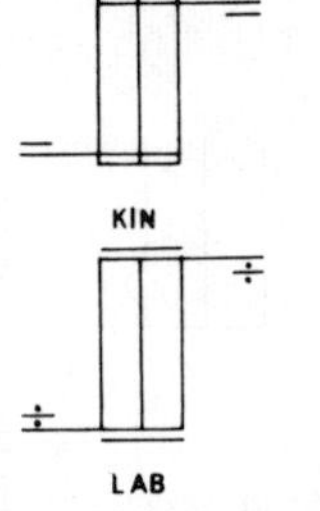

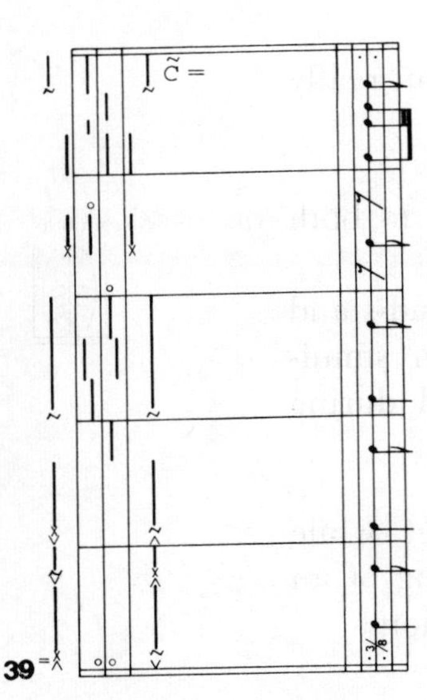
39

Motif 39 forms a sequence of arm gestures, steps and a jump (both legs gesturing away from the ground) and a few further steps with trunk and arm motions; the rhythm of the movements 34–39 has been notated by musical notes in an adjacent stave. The bar lines of movement and music coincide.

Both movement and the accompaniment by music are repeated in graph 39.

It is possible to write dances parallel to the accompanying music, or to accompany notated movement by a drum or some other percussion instrument while reading the rhythm from the movement score.

Within the body movement several rhythms can appear, each one followed by different parts of the body. In this sense the body is to be considered as a kind of orchestra, in which arms, legs, trunk, head, hands, shoulders and all the other articulations play their parts.

In Section A we have dealt with "narrow" and "wide" movements without taking into consideration the many possible turnings and revolutions of the limbs or of the whole body towards the various regions of space.

Downwards, towards the ground, and upwards in the air are two of the regions of space that must be considered, but there are many more; in movement the most obvious ones are the sideways direction (opening-closing) and the forwards and backwards directions (advancing-retiring).

Changes of front, as in turning to the right or to the left until one faces in a new direction, necessitate the indication of such movements with special signs.

From the weight-level and directional viewpoint, all movements can be understood as a series of definite positions in space. This applies not only when a simple turning towards a new direction is involved, but also when, in a series of movements, the limbs or the whole body are turned into many of the different possible directions during the motif. This will be best understood by comparing the possible body positions in space with those of statues, which may be standing; kneeling, sitting, lying or even, in jumping, flying through the air; in doing so they, with their limbs, may point to any of the regions of space surrounding them.

This comparison with statues in their various positions is applicable mainly to the art of dancing. The everyday activities of contemporary man are in general much less "plastic." But in sports, games, hunting climbing and sailing and also in certain working activities a great amount of movement plasticity can still be observed.

In dancing, as well as in everyday gait, in work and in the manner of carrying the body, a great variety of movement levels is noticeable; some people bend their back and knees habitually, while others walk and move in an erect fashion, as if stretching upwards.

These differences between the habitual weight-levels of the body are of interest to the movement notator.

The direction into which every single movement leads can be compared to the "pitch" of a melody. The detailed prescription of these directions will be discussed in the next Section.

SECTION B

The notation of weight-level and the directions of movement

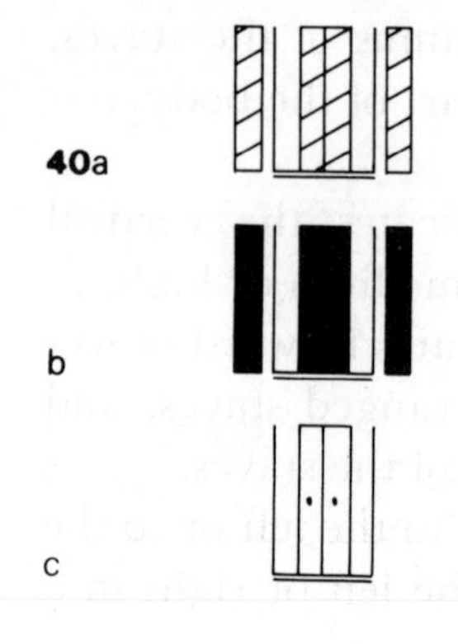

DURATION strokes broadened into blocks of three different shades indicate three levels of height towards which a movement can be orientated.

40 (*a*). This shading of the block-sign by strokes means a *high* level. The example shows: Standing elevated on the balls of the feet, with straight knees. Both arms are raised high.

(*b*) Shading by blackening the whole block means *deep* level. The example shows: Standing on the whole feet with lowered (bent) knees. Both arms are directed downwards by the sides of the body.

(*c*) Shading with a dot in the centre of the block means *medium* level. The example shows: Standing on the whole feet with straight knees.

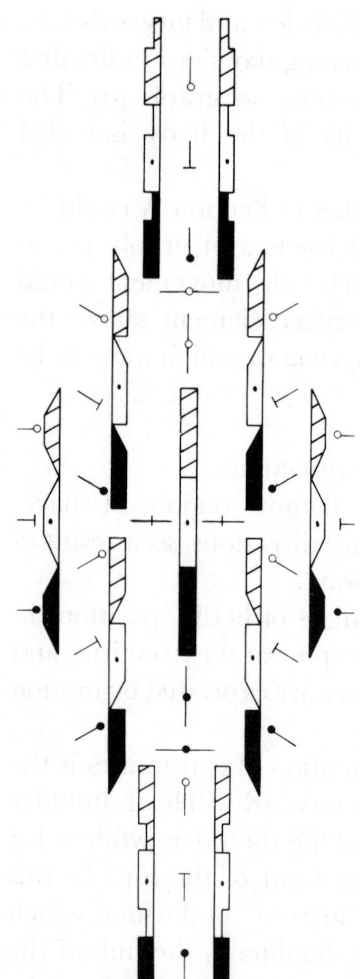

41. In graph 41, two sets of directional signs are shown.

The larger shaded blocks, of different shapes, can be drawn longer or shorter according to the varying durations of the movements represented by them.

The smaller, pin-shaped signs point to definite directions, but have no time value and remain, therefore, always of the same size.

The block-signs, which have been developed from broadened duration strokes, are compound signs containing combined indications of the level, the direction and the duration of a movement. They are called motion characters (the letters of the lan-

"Motion characters" are now named "direction signs."

guage of movement). Written into the various columns of the staves, they indicate complex movement actions for each part of the body.

The blocks are of four different shapes:

The rectangular shape (*see* graphs 40*a*, *b*, *c*) indicates the vertical direction which is called "place." This can be low, medium or high.

The pointer shape, almost like an index finger, indicates forward movements when pointing to the top of the vertically arranged staves, and backward movements when pointing to the bottom of the staves.

The arrowhead shape (truncated triangle), pointing to the left or to the right of the writing space, indicates movements to the left or right in a sideways direction.

The diagonal corner shape indicates movements in intermediate directions: forwards-right, backwards-right, backwards-left and forwards-left.

In the centre of graph 41 are written the rectangular signs indicating the three levels, high, low, and middle or medium (*see* graph 40). The spot on the floor under the centre of gravity of the body is called "place."

Theoretically any one of the duration strokes in Section A could be replaced by one or several of the motion characters of graph 41; in this way an indication of the direction and level of the movement would be given. However, the exact control of the space element allows the definition of certain significant patterns of movement which have to be discussed.

Such patterns are:

Floor patterns, built up from *steps* of definite directions.

Air patterns, designed by arm gestures into definite regions of space.

Changes of front, facing towards varying space directions, as a result of turns, or runs along circular or curved pathways.

Variations of motifs based on significant changes of bodily positions in space. The positions of the articulations of the spine and extremities and of their turnings towards definite regions of space are expressed by motion characters and pin-signs.

An important conception of the space orientation of extremities is the hub or centre of direction. An arm movement forward will lead shoulder high (the natural level of the hub), in front of the shoulder, while a leg movement forward will lead at hip height in front of the hip. In this way many forward directions exist, each one "in front" of the joint which is the hub of the directional movement. The shoulder is the hub of the arm, the elbow is the hub of the forearm, the wrist is the hub of the hand; and similarly the hip is the hub of the leg, the knee of the lower

part of the leg, and the ankle of the foot.

As will be shown, the exact indication of movement directions offers the possibility of recording a rich variety of movement patterns.

Each example shown in Section B allows almost unlimited variations, which can only be briefly indicated in this short survey of the principles of dance and movement notation.

A very large number of possible combinations of linear and plastic patterns can be built up from directional indications. Floor patterns of steps can be combined with air patterns. Both floor patterns and air patterns can contain twists and turns, or be performed in straight directions. Combined linear patterns can become plastic, if the simultaneous movements follow different directions. The pattern of movement can be interrupted at any place by pauses in definite positions. Such positions, in which the movement stops, can be assumed by the whole body or by any single part of it. Variations in the length of the directional signs allow any part of a pattern to be speeded up or slowed down, so that the pattern can be performed with any imaginable rhythm. Indications of deviated or diverted direction can give the pattern a great range of sizes and variations in shape. Manifold possibilities exist of touching, gripping, or carrying objects or a person, either while stationary or while moving along a floor-pattern path; these actions can be combined with suitable air patterns.

These various combinations of movement have their own logic; the possible variations are restricted in several ways. The human body can hover in the air only for a very short moment, during a jump. The body or its limbs frequently form a kind of obstacle on a directional path, and this obstacle has to be circumvented. The smaller articulations of the body, as, for instance, the fingers, have their own restricted orbit of movement. These logical considerations of what is possible or impossible for a normally functioning body are reflected in certain rules of the graphical representation of movement.

The graphs of Section B show some typical combinations of directional indications.

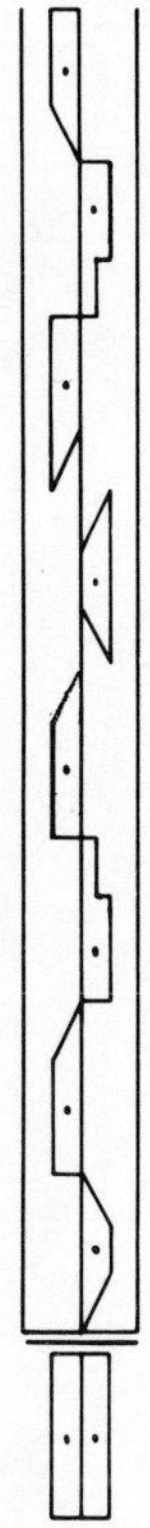

42. Steps in different directions create *floor patterns*. The front of the body remains facing the same direction. The steps are all at a medium weight-level.

With each step a new *stance* is reached from which, as a *centre*, the direction of the next step is reckoned.

In the first right step, the weight will be transferred to the right foot; a left step then crosses from this new stance-centre diagonally right and forwards. Again a new stance is reached, from which the next step forward is made with the right foot, and so on, until the last left step returns near to the starting place. If the steps become increasingly shorter, say: 1st step very long (double length), 2nd step long, 3rd step normal extension, 4th step short, 5th step very short (half the 4th), and 6th, 7th and 8th steps extremely short, a successively narrowing pathway would be formed.

A successively widening pathway would be formed through increasingly lengthening steps (starting with very short ones). A great number of variations of floor patterns can be described through the combinations of steps of different directions and extensions.

Now the starting position is always enclosed in the stave as follows

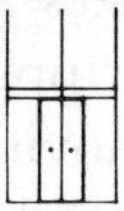

42

Note: In this sequence of steps the changing of the direction of the fourth step (from right diagonal forwards to left diagonal forwards) would alter the floor pattern into a circular path. The method of describing the following of a circular path with a continuous change of front is shown in graph 55.

43. Arm or leg gestures made in different directions create *air patterns*.

In the example given a line similar to a figure S is drawn in the air by the right arm.

The sequence of the motions shows changing weight-levels.

The arm is swinging around the right shoulder as its hub or *centre*, from which all the directions radiate. No steps are made during the arm movement, but as the level is changed, the knees are accordingly bent or stretched. (*See* graph 40.)

Note that in the two final movements the arm will reach behind the back.

43

44. Smooth transitions from one weight-level to another are indicated by *double-shaded* motion characters.

The direction is indicated by the *whole* sign. The level changes during the transference of the weight of the step. The graph shows a sequence of steps in which, during the first step, the knee is first bent and then stretched. In the second step, the level falls from the balls of the feet to the whole foot, but the knee is still stretched. In the next step, the level falls from high to low, the latter involving the bending of the knee, while in the last step the level falls from medium to low.

44

45. A leg gesture with mounting level precedes two steps of different levels.

The direction signs are now written narrower in relation to the staff columns. In this way there is more room between the signs making the kinetogram more readable. A new rule has also been adopted. The resting of the weight on the supporting leg must each time be confirmed (retention sign).

46. Three steps, each remaining on one level, are accompanied by one slow arm gesture (sideways right), the level of which is changed twice, gradually mounting from low through medium to high. The arm gesture is ended with a quick zigzag of varying "width" in three directions, the middle one of which is an intermediate direction.

Note that target points between two neighbouring directions can be indicated by writing the two directions and connecting them with a small vertical simultaneity bow with a dot in it. In this way one can, for instance, express an intermediate direction, say, between forwards and high left forward, etc.

45

The intermediate directions are now also written with the help of pin signs inserted into the direction signs, allowing a three-part division between two directions.

The weight centre of the body, or centre of gravity, above the pelvis region of the trunk, can be raised or lowered by stretching and bending of the supporting limbs.

In sitting and lying this is not the case. The weight centre in these two support situations is invariably on the ground. This position of the weight centre is indeed its medium height, since it can sink still lower till it is *below the support*, for instance, in hanging by the arms (or the feet, etc.) from the branch of a tree or the rung of a ladder. In standing even with bent knees, the weight centre is at a high level, above the ground.

This is important in crouching positions, when the knees are bent much more than in even a low step. In crouching,

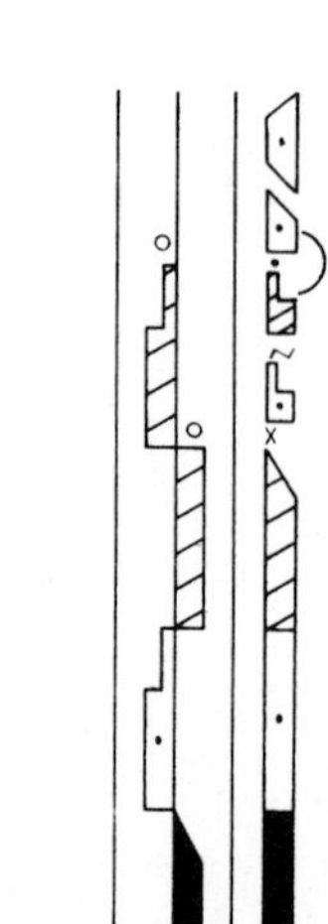

46

the weight centre comes "near" to its medium level, as in sitting, without, however, being fully on the ground which supports the body.

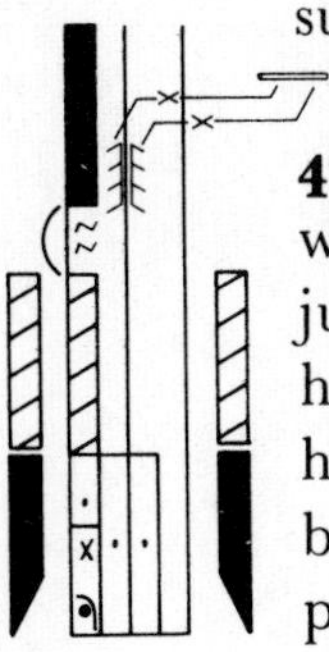

47

47. The body is at first in a crouching position, with the weight centre "near" to medium (*i.e.* to sitting). Then a jump occurs, with a transference of the support to both hands gripping the bar. (Objects touched, gripped or handled by a moving person have to be drawn or described by words. There exist no conventional signs for objects or properties used by a dancer on the stage.)

The symbol for the centre of gravity is now ●

The weight centre, having been lifted in the elevation, falls down *below* the support in hanging. In hanging on the arms the weight centre is "very deep."

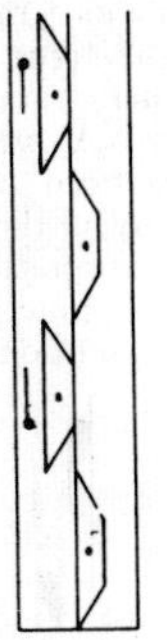

48

48. In the transition from one position to the next, a doubt can arise whether a step or an arm gesture has to pass in front of or behind the body.

In such cases, pin-shaped relation signs are used, which do not indicate by themselves any movement, but point to regions of space which are of importance to the movement, *e.g.* above or below, and in front or behind.

This graph shows several steps to the right; the left step crosses the first time in front of, and the second time behind the body.

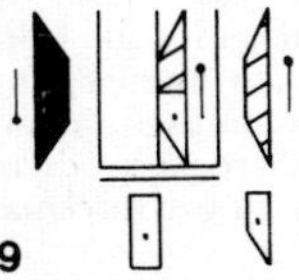

49

49. Through the pin-shaped relation sign near the motion character in question, it is made clear that the left-arm gesture passes in front of the body, the step and the right-arm gesture pass behind the body.

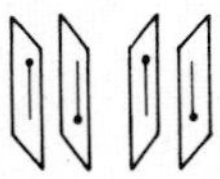

50 a b c d

50. *Changes of front* and other rotations are indicated by turning signs:

(*a*) Anti-clockwise (to the left) half-turn. The pin-sign inserted into the turning sign indicates that the new front faces in the direction which was previously backwards.

(*b*) Anti-clockwise (to the left) full turn. The pin-sign indicates that the body pivots until the old "in front" region is re-established.

(*c*) Clockwise (to the right) half-turn.

(*d*) Clockwise (to the right) full turn.

Changes of front or turns of the whole body are inserted in the support column.

Any degree of turn is indicated by a pin-sign. Changes of front of $\frac{1}{8}$, $\frac{1}{4}$, $\frac{3}{8}$, $\frac{1}{2}$, $\frac{5}{8}$, $\frac{3}{4}$, $\frac{7}{8}$, and full turns (clockwise or anti-clockwise) can be indicated.

51

51. Right step forwards, medium; clockwise quarter-turn on right foot; left step forwards, medium (in new front).

After this, a quick right step backwards, deep, followed by a quick anti-clockwise half-turn.

Note: This turn needs a strong impetus of either the upper part of the body or the free-swinging leg; no description for this auxiliary motion is given in this simplified example of notation.

In KIN the weight has to be transferred first before the turn may occur in reality. Therefore the vertical bow connecting the turn sign with a step will not be written. The pin signs now indicate the relationship of one foot to another.

Following this is a left foot step to the right, followed by a slow anti-clockwise $\frac{1}{8}$-turn.

The next movement is a right-foot step to the left connected with an anti-clockwise $\frac{3}{4}$-turn; a left step closes the left foot with the right.

Note that the pin-signs near a step are relation signs, indicating the passing of the step behind the body (*a*) and in front of the body (*b*).

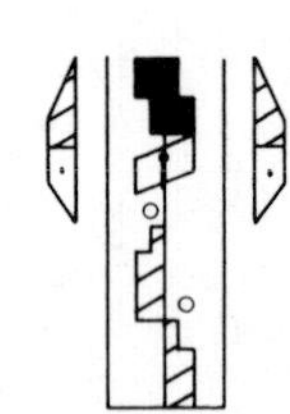

52

52. If, as in the beginning of this example, one leg maintains some support, the weight will remain on both legs. In this graph a half-turn on both legs brings the left leg into a backwards position, while the right leg comes in front.

Right and left steps are made, forwards, on the balls of the feet. The weight is carried by both legs. A half-turn to the right results in the right leg now standing forwards, in relation to the new front, both legs at deep level. Both arms are raised during the turn.

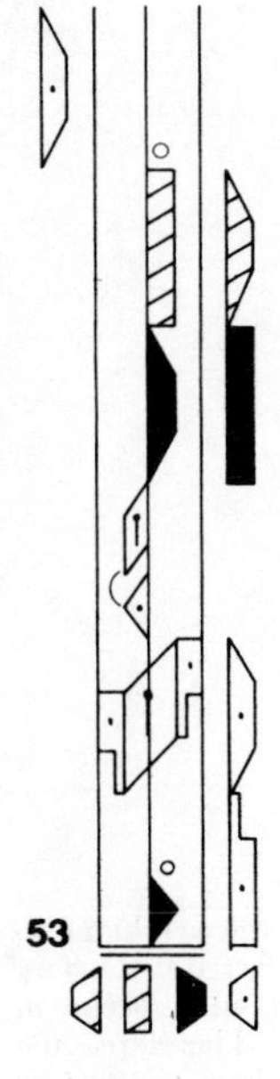

53

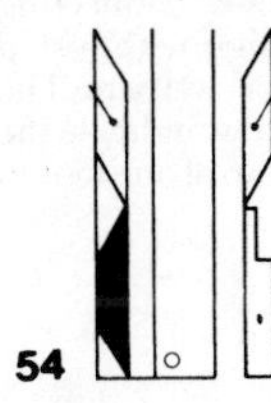

54

53. A turning jump. The right leg steps to the right. After a clockwise jumping half-turn in the air, the left foot takes over the weight a step-length to the left and completes the clockwise half-turn to a full turn.

With a stand on the right foot with bent knees, the original front is reached again in a starting position, from which the same turning jump could be repeated, but this time anti-clockwise to the left, starting with a left step.

54. *Rotations* (clockwise or anti-clockwise) of arms and legs are indicated by the turn-signs inserted in the corresponding columns.

Now white pin signs are used in the turn signs indicating out- and in-turn in relation to the body.
Black pin signs indicate out- or in-turn in relation to the last achieved position.

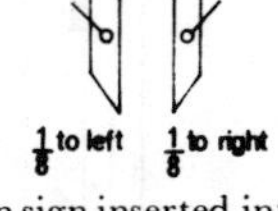

The pin sign inserted into the path sign now indicates the degree of circling in a similar way to turn signs. (In this case it is 1/4 circular path, clockwise.) The new front is now indicated with an auxiliary sign written outside the kinetogram.

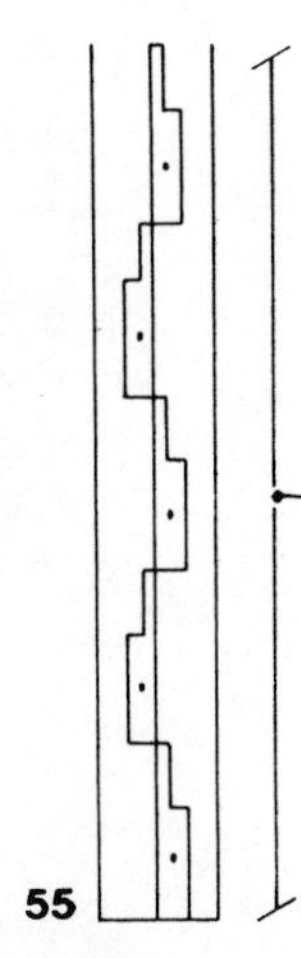

55

55. *Circular or curved path* signs refer to a series of steps which describe a circle or a part of it. Graph 55 shows five steps forward on a path representing a quarter of a circle. (To complete the whole circle would take twenty steps, each five steps resulting in a quarter circle.) The path in this example is curved. In the gap in the path-sign the final new front is inserted, which indicates subdivisions of the circle. The front of the body is continuously changing as it goes along the circular pathway.

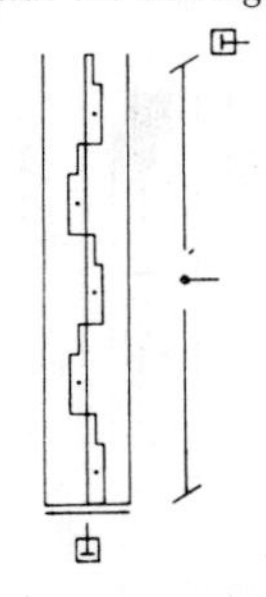

56. *Anti-clockwise circular path* (half-circle) with right sideways steps.
(Note: When stepping anti-clockwise to the right, the moving person is compelled in this example to stand and progress with his front facing towards the centre of the circular path.)

In KIN the anti-clockwise circular path sign is written on the left side of the stave. The clockwise circular path is written on the right side of the stave. In LAB all are written on the right side of the stave.

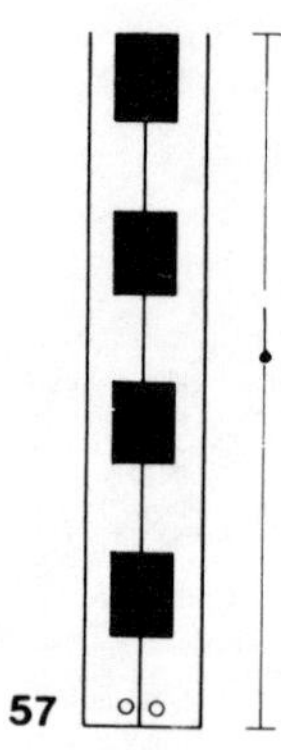

57. *Direct* or straight path-signs have in some cases to be written, *e.g.* in hopping on both feet, if a slight progression in a definite direction is made by this means.

Now the following sign is used

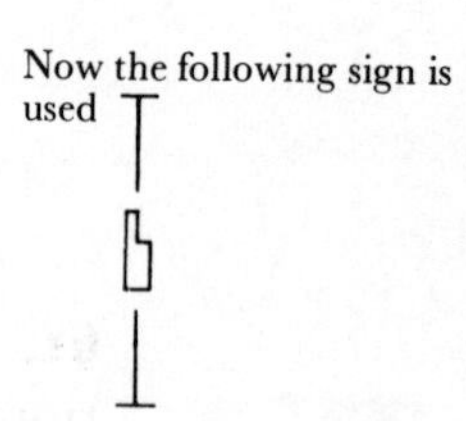

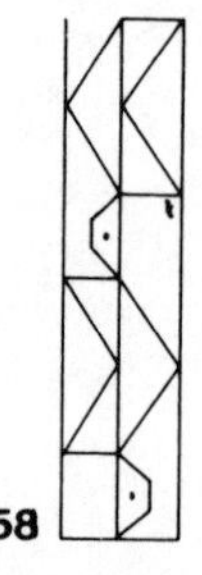

58. The rotation of the whole body in a *cartwheel* is notated with the help of a variant of the turn sign. In this graph a cartwheel to the right is followed by a cartwheel to the left.

The cartwheel sign is now written

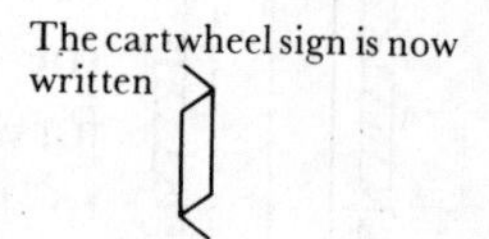

cartwheel to the right

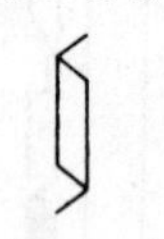

cartwheel to the left

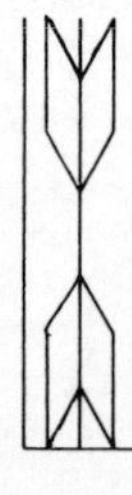

59. Other variants of rotations are the *somersault*, forwards and backwards.

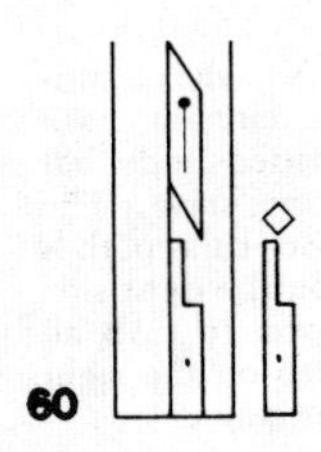

60

60. The small diamond-shaped space-holding sign after a gesture means that the part of the body thus designated remains in the same position in space while other parts are turning in different directions.

In this example, without the space-holding sign the forward-stretched right arm would follow the turn and would point "forwards" in relation to the new front. *With the space-holding sign* the arm remains where it is in space, and therefore points "backwards" at the end of the turn.

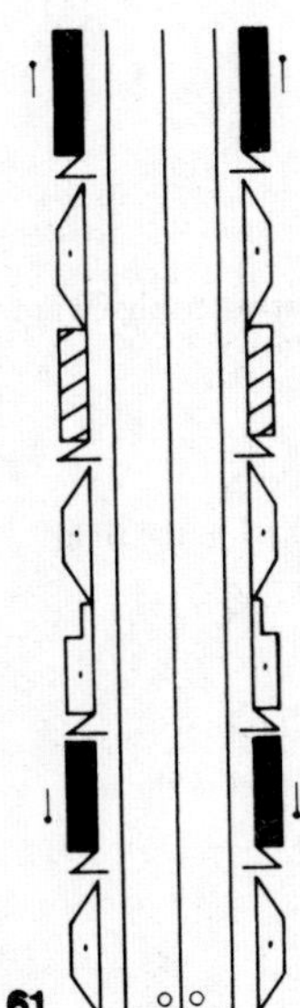

61

61. Some of the intermediate space-directions or deviations of movement-targets (*see* graph 46) are of particular importance owing to the symmetrical structure of the body. All directions originate from or are related to a hub (*see* explanations to graph 41).

The arms are frequently moved in directions which are related to the centre or to the central plane dividing the left and right sides of the body. This applies to all forwards and backwards directions of the trunk and also to its normal, vertical, low and high positions.

There are several ways of writing these directions for arm movements, in fixing definite arm positions similar to the dance positions of the feet. In movement notation I prefer a small angular bracket connecting the arm column with the trunk column. This bracket indicates that the arms have to be directed into the corresponding trunk directions. In graph 61, such deviations of the target are shown: in the directions deep, forwards and high above the head. The deep signs show the deep low positions in front of and behind the trunk. Backward targets can be deviated in the same way.

The angular bracket is no longer used.

62. This graph shows *diversions* or deflections of the movement path. The diversion signs are very small directional signs (mostly diagonals) which indicate in the example, for instance, that the first arm movement does not proceed directly from left diagonal backwards to high right, but that the movement takes a roundabout path through diagonal left high forwards. Such a diversion passes the indicated direction by deflecting slightly towards it, without really reaching it.

The diversion sign indicated is no longer used. Deviations (detours) are now written with the pin sign written into the vertical bow.

Many deflecting movements of this kind can be followed between two points of space.

The other two diversions lead:

(for the left arm) through diagonal right deep forwards to left deep;

(for the second movement of the right arm) through diagonal right high backwards to diagonal right forwards.

At the end there is a deviation of the high direction of both arms into a high position directly over the head, finishing in an ordinary sideways gesture for both arms.

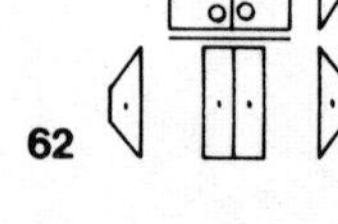
62

63–68. Amongst the significant changes of position in space, those in which opposite directions are combined into one motif play a dominant rôle.

It is important for the notator, and simplifies his task, if he can easily recognise and discern such changes.

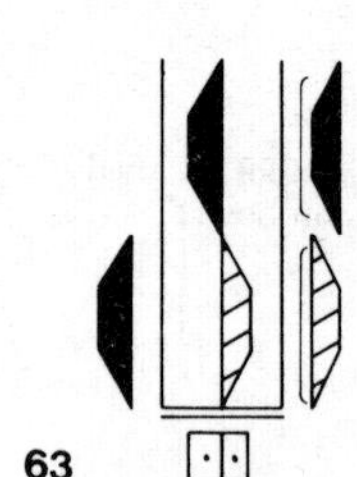
63

It is possible to distinguish regions of space which are most easily reached by one of the arms or a leg, while movements into opposite directions or regions often involve a certain contortion and strain. The simple notation of opposite directions can, in some cases of harmonious movement, replace the detailed description of the various bendings and stretchings, shiftings and tiltings, turns, twists and rotations, described by pin-signs, which are involved in the more contorted parts of a motif.

Six examples of motifs containing changes in opposite directions are shown in the graphs 63–68. It can easily be imagined that in a manner not unlike that seen in the time rhythm, which is built up from contrasting quick

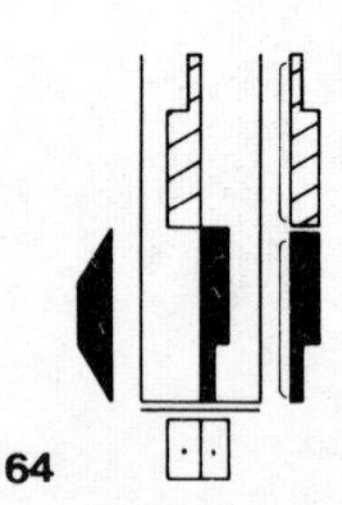
64

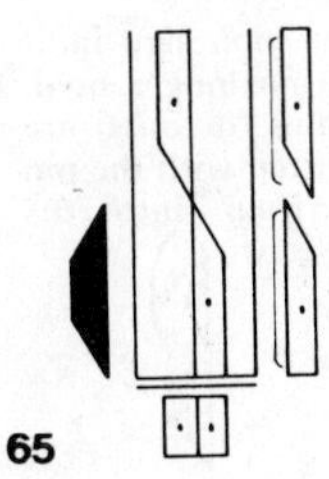

65

and slow movement durations, a space-rhythm or harmony can be discerned, consisting in principle of the alterations of contrasting movement directions. The contrasts shown here are:

63. high right *v.* deep left

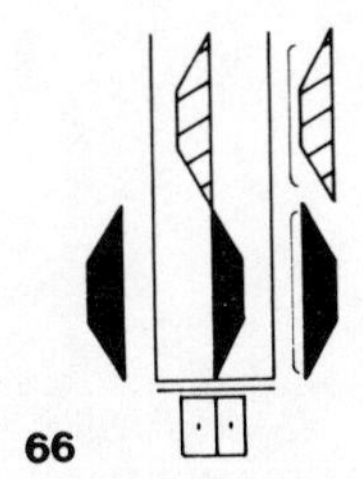

66

64. deep backwards *v.* high forwards

65. left forwards *v.* right backwards

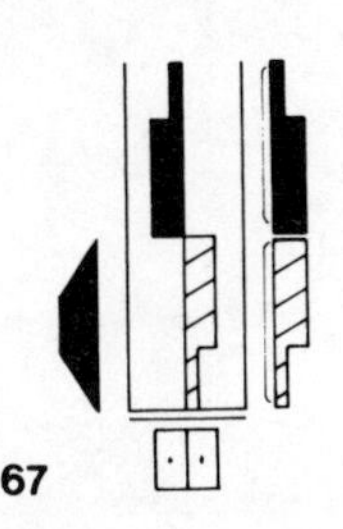

67

66. deep right *v.* high left

67. high backwards *v.* deep forwards

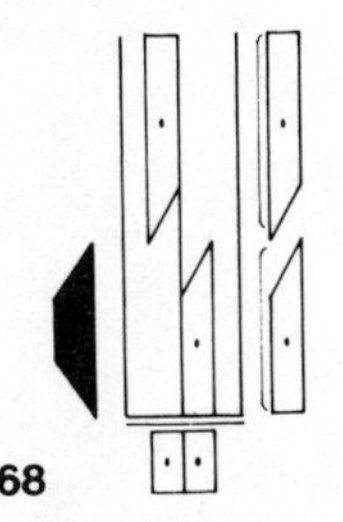

68

68. right forwards *v.* left backwards.

Note: The participation of the trunk in an arm movement is indicated in notation by an angular bow in the trunk column. See this bow in the six motifs in the graphs 63–68.

This symbol is called the inclusion bow.

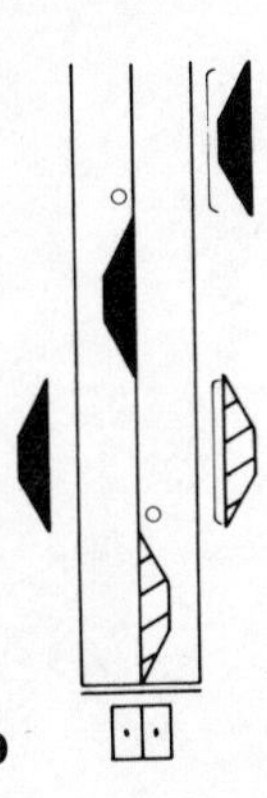

69

69. In this graph the end position of motif 63 is not reached in one simultaneous movement, but is successively developed.

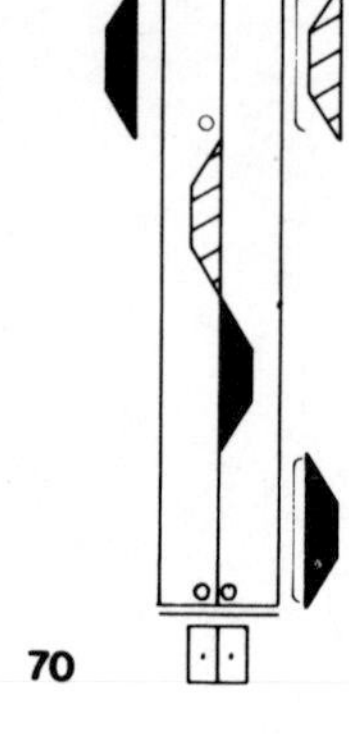

70

70. The same is the case in graph 70. The end position of motif 66 is reached here, but by successive development rather than by simultaneous movement.

Note: It is perhaps interesting for the notator to become conscious of the similarity between body positions and chords in music, while the successive development of the final position is more akin to the progression of melody in music.

The contortion and strain in one part of a motif calls for the release of such tension, which release is similar to progression or resolution in harmony, *i.e.* the re-establishment of a natural balance.

The recognition of such transitions from spatial strain to release is of great value in the observation and description of movement.

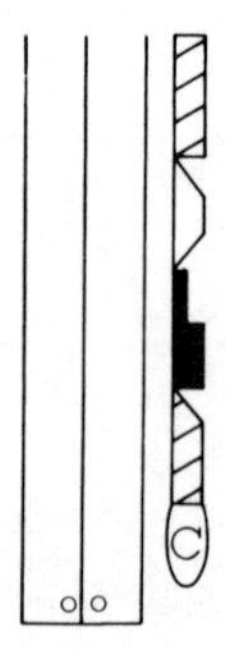

71

71. The face—signalised by a head sign in an oval frame—is oriented in space by "looking" into a definite direction.

In this graph the face "looks" into four different directions, which could not be expressed by notating all the tiltings and turnings of the head involved in this movement—some notators use a square frame around the head sign.

All notators now use a square frame with a stroke indicating the frontal surface of the head = face.

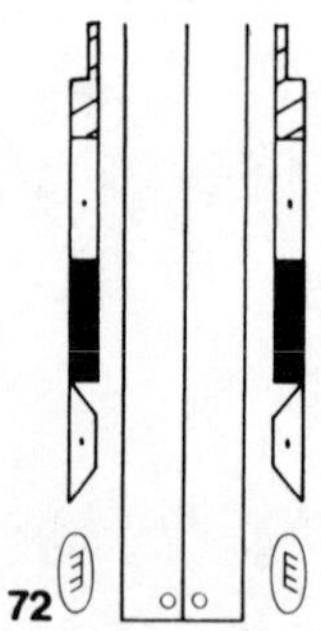

72

72. It is also possible to consider other parts of the body, such as the palms of the hands (or even the soles of the feet) as facing in some direction or, as it were, "looking" somewhere. Graph 72 shows the palms of both hands as first facing each other and then "looking" together, downwards and forwards, with a smooth transition through medium forwards to high forwards.

The palm is now written

Note: Palm "facings" should not involve arm movements if these are not especially prescribed.

The chest is also a part of the body which can be often advantageously described as facing a direction, instead of tilting towards it. In this case the chest sign has to be put into a square or oval frame.

All notators now also use square frames for the chest sign

70a. The same as paragraph 70. The end position of motion is reached here, too, by successive development rather than by simultaneous movement.

Note. It is more interesting for the student to make comparison of the similarity between body positions and chords in music, while the successive development of the final position is more akin to the progression of melody in music.

The concrete understanding that part of a melody can be a series of such elements, which, [illegible] simultaneous compositions, [illegible] of [illegible] balance.

The recognition of [illegible] is of great value in the observation and description of movement.

71. [illegible] indicated [illegible] by the 'looking' upon a definite part.

In [illegible]

72. It is also possible to consider other parts of the body, such as the palms of the hands (or even the soles of the feet), as being the guiding direction [illegible] 72 and 72a show the palms of both hands as first facing [illegible] and then the 'looking' together downwards and forwards, with a smooth transition through the [illegible] which [illegible]

Note. [illegible]

The first [illegible] which [illegible] often [illegible] In this case the [illegible] has to be put into a square or a [illegible]

SECTION C

The notation of the stresses of movement

As has been seen before, in movement notation the accentuation of the first movement in regular beats can be expressed by inserting bar lines, as in music.

Apart from this, the particular stress laid on a part of a motif is indicated in movement notation by an accent comma which is used in two shades:

A black comma for particularly "strong" movements.

A white comma for particularly "light" movements.

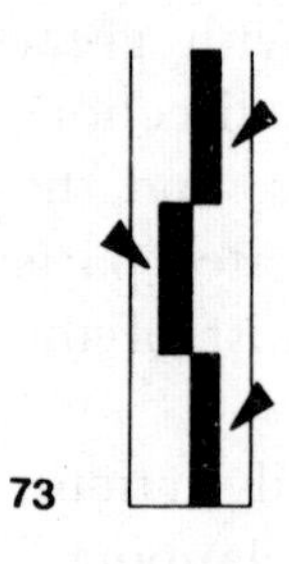

73. This graph shows three low stamping steps on "place" (*see* explanation to graphs 40 and 41) which will produce a more or less audible sound or noise.

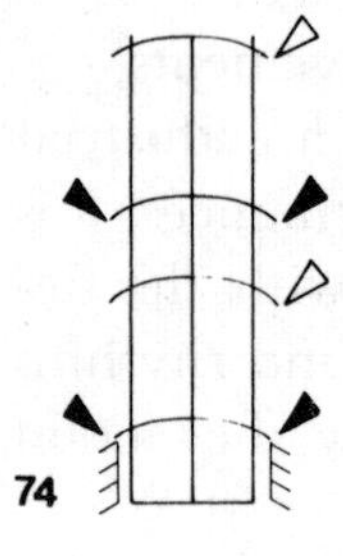

74. Stressed arm or hand movement can also produce a sound. In this graph a clapping of hands is notated. In the first and third strong claps, both hands are *hit* together. In the second and fourth light claps, the high hand alone hits the immobile left hand.

Note: the distances between the hits indicate different durations, so that a definite rhythm comes about.

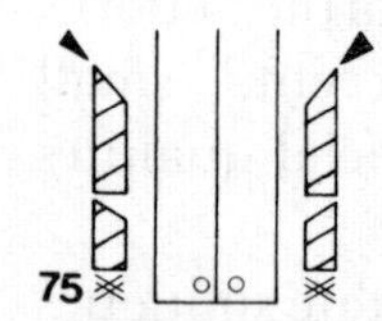

75. A stressed arm movement in the air in which no sound is produced. This graph records a "punch"-like *thrust* in which both arms stretch in a direct line diagonally upwards.

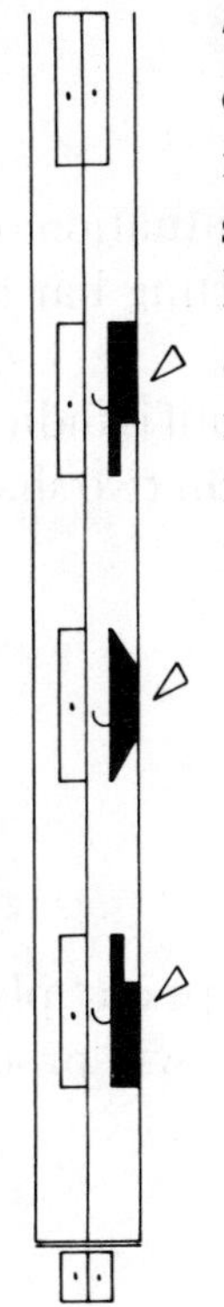

76

76. This graph shows a hopping on the left foot, tapping or *dabbing* at the same time lightly with the toes of the right foot on the ground. The taps are made, first in front; second, on the right side; and, third, behind. In the last hop both feet join together on "place." A hook connecting a leg gesture with the support column indicates that the foot touches the floor. Such floor touch signs pointing forwards mean touching with the toes, pointing backwards with the heel, pointing forwards and backwards with the whole foot.

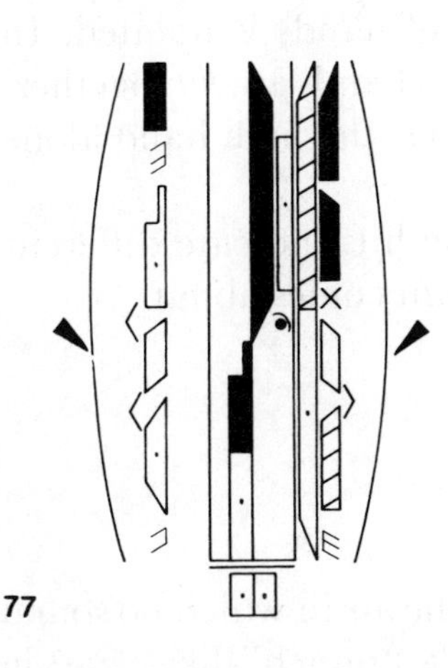

77

77. All the movements of this motif are strongly stressed, *i.e.* performed with great muscular energy. As a result of the directions of the steps and trunk movements, and the simultaneous rotations of the indicated parts of the arms, a "wringing"-like twist of the whole body takes place.

Note that in the graphs 73–77 bodily actions, such as "stamping," "hitting," "clapping," "tapping," "dabbing," "punch-like thrusting" and "wringing" have occurred.

In the notation of everyday movements, *e.g.* some of the actions occurring in industrial operations, or in dramatic performances, it is sometimes possible to dispense with the detailed description of the shapes and rhythms and to record more briefly only the action character of the movement.

For industrial purposes a more elaborate notation of the details of stresses is normally used. This is described in my book *Effort* (Macdonald & Evans Ltd., London).

To the central diagonal stroke of the "effort" signs, which represents the "accent," small affixes are added, indicating special qualities of the accent.

As it is sometimes useful to notate subtleties of accent-combinations also in recording

dances, abbreviated signs have therefore been introduced which are shown together with the original industrial signs in the graphs 78, 79, 80, 81.

These are adjustments of the standard effort signs to be used in conjunction with movement notation.

In the left vertical columns (*a*, *b*, *c*, *d*) some fundamental industrial effort signs are represented, while in the right vertical columns (a_1, b_1, c_1, d_1) the corresponding abbreviations used in dance notation are shown.

Note: The key to the abbreviation signs is:

(1) If the main diagonal stroke of the accent sign is inclined to the right the stress is "direct."

(2) If the main diagonal stroke is inclined to the left the stress is "flexible" (roundabout).

(3) A single diagonal stroke indicates a "light" stress.

(4) A double diagonal stroke indicates a "strong" stress.

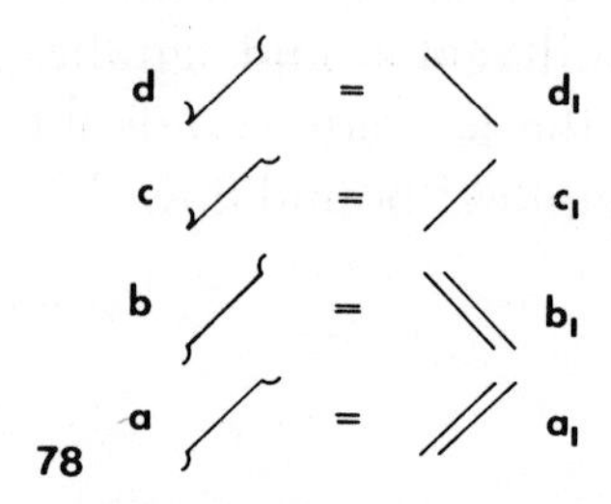

78. 78*a* and a_1 indicate a strong and direct stress.

78*b* and b_1 indicate a strong and flexible stress.

78*c* and c_1 indicate a light and direct stress.

78*d* and d_1 indicate a light and flexible stress.

The graphs shown in 79 are the same as in 78 with a small horizonal stroke added at the left side, which stroke is the sign of sustainment. With this addition a series of basic actions can be characterised.

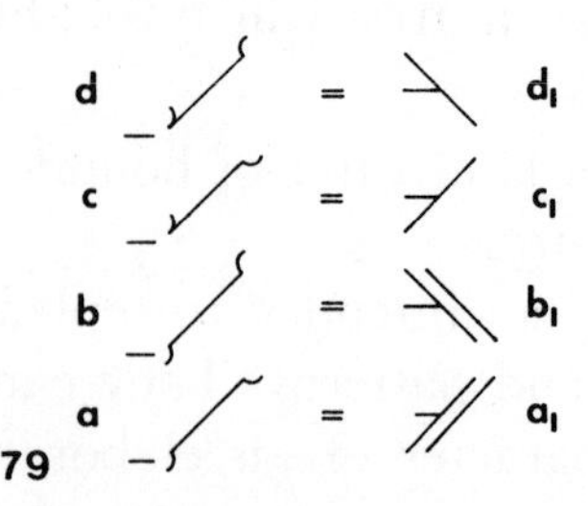

79. 79*a* and a_1 indicate "pressing," which is strong, direct and sustained.

79*b* and b_1 indicate "wringing," which is strong, flexible and sustained.

79*c* and c_1 indicate "gliding," which is

light, direct and sustained.

79*d* and d_1 indicate "floating," which is light, flexible and sustained.

The graphs shown in 80 are again the same as in 78, but the small horizontal stroke is added at the right side, which stroke is the sign of quickness. With this addition another series of basic actions are characterised.

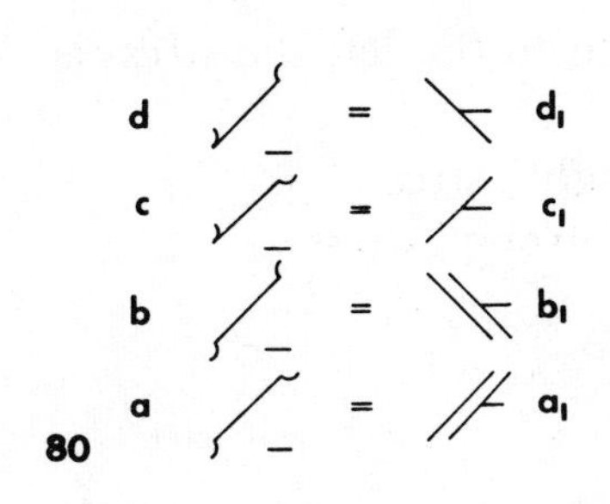

80. 80*a* and a_1 indicate "punching," which is strong, direct and quick.
80*b* and b_1 indicate "slashing," which is strong, flexible and quick.
80*c* and c_1 indicate "dabbing," which is light, direct and quick.
80*d* and d_1 indicate "flicking," which is light, flexible and quick.

The graphs shown in 81 have as an affix to the four fundamental forms of 78 a slightly longer horizontal stroke. This stroke is immediately connected with the lower end of the main diagonal and signifies the "flow" of the stress. This affix written on the left side stands for "free flow." Written on the right side the affix signifies "bound flow."

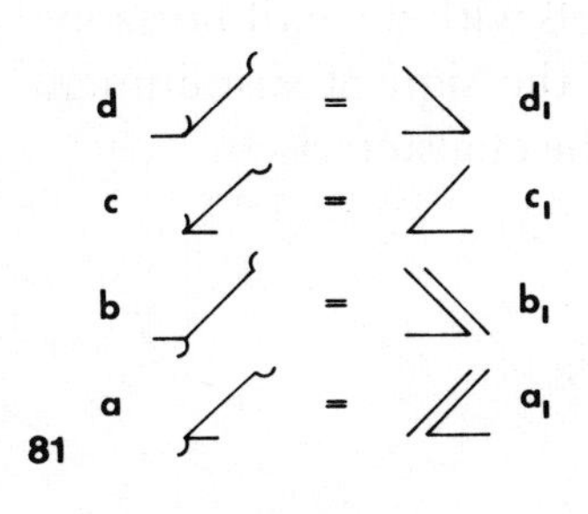

81. 81*a* and a_1 indicate a stress which is strong, direct and bound.
81*b* and b_1 indicate a stress which is strong, flexible and free.
81*c* and c_1 indicate a stress which is light, direct and bound.
81*d* and d_1 indicate a stress which is light, flexible and free.

Note: An additional flow indication of either kind—free or bound—can be added to any other simple or combined stress.

Accent or stress signs in dance notation are not intended to replace the exact description of body parts, rhythm, and patterns. They can, however, express briefly the whole action-character of an elaborate

motif. Thus, for instance, the whole character of graph 77 could be summarised by the stress sign for "wringing," which would enable the reader to realise this character at one glance.

The stress and action factors of Section C are of great interest in the study of the psychological implications of movement.

SECTION D

Some examples of the practical application of the script

82–86. *A series of 5 fundamental jumps*

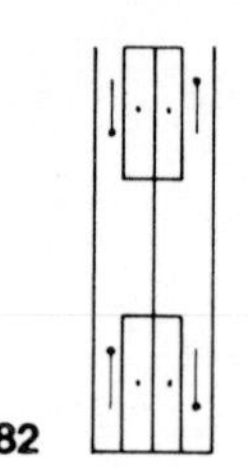

82. A jump from both feet, ending with both feet on the same spot, but changing the position of the feet from right foot in front to left foot in front (*"changement"*).

Note: the pin-shaped signs show the relative position of the feet. The jump is indicated by the gap between the two steps. The gap shows that the body has no support, and therefore must, for a moment, hover in the air. The time in the air is determined by the length of the gap.

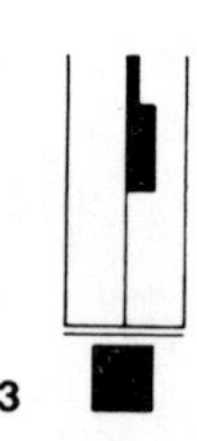

83. A jump from both feet ending on one foot, travelling forwards ("*sissonne*" form).

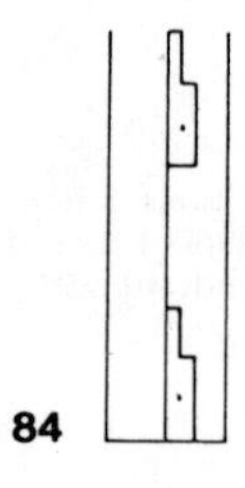

84. A hop from one foot on to the same foot, travelling forwards (*"temps levé"* form).

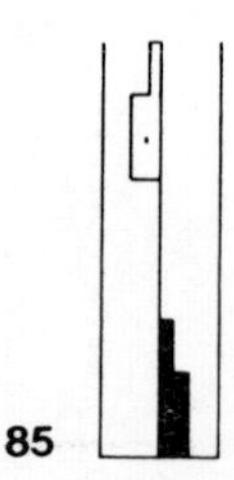

85. Leaping forwards from the right to the left foot (*"jeté"* form).

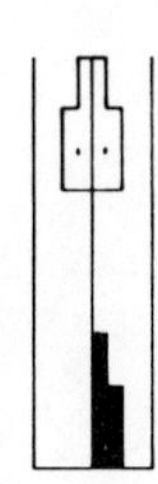

86

86. A jump from one foot on to both feet, travelling forwards ("*assemblé*" form).

87–91. *The five basic foot positions.*

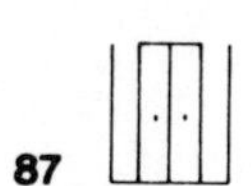

87

87. First position; the feet are together side by side.

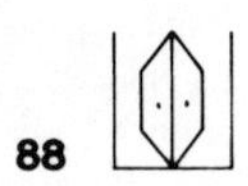

88

88. Second position: the feet are set apart sideways, usually with a foot-length distance between them.

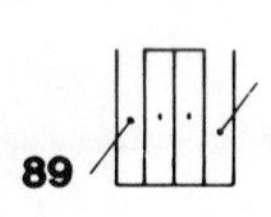

89

89. Third position: the feet are together, the right foot half way across in front of the left.

Note: the left foot can similarly be in front of the right, in which case the pin-signs will have to be altered accordingly.

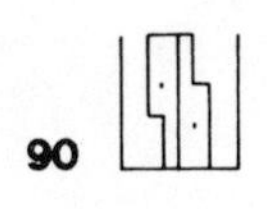

90

90. Fourth position: the feet are set apart in a forward-backward position, usually with a foot-length distance between them.

In open positions, a step-length's distance between the feet is understood.

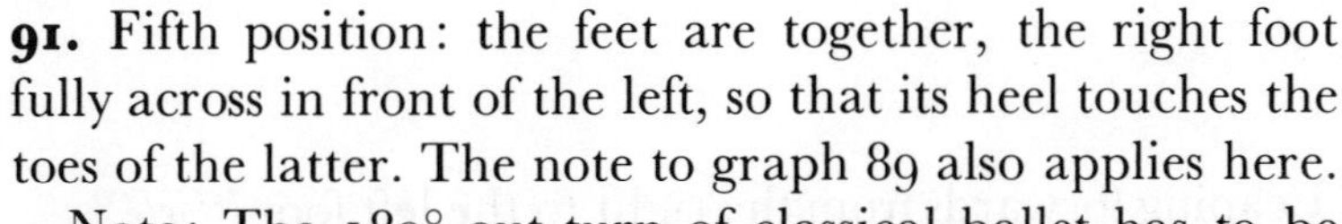

91

91. Fifth position: the feet are together, the right foot fully across in front of the left, so that its heel touches the toes of the latter. The note to graph 89 also applies here.

Note: The 180° out-turn of classical ballet has to be indicated by turn and rotation signs in the leg gesture column. In- and out-turns used in special dance styles are not included in the basic movement positions.

92–97. *Further details of positions, jumps, etc.*

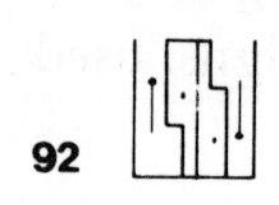
92

92. A fourth position, right foot in front, in which the feet stand in exactly the same relationship as in the fifth position, namely across one another, but are separated by the length of a foot.

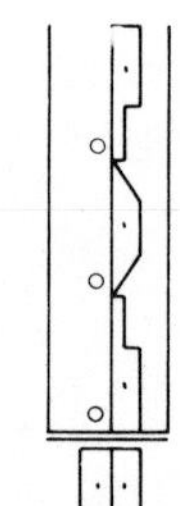
93

93. The left foot supports part of the weight throughout, while the stepping leg goes from first position to fourth in front, and to second and to fourth behind.

Now two retention signs are necessary, (*see* graph 45).

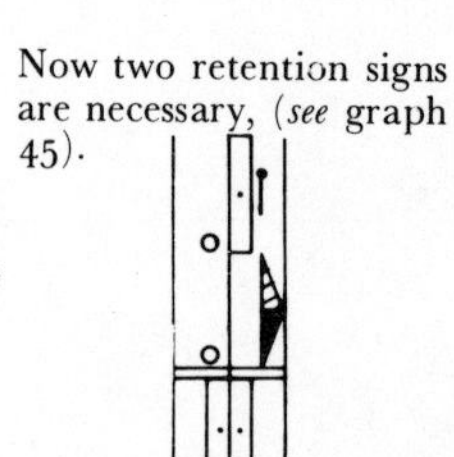

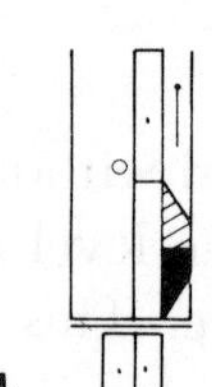
94

94. The right leg closes behind the left foot in fifth position after a high gesture to the right ("*grand battement*" form).

95. Open (second) position; the right foot closes up to the left, taking over the whole weight. The square vertical bracket links the right step to the left foot, indicating that the right foot goes beside the spot where the left was.

95

In LAB this sign is called the "staple." In KIN it may be written, but generally there is no need for it.

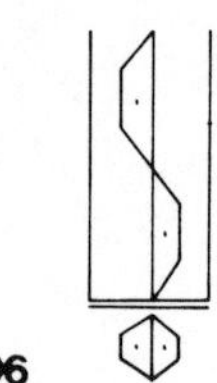
96

96. Swaying the weight of the body from second position over to the right and then to the left foot. The sideways steps go to the same spots where the feet were in the second position.

97

97. Hopping to the left on the right foot. At the start, the left leg is already lifted, so that when the standing leg comes off the floor a jump is made.

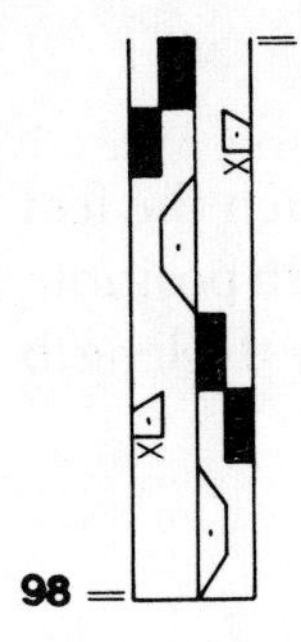

98–100. *Three simple National Dance steps.*

98. A Tarantella step; during the hop the free leg is lifted bent across the other side. Notice the repetition signs, used also in 99 and 100.

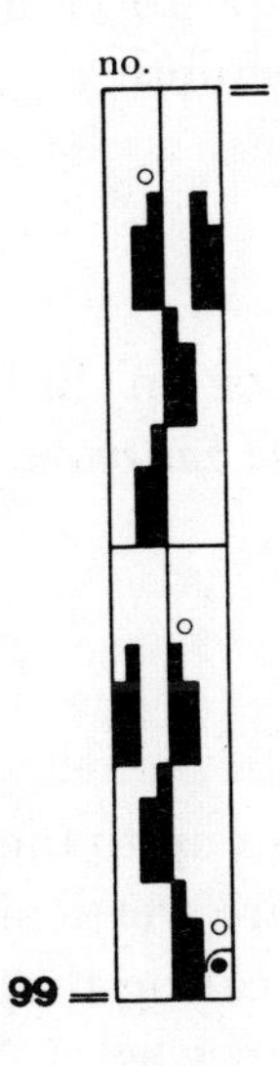

99. A Czardas step: the movement is performed without rise and fall. During the low steps forward, the level of the centre of gravity remains strictly the same. This is indicated by the "hold" after the pelvis sign.

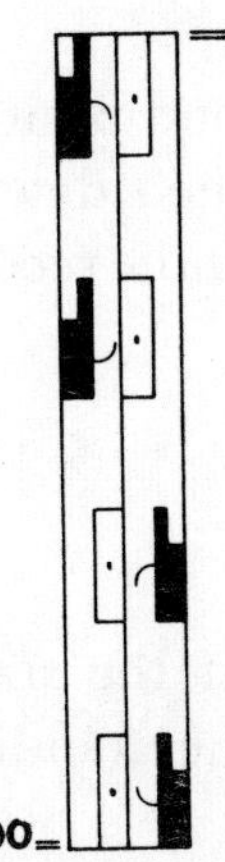

100. A typical dance step, hopping and touching the floor first with the toe and then the heel.

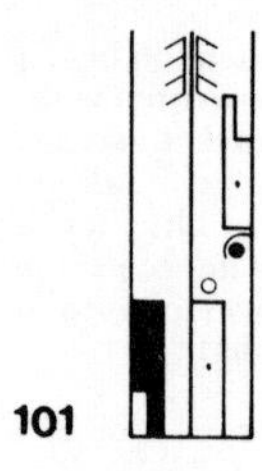
101

101–108. *Examples of various motifs displaying agility.*

101. Falling forward on to both hands.

Note: falling or loss of balance results when the centre of gravity is for a moment not above the feet, *i.e.* not in a vertical line with the support.

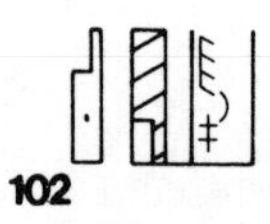
102

102. "Arabesque"-like position, the body being supported by the right knee and hand.

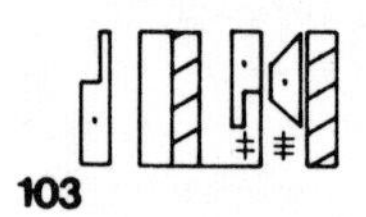
103

103. The basic movement directions of a typical classical ballet "attitude."

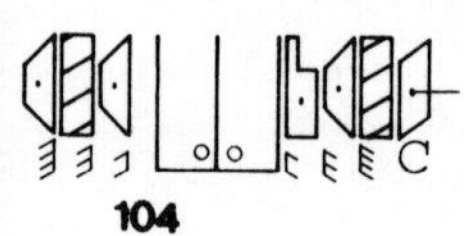
104

104. A stylised angular position, such as might appear in oriental dances or frescoes of ancient Egyptian movement. The position is a complex one, and the graph is inevitably complex also.

Note: Remember that when the elbow sign is written, it is the upper arm that moves in the direction stated; when the wrist sign is written, it is the lower arm that moves. The same applies for the various parts of the leg: when the knee sign is written, it is the thigh that moves so that the knee points into the direction stated; when the ankle sign is written, it is the lower part of the leg that moves.

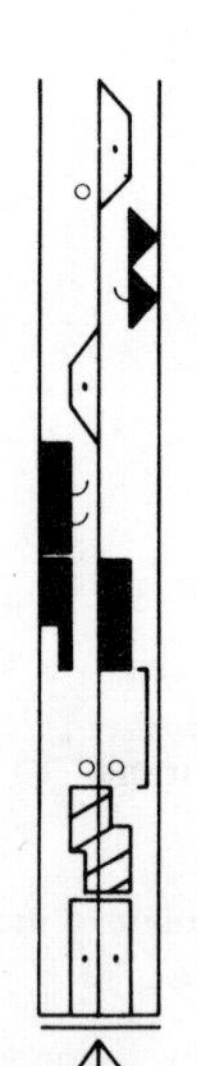
105

105. A dance step sequence in which the motif of sliding the feet over the floor alternates with leg gestures, the legs being lifted from the floor.

Starting position: legs astride, medium level stance. Without elevating them into the air (since there are no jumping gaps) slide the feet together into first position

medium level, then apart into fourth position high level, right foot front. After a pause for one beat the weight is lowered on the right foot and the left lifted off the ground behind. Notice the angular vertical bracket in the right leg column which shows that "place" (*see* explanation to graphs 40 and 41) is the spot where the right foot stood previously, although the weight is shifted forward when the left foot is released.

The movement on beat 4 may also be written without the bracket (staple, *see* graph 34), but an indication of direction is needed. (The centre of gravity moves forward in this example.)

Now the tip of the left foot slides through the first position (two floor touch signs connected with one gesture means sliding) and the weight is transferred left sideways on to the left leg. The right foot performs a short touch of the floor before stepping out to the right, while the left leg retains weight, thus ending in a second position.

Whilst the one leg is gesturing the other one has to take the weight. For this reason a retention sign is needed on beats 5 and 7, (*see* graph 17).

106

106. The legs beat together in the air ("*cabriole,*" "*assemblé battu*").

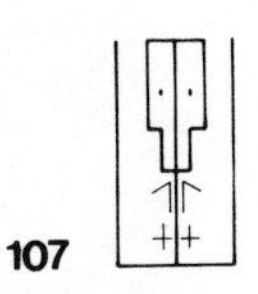

107

107. Lying on the back, supported on seat (two hip signs) and shoulders.

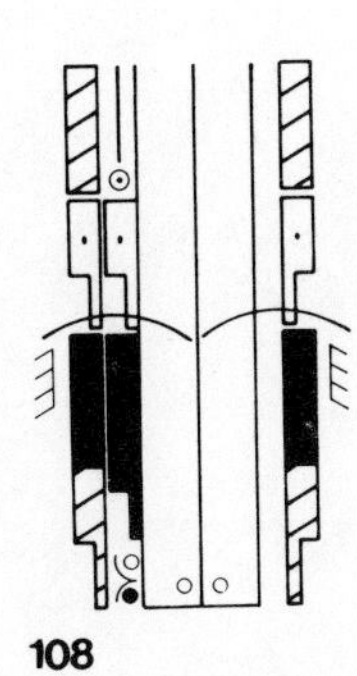

108

108. Bending backwards to touch the floor with the hands (bridge), and coming up again. For the return to the upright the usual directional sign "high" may be used in the trunk column. Here a special "return to normal" sign (last sign in the left trunk column) is shown.

One now uses to indicate the trunk.

Note: This sign (circle with a dot) is used for any part of the body when it returns to its normal carriage from a special position. The duration line after the sign indicates the relative length of the time used for this return.

This is still used in LAB. KIN uses as the general "back-to-normal" sign.

109–114. *Examples of partners moving together.*

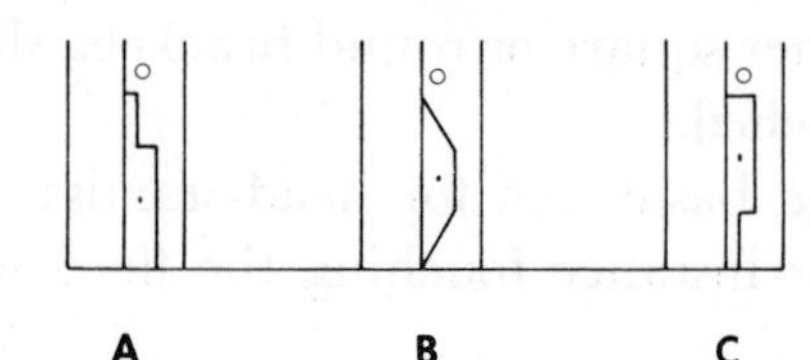

109. Three people move together, each stepping in a different direction. If several people move in a different manner at the same time, each is given an individual staff which is joined by a straight line to the others, thus forming a group score.

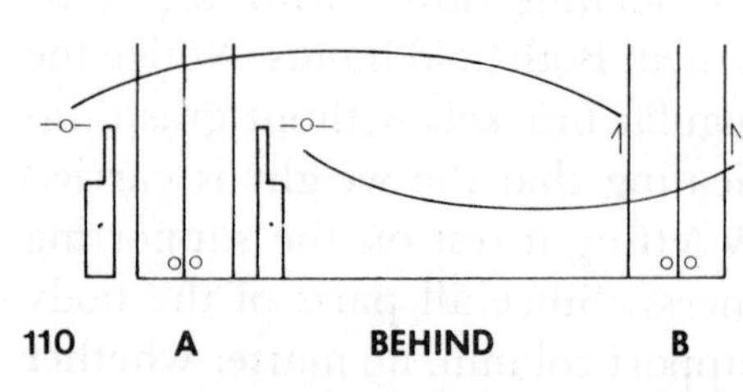

110. Two people standing together. Partner A stretches his arms forward and touches B's shoulders. The signs with two ends with white centres, indicate that A touches B's shoulders "from above," right hand on right shoulder, left hand on left shoulder.

Note: If no particular part of the limbs is mentioned, it is the end which touches, *i.e.* hands or feet.

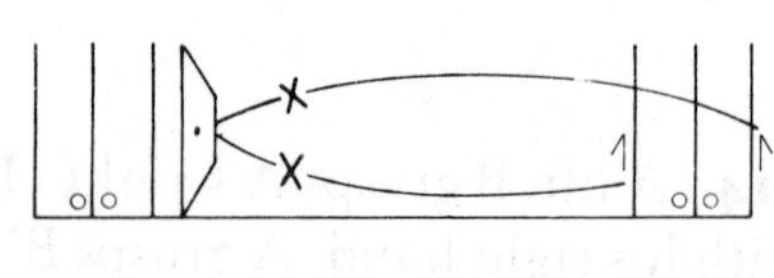

111. A holds B with his right arm round both shoulders. The narrow sign in the bracket means that the arm is bent and *embraces* the partner's shoulders. It is written near the active part, which is in this case A's right arm.

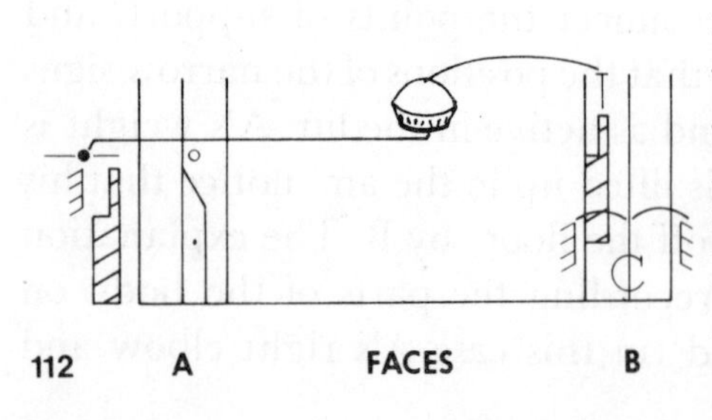

112. A holds a basket high and forwards, carrying it from underneath with his flat left hand without gripping with his fingers. B stands on his head and touches the basket from behind with his left foot. The angular brackets (in A's staff) indicate that the weight of an object or person is

carried, as opposed to the curved brackets (in B's staff) (touch signs) showing that no weight is taken. B also touches the floor with his hands. The pin signs, in connection with either square or round brackets, show from which side the object is approached.

B's head-stand is recorded by the basic sign for head-stands; any further details of the position, as for instance touching the floor with both hands, must be added.

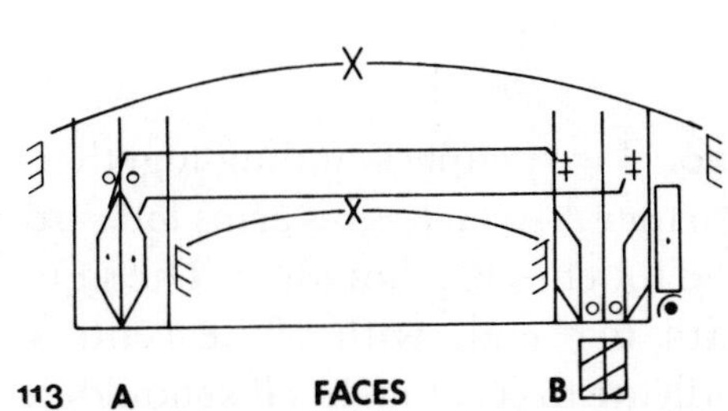

113. Standing on a partner's knees. A's weight is carried on B's knees, B crouching down with legs out-turned. Both hold hands. Notice the angular brackets without grasp, indicating that the weight is carried by letting it rest on the supporting parts of the body (in this case B's knees). Since all parts of the body carrying its weight are written in the support column, no matter whether the weight is carried by the floor, or by objects, or by other persons, A's position with legs astride, on B's knees is shown in the support column. The narrow sign in the centre of the curved ("touch") brackets indicates that both partners grip the hands of the other in the touch.

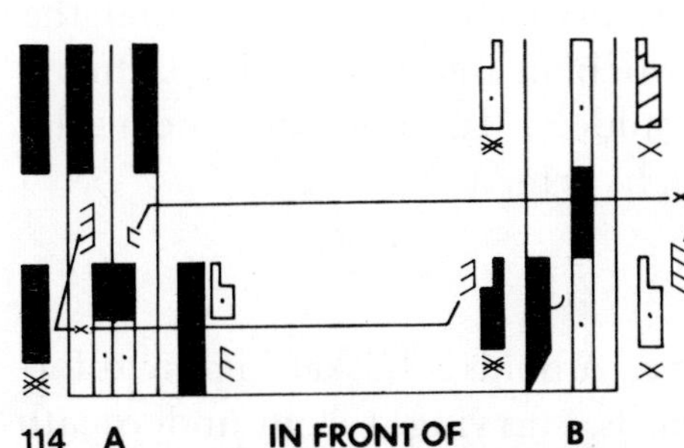

114. A lift. B grasps A's right elbow with his right hand. A grasps B's left wrist with his left hand. The angular brackets with the narrow sign indicate carrying with hand grasp. Notice also that the angular brackets connect the points of support, and that the positions of the narrow signs show A's left hand and B's right hand as active in the lift. A's weight is supported by these two grasps and is lifted up in the air (notice that his two legs are shown as being finally off the floor) by B. The explanation of graph 33 shows the method of recording the parts of the body on which the body weight is supported (in this case A's right elbow and left hand).

Note on Staging Signs.

The place of a person on a definite spot in space, say, on the stage, can be inserted in the form of a floor design and made more precise by additional notes in words. The same is the case with positions in relation to a partner or a group. (*See* graphs 110–114, where it is indicated by words whether the person A stands behind the person B, or facing B, or in front of B.)

Special group movement signs belong to the category of staging signs. The ingenious system of group movement symbols, which has been developed by Professor A. Knust, can be highly recommended. The details of staging signs fall however outside this introduction into the principles of body movement notation.

New symbols for all these circumstances are used. Area signs indicate the area, *e.g.* the central area of the floor

the forward central area of the floor, etc.

Relationship signs indicate the relation of the partners to each other, etc. *e.g.* the boy is standing behind the girl

the girl is standing in front of the boy.

each boy has one girl on his right

each girl has one boy on her left

INDEX A

List of Signs in Alphabetical Order

INDEX B

List of Movements in the Order of Graph Numbers

Graphs	*Movement*
1–8	Trunk, arm and legs—gestures; steps (transfer of weight) without and with stops.
9–12	Narrowing and widening of movement.
13–16	Touching and gripping.
17	Rebouncing movements.
18	Active and passive movements.
19–25	Successions of arm, trunk and leg articulations.
26–27	Finger movements.
28–30	Combinations of articulation sequences and narrowing and widening movements.
31–38	Transference of weight to various parts of the body.
39	Rhythmical motif (with music notation).
40	Elevation levels on "place."
41	Table of elevation levels in various directions of space. (This table comprises space-relation signs.)
42	Steps forming floor pattern.
43	Arm gestures forming air pattern.
44–45	Smooth transitions between varying levels.
46	Changes of levels and an example of an intermediate direction.
47	Hanging on arms (support above centre of gravity).
48–49	Passing in front of or behind the body or a part of the body.
50	Clockwise and counter-clockwise turns.
51–52	Combinations of turns and steps.
53	Turning jumps.
54	Twist, turns of legs and arms.
55–57	Steps and hops along curved and straight pathways.
58–59	Cartwheels and somersaults.
60	Immobilising an arm in space during a turn.
61–62	Deviations and diversions of the directions of arm movements.
63–68	Body positions reached by a simultaneous movement of the whole body.
69–70	Body positions reached by successive movements of one part of the body after another.
71–72	Face (71) and palms (72) "looking," i.e. turning towards definite directions.
73–76	Stresses of movement causing stamping with the feet (73), clapping hands (74), thrusting with arms (75), dabbing with one foot on floor (76).
77	Twisting of arms in opposition to trunk movement, limbs and steps, resulting in a "wringing" movement of the whole body. (Compare 79b, the simple stress sign indicating "wringing.")
78–81	Various stresses of movement (without indication of definite directions of body parts).
82–86	Five jumps. From *both* legs to *both* legs. From *both* legs to *one* leg. From *one* leg to the same leg. From *one* leg to the other leg. From *one* leg to *both* legs.
87–91	Five positions of feet, (first, second, third, fourth and fifth positions).
92	Variant of fourth position.
93–97	Various detailed positions, jumps, etc.
98–108	National dance steps, movements and motifs displaying agility.
109–114	Examples of partners moving together.

Introduction

WHEN MY HUSBAND DIED in 1957 and bequeathed Waddesdon Manor to the National Trust, their first care was to enable the public to visit the house as agreeably as possible. Their second priority was the longer-term objective of producing a complete catalogue of the contents of the house.

During the 21 years since the catalogue was first mooted, ten volumes have been published out of an anticipated total of seventeen. Yet although the complete series will one day give all the known provenance of the works of art in the bequest, the story of the house itself and of those who lived in it will still be missing.

I am trying to fill this gap because, by good fortune, I have probably learnt rather more than most about the people who created Waddesdon, who lived in it and transformed it, stage by stage, into what it has now become.

For 56 years I have been closely associated with many of its inhabitants and thanks to the date of my birth and marriage I became a member of the Rothschild family at a time when many of an older generation were still alive. They could clearly remember events which now seem infinitely long ago and were kind enough to share their memories with me and pander to my eagerness to learn all that they could tell me. In this way I was given the opportunity of understanding at least a few of the factors which impelled some of the family to reach decisions which have had a great impact on my own life. But my main source of information was my husband whose interest in his family was intense and whose knowledge of it was unrivalled.

The story of Waddesdon Manor divides itself naturally into its four different periods of ownership. They are those of three Rothschilds, Baron Ferdinand, his sister Alice and their great-nephew James; and finally, the National Trust in whose possession Waddesdon will, I hope, as in a fairy-tale, live happily ever after.

D. de R.

Baron Ferdinand de Rothschild 1874-1898

THE FIRST ROTHSCHILD to be known as an inhabitant of Frankfort lived there in the mid sixteenth century; the first to be known as a collector of works of art was Mayer Amschel (1744–1812), the founder of the banking firm whose influence on international finance derived from his appointment as financial adviser to the Elector of Hesse in 1801. It was Mayer Amschel's collection of rare coins and his skill as a chess player which first aroused the interest of the Elector, who later placed all his financial concerns in his hands. Mayer Amschel had five sons; the eldest remained in Frankfort, but the other four were sent to open banking houses in what were then, financially, the four most important countries of Europe—Austria, England, France and the Kingdom of the Two Sicilies. The five brothers were closely knit as a family and they operated their banks as a single unit, but with the passage of time these banks have lessened in number. The first to go was the Naples branch which was closed in 1869 after the Bourbons had had to leave the city; the next was Frankfort which ceased to exist in 1901, when Baron Willy, the Rothschild in charge of it, died leaving only two daughters. From that date the remaining banks became independent entities. Finally, the Vienna branch closed when Hitler invaded Austria. Now, only the London and Paris houses remain.

The five sons of Mayer Amschel all married; only his eldest son, Amschel, had no children. In the course of time the progeny of the other four sons intermarried continuously—in some cases for three succeeding generations. Such intensive inbreeding seems to have sustained a natural aptitude for finance as well as a distinct scientific bent. Common to all was a flair for quality and a love of collecting, whether it was of works of art, books or butterflies.

I knew intimately the youngest son of Mayer Amschel's youngest son; he was my father-in-law, Edmond. I also knew quite well the widow of Salomon, one of his elder brothers. Edmond himself married Adelaide, the grand-daughter of his father's brother Mayer Carl of the Naples branch; her range of family knowledge was singularly complete. Most people have eight great-grandfathers: my husband, thanks to intermarriage, had only one—Mayer Amschel. Whenever I am asked what

Baron Ferdinand de Rothschild

relation he was to any other Rothschild it always seems simpler to say he was a cousin. This answer has the merit of truth but in most cases it would be possible to say that he was also an uncle or a nephew or a great-nephew. This multiple relationship sometimes played havoc with the mode of address used by members of the family, in the old days, outside England. My father-in-law told me that since his earliest youth he had been accustomed to '*tu-toyer*' his well-liked cousin Mathilde; on his marriage to her daughter he found it not only embarrassing but quite difficult to remember to conform to the rigid convention of the day and refer to Mathilde, thereafter, as '*Ma chère Belle Mere*' and employ the more formal 'vous' whenever he spoke to her.

Baron Ferdinand de Rothschild, who was alone responsible for the existence of Waddesdon Manor and its surrounding estate, was a great-grandson of Mayer Amschel. Born in Paris in 1839, he was a younger son of Baron Anselm who had married Charlotte, a daughter of N. M. Rothschild of London. Shortly after his birth his father was sent, first to Frankfort and then to take charge of the family bank in Vienna. Baron Ferdinand's childhood in Frankfort and Austria was uneventful, interrupted only by a hugely enjoyed expedition to visit the 1851 Great Exhibition in London. His relations with his father were always distant: they never understood each other. However, his adoration for his mother was unlimited. To quote his own words: 'Children, like dogs, feel instinctively who it is who genuinely loves them. All my love went to my mother, who indeed sacrificed the whole of her short life to the care and tuition of her young family. I could hardly bear to be out of her sight; my happiest moments were when I was recovering from an illness and she nursed me and stayed at my bedside, telling me stories of which I never tired. My mother was my guardian angel, the one being around whom my existence revolved'.

Both his father and his mother contributed to his early awareness and love of works of art, which became the overriding interest of his life. Writing of his childhood he said: 'In the early forties we resided in Frankfort, spending the winters in the town and the summer at a villa close by. As soon as the swallows made their appearance my father's curiosities were packed and stored away in a strong-room, where they remained until the cold drove us back again from the country. It was my privilege on these occasions to place some of the smaller articles in their old leather cases, and then again in the winter to assist in unpacking them and rearranging

* Baron Ferdinand de Rothschild's unpublished *Reminiscences* written in 1897.

Baroness Anselm de Rothschild (1807–1859), mother of Baron Ferdinand, after a portrait by Sir Thomas Lawrence

them in their places. Merely to touch them sent a thrill of delight through my small frame. Long before I was born my father had acquired a collection of Dutch pictures from Holland. Day after day I would reverently study them, learning under my mother's tuition to distinguish a Teniers from an Ostade or a Wouvermans from a Both . . . But my happiness was greatest when Professor Oppenheim was announced. He was a painter of no special merit but he was a friend of the family, and all we children had to sit to him for our portraits—which in days not far distant will probably adorn the steward's or the housekeeper's room. I readily forgave him the severe trials of patience to which he subjected me, because he was one of my father's chief purveyors of works of art. In those days there were no curiosity dealers in Frankfort worthy of the name, but his work took Professor Oppenheim into many private houses, where he occasionally discovered and picked up a fine old German cup, which he then brought to my father. I cannot describe the joy I felt when he unpacked some quaint Nuremberg or Augsburg tankard, or the figure of a man, a lion or a stag, which was weighed and bought by the weight. Oh! for those good old days when the artistic merit of a cup was of no account to its possessor, and he merely valued it according to the number of ounces it contained.'

The first tragedy of Baron Ferdinand's life came when his mother died in 1859; he was then nineteen years old. He was deeply attached to his two brothers and four sisters, but after his mother's death he felt he had no future in his father's austere house. England beckoned him as being in some way a link with this mother; within a few months he journeyed to London and then decided to stay there. His father, Baron Anselm, made no effort to force his son to take an active part in the family firm; he appears to have contemplated this son's interest in the arts and his lack of interest in banking with toleration. Baron Ferdinand, however, viewed his father's somewhat sporadic activity as an art collector with less equanamity. 'My Father might have formed a matchless collection' he wrote 'as he lived in a country where for years old works of art were deemed worthless. But his taste was limited to a small range as he cared for minute articles only, besides his time was too much occupied with business to devote much of it to other pursuits. When I left Vienna for London in 1860, I had many opportunities of offering him works of art, but he rarely availed himself of them. Many and many a time dealers showed me some fine article for which I had not space in my humble lodgings or which I had not the means to acquire and which I then offered to my Father—but as a rule he declined them'. Despite Baron Ferdinand's feelings of frustration, some thirty works of art which are now at Waddesdon come from Baron Anselm's collection; the majority are indeed snuff-boxes, miniatures or other 'minute articles'— not very helpful when the time came to furnish large empty rooms.

Baron Ferdinand's decision to settle in London proved to be a happy one; he fell in love with his first cousin Evelina, the daughter of Baron Lionel de Rothschild of the English branch, and his mother's niece. He became a British subject at the joint wishes of both himself and his prospective parents-in-law and, in July 1865, he and Evelina were married, with

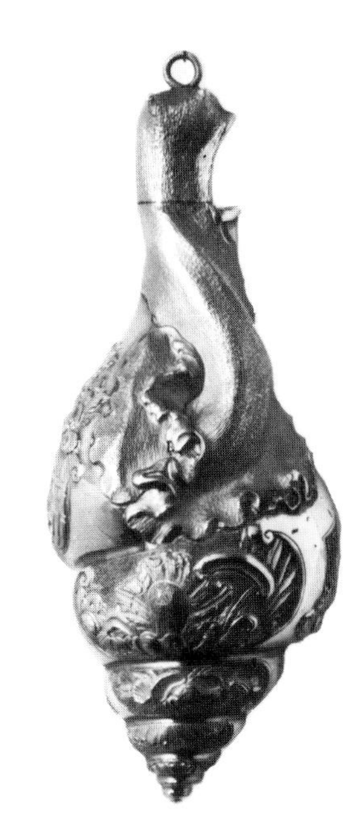

3-inch high gold flask in the shape of a shell. c. 1740

Egg in gold, agate and enamel inscribed 'Rien d'agreable Eloignez de Vous'. The mis-spelling of 'éloigné' makes it probable that it was made in England, rather than France, c. 1760

Disraeli making a particularly felicitous and flowery speech at the wedding. They bought a house in Piccadilly and for eighteen months Baron Ferdinand learnt what perfect bliss could be, but it was not to last. His wife was injured in a railway accident and, as a result, died while giving birth to a still-born son. The inscription he placed on her grave, inspired by the Psalms and the Proverbs, may give the key to his feelings:

'If I ascend up into heaven, thou art there
If I lie down in the grave, behold I find thee.
Even there, thy hand leads me and thy right hand supports me.
She opened her life with wisdom and in her speech was the law of kindness.
My darling wife'.

Once again he was forlorn and lonely and the fact that he had glimpsed paradise only enhanced this feeling.

He had evidently planned with his wife to play a useful part in life from the background of a beautiful home, but although his sister Alice, then a girl of nineteen, decided to devote her life to his to relieve his loneliness, for some eight years he was numbed by sorrow. Doubtless he was advised that new sights and sounds might take his mind off his misery. He travelled to Russia alone and spent some time there in evident despondency. Even when pressed to take his pick of many wonderful works of art belonging to a Princess Galitzine which were shortly afterwards to be put up for sale, he was unable to rouse himself from his sorrow. In his *Reminiscences* he records: 'On entering the Princess's Palace and seeing the many fine pictures, the furniture, the sixteenth century works of art, I lost my breath. No amateur ever had such an opportunity, and possibly will never have the like again . . . I alas was still very inexperienced, moreover I was bewildered and hustled, and finally being in deep mourning I was not in the mood to take advantage of the opportunity'. All he bought was a topaz cup as a present for his father-in-law and 'a very inferior picture of the School of Snyders' for himself. Within a short time the majority of Princess Galitzine's possessions had found their way through dealers to the Wallace Collection.

On his return home he busied himself in planning and building the Evelina Hospital for Children in Southwark as a memorial to his wife. The hospital, which he purposely placed in one of the most crowded and poorest parts of London, had beds for a hundred children. It was formally opened by the Lord Mayor of London in 1869 who, in his speech,

A group of gold boxes
Top row left to right:
Gold Piqué snuff box with miniature after Nattier, 1760
Gold & enamel travelling inkpot, c. 1750
Bonbonnière in gold, enamel & mother of pearl with miniatures of the Bombelles Family.

Bottom row left to right:
Swiss snuff box in gold & diamonds, late 18th century
Gold enamel needlecase, c. 1765
Double snuff box in gold & agate, mid 18th century.

stressed that it was the first establishment for the cure of the sick which he had seen where emphasis had been put on the provision of light, air and space. Possibly through the building and the maintenance of the Evelina Hospital Baron Ferdinand became interested in the support of other hospitals. He was a generous donor, particularly to the Hospital for Consumptives in the Brompton Road, and St. George's Hospital at Hyde Park Corner, which was within a stone's throw of his own house in Piccadilly.

His sister Alice, having decided to live permanently in England, began by renting a house on Wimbledon Common, but joined her brother during the winter months at Leighton House, Leighton Buzzard, from where they hunted with the Whaddon Chase and the Tring Staghounds. Before long, the house next door to Baron Ferdinand's in Piccadilly became available and Miss Alice (as she was always known) seized the opportunity to become his near neighbour in London. Indeed they pierced a communicating door between the two houses, thus establishing the future pattern of their lives, separate but together.

At his death Baron Ferdinand left all his correspondence to his sister, it is thought with instructions that she should destroy it. Apart from the scarce family anecdotes of the period it is therefore only through reports issued by various charities,

Page from Baron Ferdinand's
Livre d'Or

Aerial view of Waddesdon

through memoirs and diaries of the time, and from snippets from the newspapers that it is possible to find any clue as to the sort of life Baron Ferdinand led during the eight years following his wife's death. It is obvious that he was active in various charitable fields and that he was making an increasingly wide circle of friends in London. Some of them were leading figures in the literary and artistic world. In 1873, he started keeping a *Livre d'Or*—an album in which he asked his friends to write or draw something. Among the first to do so were Anthony Trollope, Robert Browning and Sir John Millais. He was also making political friends; Gladstone and, of course, Disraeli added their contributions in 1873, as did John Lothrop Motley, then American Minister in London, who was famous as the author of the *Rise of the Dutch Republic.**

It was while hunting that Baron Ferdinand first saw the magnificent views which can be glimpsed from the top of the hill on which Waddesdon Manor now stands, and, when his father died in 1874, he found himself provided with the funds

* The present Lord Rothschild reproduced Baron Ferdinand's *Livre d'Or* as his Roxburghe Club book (Cambridge University Press, 1957).

to build a house there and realise the plans he had first formulated with his wife.

The best and most detailed account of the building of Waddesdon Manor was written by Baron Ferdinand himself only about a year before he died. He said he wrote this because of the many enquiries he had received from his friends who wanted to know how he had managed to tackle such a vast enterprise in such a comparatively short time. If I were asked for my own views on *why* he did so I think, in racing parlance, I would say it was out of Loneliness by Artistic Craving. I can, however, think of no better way of describing the building of Waddesdon than by quoting from Baron Ferdinand's own account. This is what he wrote:

> 'In the autumn of 1874 I purchased from the Duke of Marlborough, by private treaty, his estate of Waddesdon and Winchendon, which had been put up for sale at Tokenhouse Yard in the spring of the year but withdrawn as the reserve price had not been reached. It then consisted of 2,700 acres to which I have since added about 500 acres. I had been looking out for a residential estate for some time, and could I have obtained one I should not have acquired this property, which was all farm land, chiefly arable, with neither a house nor a park, and though comparatively near London, was at a distance of six miles from Aylesbury, the nearest railway station. But there was none other to be had; there was not even the prospect of one coming into the market, and I was loath to wait on chance. So I took Waddesdon with its defects and its drawbacks—of which more hereafter—perhaps a little too rashly. I was buoyed up with the illusions and beguiled by the belief that within four years it would be connected with Baker Street by a direct line of railway, the first sod of which had not yet been turned. This much could be said in its favour; it had a bracing and salubrious air, pleasant scenery, excellent hunting, and was untainted by factories and villadom.
>
> As soon as the contract was signed I set out for Paris in quest of an architect, and decided on the late M. Destailleur, whose father and grandfather had been architects of the Duke of Orleans, while he himself had risen to fame by his intelligent and successful restoration of the Château de Mouchy. M. Destailleur accompanied me back to England to choose the site for the house. This being settled, he left me fully supplied with instructions, while Monsieur Lainé, a French landscape gardener, was bidden to make designs for the terraces, the principal

roads and plantations. It may be asked what induced me to employ foreign instead of native talent of which there was no lack at hand? My reply is, that having been greatly impressed by the ancient Châteaux of the Valois during a tour I once made in Touraine, I determined to build my house in the same style, and considered it safer to get the design made by a French architect who was familiar with the work, than by an English one whose knowledge and experience of the architecture of that period could be less thoroughly trusted. The French sixteenth century style, on which I had long set my heart, was particularly suitable to the surroundings of the site I had selected, and more uncommon than the Tudor, Jacobean or Adam of which the country affords so many and such unique specimens. Besides, I may mention that M. Lainé was called in only after Mr Thomas, the then most eminent English landscape gardener, had declined to lay out the grounds for reasons he did not deign to divulge.

By the side of the grand *châteux* of the Touraine, Waddesdon would appear a pigmy. The castle of Chambord, for example, contains 450 rooms, the smallest of which would dwarf the largest at Waddesdon. But its main features are borrowed from them; its towers from Maintenon, the château of the duc de Noailles, and its external staircases from Blois, though the latter, which are unglazed and open to the weather, are much more ornate. Though far from being the realisation of a dream in stone and mortar like Chenonceaux, M. Destailleur's work had fairly fulfilled my expectations.

M. Destailleur was a man of the highest capacity in his profession. He was a purist in style, painstaking, conscientious, and of the most scrupulous honesty. During the eighteen years of my relations with him there was never the smallest difference between us. But he was dilatory and unpractical. He had not the faintest conception of the needs of a large establishment, sacrificed the most urgent household requirements to external architectural features, and had the most supreme contempt for ventilation, light, air and all internal conveniences. This, perhaps, need not have surprised me, for he and his numerous family lived huddled together in a small and musty house in a dingy back street which I never entered without a shudder. It took me many an hour to convince him that ladies need space for their gowns and their toilette, and men want rooms in which they can move at their ease and perform their ablutions. The delay in the first start, however, was only partly his fault. He submitted a plan to me at the end of a year on a scale of such grandeur that I begged him to reduce it, and another long year was spent on the preparation of a second and more modest proposal. This I sanctioned, though it did not quite satisfy me. 'You will regret your decision' he said to me at the time; *'one always builds too small'*. And he prophesied truly. After I had lived in the house for a while I was compelled to add first one wing and then another; and a greater outlay was eventually incurred than had the original plan been carried out, not to speak of the discomfort and inconvenience caused by the presence of the workmen in the house. Though more picturesque the building is less effective, and while spreading over so much ground it is less compact and commodious.

As soon as the architect, the landscape gardener and the engineers had settled their plans, we set to work, but at the outset were brought face to face with a most serious consideration. This was the question of the water supply, as the few springs in the fields were not to be relied on in a drought. The Chiltern Hills fortunately contain an inexhaustible quantity of excellent water, which an Aylesbury company works with much skill to the advantage of the immediate neighbourhood and profit to its shareholders. Not a moment was lost in coming to terms with the Company, laying down seven miles of pipes from the county town to the village and thence to the projected site of the house, and building a large storage tank in the grounds. This subsequently proved insufficient for our wants, as one dry summer the supply failed, and but for the Manager's energy, who sat up all night at the Works sending us up water, we should have been compelled to leave the next day. To obviate the recurrence of a similar difficulty another and larger tank was constructed.

Then we had some trouble with the foundations of the house. We planned to build it on the crown of Lodge Hill, as it is called; small, but steep with its highest point being 64 feet above sea-level, it commands a panoramic view over several counties. The part of the hill we had selected as the site of the house consists of sand, and the foundations having been proceeded with for some months proved not to have been set deep enough, as they suddenly gave way. The whole of the brickwork had then to be removed and thirty feet of sand excavated until a firm bottom of clay was reached. I now began to realise the

Opposite Destailleur's elevation of the North front

The North front as it was built

Overleaf Preparing the site. Landscaping the Park. Laying the foundations of the house

importance of the task I had undertaken. But the difficulty of building a house is insignificant compared with the labour of transforming a bare wilderness into a park, and I was so disheartened at first by the delay and the worry that during four years I rarely went near the place. Slowest and most irksome of all was the progress of the roads, on which the available labourers of the neighbourhood were engaged supplemented by a gang of navvies under the direction of Mr Alexander, a London engineer, and M. Lainé. The steepness of the hill necessitated an endless amount of digging and levelling to give an easy gradient to the roads and a natural appearance to the banks and slopes. Landslips constantly occurred. Cutting into the hill interfered with the natural drainage, and despite the elaborate precautions we had taken, the water often forced its way out of some unexpected place after a spell of wet weather, tearing down great masses of earth. Like Sisyphus, we had repeatedly to take up the same task, though fortunately with more permanent results. The stone for the house which came from Bath, and most of the bricks which came from all parts of the country were conveyed

Stonemasons working at Waddesdon, c. 1876

Chimneys at Waddesdon

on a temporary steam tram from the railway direct to the foot of the hill, up which the trucks were drawn on rails by a cable engine. Other materials for the building, as well as for the farmsteads, cottages and lodges, and the trees and the shrubs, had to be carted some miles by road. Percheron mares were imported from Normandy for this purpose, and they proved most serviceable, for though less enduring they travelled faster over the rough ground and were much cheaper than Shire horses.

The Percherons were employed principally in connection with the cartage of large trees which were brought from all parts of the neighbourhood, and for the moving of which into the highways the telegraph wires had to be temporarily displaced. They were transplanted with huge balls of earth round their roots, and were lowered into the ground by a system of chains, having been conveyed to the required spot on specially constructed carts, each drawn by a team of sixteen horses. The trees answered their purpose for a time, for they quickly clothed and adorned the bare hill. But if I may venture to proffer a word of advice to anyone who may feel inclined to follow my example—it is to abstain from transplanting old trees, limes and chestnuts perhaps excepted, and even these should not be more than thirty or forty years old. Older trees, however great may be the experience and skill of

The South front seen from the foot of the hill

Opposite Exterior of the Morning Room

the men engaged in the process, rarely recover from the injury to their roots, or bear the change from the soil and the climatic conditions in which they have been grown. Young trees try your patience at first, but they soon catch up with the old ones, and make better timber and foliage.

In 1880 I first slept in the so-called bachelors' wing, and in 1883 in the main part of the house. We had a grand housewarming in the month of July of that year, though the stables were not yet built, and the horses and carriages we required had to be accommodated in tents and in the village inns. The stables were built the following year from plans made by my stud groom, my builder, Mr Condor—than whom I have never met a more trustworthy businessman—and myself. Only the elevations were designed by M. Destailleur, and no other architect was ever called in for the alterations and additions subsequently carried out at Waddesdon. The whole credit of the work is his. I must take my full share of whatever blame there be. 'You should always begin with your second house', a lady once wittily said to me. But could this paradox be put into practice the second house would be as much open to criticism as the first. However great

your experience may be, you cannot arrive at perfection. I was anxious from the outset to sacrifice every consideration to ensure comfort, and for this reason determined against the introduction of a central hall, which, in my opinion, is fatal to all comfort; or, if made into a cosy and liveable apartment, condemns every other sitting-room to complete solitude. But a hall is, nevertheless, an indispensable feature in a country house of any size, and the want of a large room where my friends could all meet and read and write without disturbing each other was so much felt, that in 1889 I built one of this kind, which though not in a central position has to some extent at least redeemed the error I had made.

A word may be expected from me concerning the internal decoration of the house. In this M. Destailleur took but very small part. I purchased carved oak panelling in Paris for several of the rooms to which it was adapted by various French and English decorators. Most of this panelling came from historic houses; that in the Billiard Room from a château of the Montmorencis; that in the Breakfast Room and the Boudoir from the hôtel of the Maréchal de Richelieu in the street which was named after his uncle the great Cardinal and which has now been transformed into shops and apartments; the Grey Drawing Room came from the convent of the Sacré Coeur, formerly the hotel of the duc de Lauzun, who perished on the guillotine; and the Tower Room from a villa which was for some time the residence of the famous Fermier-Général Beaujon, to whom the Elysée also belonged.

The ornamental ceilings are either replicas of those of the rooms from which the panelling was taken, or copied from ones still in existence in Paris. The old mantel-pieces I secured from houses for which they were made; the one in the East Gallery was in a post-office, formerly the residence of the celebrated banker, Samuel Bernard. The modern mantel-pieces are copied from old models.

My grateful thanks are due to those who from first to last assisted me in my undertaking. They, too, may have remembered me kindly. M. Destailleur was entrusted by the Empress Eugénie with the construction of her house and church at Farnborough, and M. Lainé by the King of the Belgians with important works on his estates. These commissions they owed—the former indirectly, the latter directly—to me. Of M. Lainé I have nothing to say but praise. Still, I may be pardoned for mentioning that he only designed the chief outlines of the park; the pleasure

The breakfast room. The panelling came from the duc de Richelieu's house in Paris, demolished in the nineteenth century.

WADDESDON HALL

grounds and gardens were laid out by my bailiff and gardener according to my notions and under my superintendence; while all the farm buildings, model cottages, and lodges were built by a local architect, Mr Taylor of Bierton.

Waddesdon now has its hotel, its village hall and reading-room, its temperance and benefit societies, and its inhabitants are prosperous and contented. The Metropolitan, now called the Great Central Railway, sets down passengers at a station not a mile from the park gates, and my visitors are spared the tedious drive from Aylesbury, on which I expended many an epithet during twenty-two long years. A few more plantations are required to furnish the park, otherwise, save a judicious 'Keep', there is little the hand of man can still do. Time must be relied on to improve the house by colouring the masonry and giving it that rich mellowness of tone which age alone can produce, and beautify the grounds by allowing the trees to grow and expand. A future generation may reap the chief benefit of a work which to me has been a labour of love, though I fear Waddesdon will share the fate of most properties whose owners have no descendants, and fall into decay. May the day yet be distant when weeds will spread over the garden, the terraces crumble into dust, the pictures and cabinets cross the Channel or the Atlantic, and the melancholy cry of the night-jar sound from the deserted towers.'

Waddesdon proved to be the ideal focus Baron Ferdinand needed for the expression of his undoubted talents—not only artistic, but organisational, and incidentally gave him limitless opportunity for his love of ameliorating the life of others in a practical way. His wish to share at least some of the good things of life with his immediate neighbours became apparent as soon as the work at Waddesdon was started. The *Bucks Herald* reported with some amazement that when piping the Chiltern Hills' water to Waddesdon for his own use he should have arranged for the village also to be provided with 'the first pure and clean water it had ever had'. Equal surprise seems to have been evoked by the repeated celebrations Baron Ferdinand organised to mark the completion of each stage of the building of his house. Detailed reports exist of the dinners he gave—followed by fireworks—to all those who had taken part in the building work and the creation of the park. The first of these festivities, to celebrate the placing of the cornerstone, was held in a marquee from which this essential bit of masonry could be admired. 'The well loaded tables presented

Cottages at the entrance to the stable drive before they were rebuilt by Baron Ferdinand

The Village Hall at Waddesdon, built by Baron Ferdinand

a nice appearance before they were attacked' we are told, and 'a very substantial repast was served hot'. One wonders how this culinary miracle was achieved, for some hundreds of people, on a bare hill-top, nearly a mile from the village.

These celebrations were only equalled in size and apparent jollity by the annual 'School Treats' the Baron now instituted for the children of the surrounding villages and their parents. Within a few years these were so heavily attended that the *Bucks Herald,* while stressing the pleasure given by the tea, games, military bands and prizes provided on these festive occasions, warned that when they took place all roads to Waddesdon were so choked with horse traffic as to be a danger to the *bona fide* traveller.

Evidently, Baron Ferdinand very quickly learnt the truth of his architect's warning 'One always builds too small'. As the house was first designed, both he and his sister each had a bedroom and sitting-room on the first floor, and this would have left only five bedrooms free for guests in the main building and three more in the bachelors' wing. Even allowing for marital bed occupancy, this must have soon seemed inadequate for the size of house-party which was fashionable in the hey-day of the Marlborough House period of entertainment.

There was almost certainly another reason for the continual 'improvements' Baron Ferdinand made to his house; this was his craving for works of art which, in their turn, called for space. Many were bought direct from other private owners or from such trusted dealers as Agnew, Colnaghi and Wertheimer, but in the eighties and nineties of the last century opportunities for acquisition from all sorts of sources were endless, and indeed Baron Ferdinand was besieged with offers which he found irresistible and which often inconvenienced his finances. Being a sleeping partner in the family bank, he was dependent on its senior partners' decisions as to when the distribution of any profits should be made, and I remember my father-in-law's description of Baron Ferdinand impatiently panting to receive the wherewithal in order to be able to acquire some particularly longed-for work of art.

He had begun collecting when he was a very young man. His first major purchase was a Sèvres *Vaisseau-à-Mat,* one of the magnificent *pot-pourri* vases in the shape of a sailing ship which were so difficult to fire that only eleven were ever made by the royal factory. This acquisition, which is now one of the glories of the Grey Drawing-room, was quite beyond Baron Ferdinand's financial resources at the time. He records: 'I was unable to pay ready money for this piece of china—the best I possess—and blush to confess that I discharged my

Sèvres *vaisseau-à-mat*. Only eleven of these 'ships' are known to exist, of which three are at Waddesdon.

debt by instalments extending over two years. During these two years, I hid the 'ship' in a cabinet afraid to own it lest I should be scolded for my extravagance by my Uncles, of whom I stood in considerable awe'. It was not until his father's death in 1874 that he inherited the means to build Waddesdon or buy most of the works of art with which he furnished it including, eventually, two more Sèvres *Vaisseaux-à-Mat*.

In choosing pictures and furniture for Waddesdon Baron Ferdinand was guided not only by a sure feeling for quality but also by his sense of history and a particular knowledge of France in the eighteenth century. Through his purchase of objects made by the superb Parisian craftsmen of that time he was able to bring to life, to a remarkable extent, one of the most civilised phases of European history. He was successful in mingling French pictures and furniture with eighteenth century English portraits, for which he had a special liking.

Today, the propinquity of Gainsborough's 'Pink Boy', for instance, and the writing table made by Benneman for Louis XVI seems particularly happy, as does the same artist's portrait of Lady Sheffield in the neighbourhood of a Savonnerie carpet and Riesener *commodes*. But the Baron did not confine himself to English and French pictures; he also loved and bought the works of Dutch masters and the paintings of Guardi. Often it was not only beauty but historical association which appealed to him. I am sure that he derived much pleasure in acquiring such things as the writing table presented to Beaumarchais by his friends in 1781, or the essay on the rivers of France written by Louis XV, when he was a child, which was then printed and bound under the boy's own eyes, so that he should understand the intricacies of book production.

Baron Ferdinand had very definite ideas about the decoration of the rooms in which his purchases were to be placed. In his 'Reminiscences' he wrote: 'From the fall of the old regime in France until the beginning of the Second Empire the style of the decoration of French houses of the seventeenth and eighteenth centuries was condemned or ignored. In England, the early Italian, the Queen Anne or no style, had long been preferred; pictures, cabinets and china of all periods being usually placed against a damask or plain background. It was lavish or simple, often its merits were great, but the decoration was never 'French'. In France the style of decoration remained French, but it was a bastard nineteenth century style, graceless and tasteless, borrowing hardly a single feature from its predecessors. Whether it is to the credit of my family or not may be a matter of opinion, but the fact

The Green Boudoir. This is one of the three rooms at Waddesdon whose panelling came from the 18th century house in Paris of the Maréchal duc de Richelieu.

The South front seen across the garden

remains that they first revived the decoration of the eighteenth century in its purity, reconstructing their rooms out of old material, reproducing them as they had been during the reigns of the Louis'.

Baron Ferdinand was particularly fortunate in building Waddesdon just at the time when much of the 'old material' to which he refers was available for purchase. In the 1860's Baron Haussman, the Prefect of the Seine, had almost completed his work of driving great new streets through the heart of Paris. In making these wide boulevards many old houses had been knocked down and the superbly carved eighteenth century panelling with which some of them had been decorated was on the market. The beauty of the furniture and pictures at Waddesdon seems to me to be immeasurably enhanced by being seen against this background which Baron Ferdinand imported from France.

His overwhelming interest in the manner of life and decorative ideas of past centuries also led him to collect such things as eighteenth century book plates and trade cards as well as illustrated books of that period, many of which give instruction in such minor arts as ironwork, penmanship, hair-dressing and horsemanship. They indeed bear witness to the extraordinary scope of his historical interest. The older he got, the earlier became the period by which he was attracted. One

Some of the gardeners

of the dealers from whom he bought told me that it was only in the last years of his life that he turned his attention to the collection of the Renaissance objects which are now in the British Museum.

In his career as a collector he did not, of course, have the field to himself. Quite apart from several members of his own family in England, Germany, France and Austria, who were eager to acquire works of art of all kinds, there were many

The stable staff, c. 1900

Miniature of a lady, c. 1640 in contemporary gold and enamel frame. English

Gold and tortoiseshell bonbonnière with miniature by Peter Adolf Hall

formidable rivals, when he was a young man, such as Lord Hertford. Later, in England, he found many competitors in the auction rooms, like Lord Dudley or Mr. Mills (later Lord Hillingdon).

But many things were not bought at auction. There was an accepted routine in the Art Dealers' world which, I believe, was practised with notable success. As soon as some particularly desirable object had fallen into a dealer's hands, it was his habit to call on one of his more notable clients at a convenient moment, and start a conversation, I gather, on these lines: 'I have brought this to show *you*, Baron, as I would like *you* to have it. I know XYZ would buy it immediately, but I wanted you to see it first, as I think it would look so well in your house. But please treat this confidentially, as I would not like it to be known that I have given you first refusal'. If such a goad to rivalry did not happen to be successful the dealer would then pass on to the next most likely buyer, with just the same story, suitably adjusted.

On some occasions Baron Ferdinand did not buy alone but combined with other members of his family to make and share some major purchase. My father-in-law and Baron Ferdinand were two of a consortium of cousins who bought the outstanding Van Loon collection which included the lovely paintings by Metsu and Willem van de Velde which are now at Waddesdon; and Baron Ferdinand and his cousin Mayer jointly instructed the dealer Alexander Barker to buy from the hôtel de Villars in Paris the carved mirror surrounds by Nicolas Pineau which were numerous enough to provide the decoration of the dining rooms at both Waddesdon and Mentmore.

As soon as Waddesdon was in any way habitable and furnished, Baron Ferdinand started asking his friends to stay. A careful study of his visitors' book reveals the growing size of his house-parties, and it was not long before he began to build again, adding more bedrooms for guests and others for their personal attendants. Increased facilities had also to be provided for the production of food. Incredible though it may seem today, not only was a Still Room added to the kitchen—for the production of breakfast rolls, home-made jam, tea, coffee and soft drinks—but a further kitchen had to be provided for the use of a pastry cook who specialised in puddings, ices and sweetmeats. In yet another kitchen, a baker made bread only. The preservation of food had also to be considered before the days of frigidaires and deep freezers. In the middle of a plantation on an eminence just off the Stable Drive, which still goes by the name of 'Ice House Hill', ice was preserved on the shelves of a stone hut put up on this completely shaded site. In place of the high windows of the northern wall of the kitchen—now the public tea-room—there was a cluster of larders. The largest had its walls pierced with tiny holes, sufficient to aerate, but small enough to debar flies; partitioned down the middle, one side was kept for meat, and the other for fish. The larders themselves were concealed by a high grassy bank, planted with tall trees and flowering shrubs. Finally, a laundry was installed behind the stables. This included ample living accommodation for five laundry maids who were expert in wielding antediluvian irons and mangles—doubtless the most up-to-date of their kind at the time—to produce an endless supply of pristine sheets with frilled edges which, for the feminine guests, were adorned with lace and ribbons. The drying ground of the laundry was marvellously conceived, concealed from all prying eyes by a huge hedge surrounding the grass lawn on which long lines of cord, stretched from end to end, sustained the washing swaying gently in the sheltered breeze.

Roll-top desk made by Riesener in 1774 for Madame Adelaide, daughter of Louis XV

The dining room: the Beauvais tapestry was designed by Boucher: the carpet is late 18th century Aubusson

Baron Ferdinand was a perfectionist which is a costly attribute, but nevertheless, there are many instances at Waddesdon of his ingenious economies. For instance, all the vast windows have secure inner shutters made of wood. In the day-time, these are folded back and only the last panel of any shutter is visible, and this is made of beautiful oak. All the other panels are made of the plainest deal, since, by night, when the shutters are closed, they are completely concealed by the curtains drawn in front of them. Again, in all the rooms, the floors are of rough planks; only in the few rooms where the carpets do not extend from wall to wall is there a border of exquisite parquet.

In appearance Baron Ferdinand was a slight, spare, bearded man of medium height. Oddly enough, we know his weight which was only 10 stone 6 lbs when fully dressed in shooting clothes. This information is entered in the book at Sandringham in which the weight of all visitors there was recorded in King Edward VII's time. In spite of recurring bouts of illness which irked him from childhood until his early death, the Baron

Detail of one of the mirrors in the dining room at Mentmore which came from the same room in the Hôtel de Villars in Paris as the mirrors in the dining room at Waddesdon

was by no means physically inactive. He rode well although he could not walk far and certainly not uphill without the aid of a friendly push. During his 59 years he attempted much and achieved a great deal, quite apart from the visible evidence of Waddesdon.

He was Liberal Member of Parliament for Aylesbury from 1885 until he died, 14 years later. He was also an active member of the Bucks County Council; a Trustee of the British Museum and a keen Mason (hence the Ferdinand de Rothschild Lodge). He worked hard at these and numberless other part-time responsibilities. He also travelled widely, both in Europe and further afield in his yacht, the *Rona*. The diary he kept of a journey he made to South Africa in 1896 shows remarkable prescience; the conclusions he reached about the probable consequences of the treatment of the black population at the end of the last century have been proved unhappily true, some eighty years later. Yet, despite all this activity, he was an omnivorous reader; his large library of historical memoirs and diaries is a most treasured part of his successors' inheritance.

As Liberal member for Aylesbury, Baron Ferdinand did not often speak in the House of Commons, but the subjects which moved him to do so are, perhaps, indicative of his character. When the extension of the Marylebone railway line to a new goods terminal, near Lord's Cricket Ground, was hotly opposed, for the reason—among others—that smuts and dirt might sully the gowns of ladies attending the Oxford and Cambridge, or Eton and Harrow matches, Baron Ferdinand would have none of it. He made a forthright speech outlining the benefits a goods line would bring to the smallholders of Buckinghamshire who wished to sell their produce in the Metropolis. On another occasion, when there was a row about the British Ambassador in Paris being ordered not to attend the opening of the Great Paris Exhibition, because it was thought this occasion was a disguised celebration of the centenary of the French Revolution, Baron Ferdinand provided a detailed historical count-down of events which did much to clarify his fellow members' somewhat hazy notions of French history. But his most persistent political endeavour was to bring about some improvement in the pay and working conditions of the Post Office Telegraph Clerks. These men, before the introduction of the telephone, formed the vital link in any form of quick communication both within the British Isles and abroad. The Government acknowledged that all the clerks had to be qualified in some 'electrical understanding', and to be fluent in French and German, but were, apparently, quite content that they should be paid a maximum of £120 a year; that they should be required to work an average of 14 hours a day, including Sundays; that they should be given no time for meal-breaks and were, in fact, liable to punishment if they were found trying to nibble any form of food during their working hours. For five long years, Baron Ferdinand persecuted a particularly obdurate Postmaster General with questions about the Telegraph Clerks' pay and conditions. Invariably the reply was that 'the exigencies of the service' determined the hours of work, and that the Clerks' pay, their minimal chances of promotion and their occasional need to eat, were all 'under consideration'. Tiring eventually of the Government's stone-walling attitude, Baron Ferdinand, with the help of Lord Compton, managed to bring in a Private Member's Bill, in which, in effect, the Government was accused of maltreating its own servants. Baron Ferdinand believing, perhaps rightly, that Lord Compton's powers of eloquence were greater than his own, was content to second Lord Compton's masterly exposition of the Telegraph Clerks' miseries, stressing, in his own speech, the callousness of a Government which had made it seem advisable to adopt the most unusual course of promoting a Private Member's Bill to regulate the treatment of public servants. Like all his previous attempts, this one was not immediately successful; the Bill was defeated. But within a year the Government did see fit to raise the Clerks' pay by £10 a year, and to reduce their daily hours of work. Feeling perhaps, however, that he had been culpably overgenerous, the same Postmaster General with whom Baron Ferdinand had battled for so many years, decided at the same time to dock the authorised annual holidays of the Telegraph Clerks by one week. That, however, was this particular Postmaster General's swan song. The Government was thrown out, and it was a new Postmaster General who had to face Baron Ferdinand's continuing questions about why the award of an extra £10 a year made the Telegraph Clerks' need for an adequate holiday any the less.

In May, 1886, when the Liberals were once more in power, Mr Gladstone brought in his proposals for Home Rule for Ireland, to which many members of his own party were hotly opposed. Led by Lord Hartington—a frequent visitor to Waddesdon—the dissident Liberals formed the Liberal-Unionist party, and voting with the Tories, threw out Mr Gladstone's Home Rule Bill. From the names to be found in the visitors' book at Waddesdon it can, perhaps, be assumed that some of the discussions which preceded this horrendous split in the Liberal party must have taken place there; certainly, Baron Ferdinand took a prominent part in the birth of the new party.

For anyone who fondly believes in the inevitable progress of the human race, any comparison of the political questions of the Baron's day with those of our own, can only be disquieting. Separated by a distance of ninety years, the Hansards of the 1880s and the 1970s display a similar agonised anxiety about what to do about Ireland. In 1886 Baron Ferdinand took part in a debate on the reform or abolition of the House of Lords, and debates on the Fishing Industry, the optimum size of the Army and the possibility of the Government providing employment for the unemployed are common to both eras. Even a Select Committee on Gaming was set up while Baron Ferdinand was a Member of Parliament which, one feels, may well have considered questions dealt with by the Royal Commission on Gambling which has been sitting under the Chairmanship of Baron Ferdinand's relative, Lord Rothschild. Despite two world wars and the loss of an Empire, at Westminster it seems that *plus ça change, plus c'est la même chose.*

Although Baron Ferdinand's personal contributions to the great debates in the House of Commons were infrequent, it is probable that Waddesdon was often a centre for political debate outside the House. All the political lions stayed with him frequently; the signatures of Gladstone, Rosebery, Joseph Chamberlain and Balfour appear again and again in the

Two of Baron Ferdinand's parliamentary supporters

visitors' book, as do the signatures of younger men—Curzon, Asquith and Winston Churchill, whose fame, in the Baron's day, still lay before them.

On some occasions, it seems, Baron Ferdinand may have assumed the role of peace-maker when political acrimony was particularly rife. Under different administrations one finds the foremost members of the Opposition being invited to meet the leading Ministers of the day. These were often preceded by, or accompanied by their closest collaborators—Permanent Secretaries and Private Secretaries. Many diplomats figure prominently, particularly when the countries to which they were accredited were of topical concern. Often, however, there was an unexpected mixture of guests, as, for instance, in August 1886, when one finds the Archbishop of Canterbury being invited to meet the Speaker and the German and Austrian Ambassadors. What, one wonders, did they discuss? Or did they just enjoy each other's company?

Very often, however, one can at least imagine the subject of some of the conversations held in the Waddesdon dining-room or billiard room. It is remarkable how many people appeared to come to stay at Waddesdon immediately after they had taken part in some notable event. As an instance, Lord Wolseley, on reaching this country after the capture of Khartoum, headed straight for Waddesdon, as did British Ambassadors after important international conferences, or war-correspondents, hot-foot from some Balkan war. It seems more than likely that Baron Ferdinand delighted in having such interesting people to stay and enjoyed being one of the best informed of men, but he may, perhaps, have had an additional reason for seeking to acquire up-to-date knowledge from the eye-witnesses of important happenings.

For many years he had been a friend of the Prince of Wales, who had first been accustomed to stay with him while the Baron was still living at Leighton House. The Prince was a regular guest at Waddesdon from the moment it became habitable. Sir Sidney Lee, in his official biography of King Edward VII, describes in detail the Prince's many attempts to persuade his mother to allow him to see Cabinet and Foreign Office papers and thus have some inside knowledge of the events which he thought were the rightful concern of the Heir-Apparent. For many years, however, the Queen invariably refused these requests and indeed ordered her Ministers to deny any pleas for information they might receive from the Prince, on the grounds that his discretion was not to be trusted. The Prince's sense of political responsibility and consuming interest in international affairs did not allow him to let the matter rest there and

Typical party for the Prince of Wales, in July 1894. Among the guests are: Lord Cadogan (Lord Privy Seal), Sir Donald Mackenzie Wallace (Director Foreign Dept, The Times) The Hon Schomburg McDonnell (Principle Private Secretary to the Prime Minister) Count Albert Mensdorff of the Austrian Embassy, M. de Staal the Russian Ambassador, Sir Edward Hamilton (Asst. Secretary to the Treasury), Sir Henry Calcraft (Permanent Secretary, Board of Trade) and Lord Brassey (Civil Lord of the Admiralty).

it is known that he made every attempt to keep himself as well informed as possible, despite his mother's ban. It indeed seems likely that Baron Ferdinand was one of the people through whom the Prince acquired some of the information he longed for and, if the Baron acted, in many instances, as the Prince's ears and eyes this may explain the presence of some of the guests at Waddesdon and the celerity with which they made their way there from foreign parts and interesting events.

The majority of those who came to Waddesdon had predominantly political interests but some of Baron Ferdinand's visitors were more concerned with the arts than with public affairs. Writers, ranging from Guy de Maupassant, Henry James and Paul Bourget to Mrs Humphrey Ward came to stay, as did painters, sculptors and musicians. Although in almost all Baron Ferdinand's house-parties the men outnumbered the women, the latter included many of those who exerted some influence on society through their beauty and their charm, but maybe sometimes through their brains. Lady Warwick, Lady de Grey and Lady Randolph Churchill were frequent guests as were Lady Dorothy Nevill, Lady Helen Vincent and Louise, Duchess of Manchester. The last, after her second marriage, gave the

Baron Ferdinand at the Devonshire House fancy dress ball, 1897

famous fancy dress ball at Devonshire House in the year of the Diamond Jubilee, and is thus indirectly responsible for those yellowing photographs which can be found in so many great houses in which *fin-de-siècle* ladies and gentlemen are implausibly portrayed as Arthurian knights, Queens of the Nile and Renaissance courtiers.

In 1889 the Shah of Persia was visiting this country and was proving to be a somewhat awkward guest to entertain. The Prince of Wales persuaded Baron Ferdinand to invite the Shah to stay at Waddesdon, with his numerous suite, but at the same time warned the Baron that he would not be able to come himself. In place of his own invaluable presence on this rather unnerving occasion, the Prince offered his two young sons, the Duke of Clarence and Prince George (later King George V) who told me, many years later, how clearly he remembered this unusual party. He said that it got off to a poor start. On his arrival the Shah was told that the Prince of Wales would not be coming and this so displeased him that he went to the bedroom prepared for him and stayed there, refusing to come down to dinner. After a somewhat agitated discussion between Baron Ferdinand and his other guests, a message was

The Prince of Wales playing tennis

Lady Randolph Churchill dressed as Cleopatra for the Devonshire House fancy dress ball, 1897

conveyed to the Shah that—as it happened—a most excellent conjurer had been engaged to entertain him after he had dined. This bait proved successful; the Shah agreed to descend, and from that moment enjoyed the evening with gusto.

Entertaining more ordinary guests, even in a house as well equipped as Baron Ferdinand's, was not always free from pre-occupation and the Baron was obviously of a temperament to which order and due warning were dear. Lady de Grey, writing to a friend, urged her to lose no time in making up her mind about whether to accept an invitation to Waddesdon. 'You know how funny Ferdy is' wrote Lady de Grey, 'he always likes an early answer'.

The time at which guests would arrive or depart was also a matter of natural concern to the Baron. We who are used to guests appearing driving their own motors, and leaving equally effortlessly, can have little idea of the complications of arranging the transport of up to 24 guests who could approach only via the railway station where a variety of different trains had to be met or caught by means of horse-drawn carriages. Moreover, many of Baron Ferdinand's guests, unlike ours, were not bound to be back at their office desks at nine o'clock on Monday morning, and the length of time any one of them might

Tea on the North lawn at Waddesdon with the Prince of Wales

decide to stay was not always a foregone conclusion. This may explain a story told me by someone who had once, rather nervously, arrived for the first time at Waddesdon. Having been greeted by the Baron, his composure was in no way increased when he was then immediately asked 'When are you leaving?'. It took him some time to realise that this question had only been put so that the necessary orders could go to the stables; not through any oversight of his would the Baron be guilty of incommoding a guest.

But of all the occasions on which the Baron planned and plotted to meet his visitors' wishes, probably none gave him more cause for thought than the visit of Queen Victoria who came to Waddesdon for the day in May, 1890. Having lived in seclusion at Osborne and in Scotland for so many years, the news, when it became known, that the Queen might be visible to some of her subjects in Buckinghamshire when she passed through Aylesbury on her way to Waddesdon, was greeted almost with unbelief, but unbounded enthusiasm. The arrangements made for what was, after all, a private luncheon party, are so unusual from our modern standpoint, that I find Baron Ferdinand's own account of this day enthralling. In the hope that it may be of interest to others as well as to myself, here is his account in full:

> 'In November 1888 the Empress Frederick invited me to an audience at Windsor Castle. When our conversation which had ranged over a diversity of interesting topics had lasted for an hour, the clock pointed to luncheon time and I prepared to withdraw. As I was taking my leave, the Empress announced to me, somewhat to my surprise, that the Queen had requested her to apprise me of her intention to honour me with a visit to Waddesdon in the course of the following Spring. The visit, however, although all the preliminaries had been settled during the month of April, failed to come off as the Princess Beatrice, who was expecting her confinement, and by whom the Queen wished to be accompanied, was not in a condition to undertake the journey. When dining at Windsor in the summer of that year, Her Majesty's first words to me were that she had not forgotten her intention of honouring me with her presence at Waddesdon, and that she fully intended carrying it out in the following year.
>
> On the 12th of April of this year, I duly received a letter from Sir Henry Ponsonby at Aix-les-Bains, where he was in attendance on Her Majesty, stating that the Queen proposed visiting me at Waddesdon on the 14th, 15th or

16th of May. A lengthy and detailed correspondence ensued, and the visit was ultimately fixed for Wednesday, May 14th. For some considerable time, the best part of my day was employed in exchanging notes and telegrams with Sir Henry Ponsonby; settling the hours of Her Majesty's departure from and arrival at Windsor and Waddesdon respectively; the list of the guests, the number of the carriages and the servants, and last but not least, the etiquette that was to be observed on the occasion. With the one solitary exception of declining an escort of the Royal Bucks Yeomanry, which I can only attribute to her objections to the indifferent horsemanship usually displayed by Her Majesty's auxiliary forces—though from personal experience I can say that the Bucks force form a brilliant exception to the general rule in that respect—the Queen acceded to every one of my suggestions and evinced the most gracious willingness to facilitate my programme of arrangements.

Princess Louise exhibited much kindness also in aiding me with her advice, and in recommending to Her Majesty's acceptance my proposals which, indeed, were framed entirely with a view to Her Majesty's convenience.

Princess Louise, and the majority of the other guests arrived at Waddesdon on Tuesday the 13th of May. The weather was cloudy and cold and the glass was falling. Perhaps a barometer has rarely been consulted so often or so anxiously as that at Waddesdon on the day preceding Her Majesty's visit. As the Queen had never been—at any rate since her accession to the throne—in that part of Buckinghamshire in which I reside, the loyalty, curiosity and enthusiasm of the population were raised to the highest pitch by the prospect of her coming. In the small town of Aylesbury, upwards of three hundred pounds were subscribed for stands and decorations. At Fleet Marston, about half way between Aylesbury and the entrance lodge to my park, I also erected a stand, mainly for the accommodation of the tenants of some of my relatives and friends; and another at the Waddesdon Cross Roads, for my own tenants and for the inhabitants of the villages situated on my estate, while there was, of course, the usual triumphal arch.

On Wednesday morning at eleven o'clock, I left the house for the railway station, meeting on the road Lord Hartington and the Granbys who had come that morning from London to join the party at Waddesdon. The glass, meantime, had done its duty and a more perfect day for

Watercolour of Waddesdon painted by Miss Alice's governess and life-long friend, Mademoiselle Cécile Hofer.

the visit, or one better suited to the Queen's peculiar taste, could not be imagined. A brilliant sun shone from a perfectly blue sky, a crisp, cold wind tempered the atmosphere, and the dust had been laid by the rain so that we could dispense with the use of watering carts.

At the station I found Lord Rothschild, exercising on this occasion, for the first time, the official functions as Lord Lieutenant of the county. Punctually at ten minutes past twelve the Royal train steamed in to the platform, and and I was amused to notice a gaudily painted crown and cushion of iron had been placed at the base of the funnel to indicate the rank of its chief passenger. The Queen was seated in a saloon carriage, together with her daughter and son-in-law, reading the morning papers. The weather, as usual, served to initiate the conversation, but the words attributed to Her Majesty in the press, that 'I always bring fine weather with me' are not accurate. Something of that kind was said *by me*, but the Queen, instead of accepting for herself a royal influence over the elements, merely uttered a few words, which I cannot precisely recollect, but which consisted of an allusion to the wilfulness of the climate and the fortunate change the weather had undergone that morning.

To compare the decorations of Aylesbury, or the crowds provided by its nine thousand inhabitants, with those of great cities of the country on the occasion of other royal visits, would of course be absurd. But still I may say that considering the circumstances of the place, the aspect of this small country town and the spontaneous outburst of enthusiasm which greeted the procession on its way through it, were altogether out of the common; the whole scene, quite mediaeval in its picturesqueness, was stirring and effective in the utmost degree. Taste in pageantry is not, as a rule, characteristic of English country people, but whether the irregularity of the streets and buildings lent itself to the purposes of decoration or owing to a fortunate accident in the selection of the sites for decorations, so that they disguised the natural blemishes of the place while bringing into relief its quaint features, or because of the richness and profusion of the arches, banners and flags which, having been used for the Jubilee in London were cheaply obtained—from whatever reason, the general effect was most happy. We went through the town at a foot's pace, where the inevitable address was presented by Major Horwood of the Volunteers, Chairman of the Board of Health, at the foot of the steps of the Town Hall, while

Waddesdon 1885.

the equally inevitable bouquet was presented to the Queen by his daughter, Miss Horwood. The Queen's carriage led the way in the procession, preceded by Her Majesty's outriders; Lady Errol, Lady Ponsonby, Lord Rothschild and myself followed in a landau and four; Sir Henry Ponsonby and Miss Phipps coming next in a Victoria, and behind them came in a wagonette one of the Queen's Indian servants, a footman and a dresser. On reaching the Cross Roads my carriage left the procession and trotted on through the village so that I might be at the house to meet the Queen, who drove through the park. There I duly waited to receive Her Majesty together with my sister, Princess Louise and the members of my family, while the other guests were, by command, locked up in the adjacent drawingrooms.

When the Queen descended from her carriage, my sister conducted her at once to the Small Library on the ground floor, which had been transformed into a dressing-room for the occasion. Shortly after, the Royal Party entered the large Dining Room where luncheon was served to them; upon which the guests were released from their confinement and lunched with me in the Small Dining Room, while the Royal Artillery Band, which was stationed in the small conservatory which connects the two rooms, played a selection of airs. The royal appetite is proverbial, and it was not until about half past three that the Queen and her daughters re-appeared in the Red Drawing Room. Evidently my cook had done his duty, for, as I was afterwards informed by my butler, Her Majesty partook of every dish and twice of cold beef. As a further evidence of her approval of the good things provided for her, I may mention that she took away three copies of the bill of fare, and that the Royal Cook was subsequently sent to learn from mine, the secret of making three of the dishes which had been sent up. The Queen, though in black, wearing her widow's cap, which she had assumed before luncheon instead of her bonnet, was nevertheless smartly dressed, and wore various brooches and lockets containing miniatures, one of which seemed to me to be a likeness of the Princess Alice.

At last the expectant guests were allowed to sun themselves in the Royal smile, but their conversational powers were not severely taxed, as Her Majesty was only pleased to address a few stereotyped sentences to those of them with whom she was better acquainted, while those whom I had to present, had to rest satisfied with a gracious smile.

The Red Drawing Room. On the right is Gainsborough's portrait of George IV when Prince of Wales. Reflected in the looking glass over the fireplace is the same artist's portrait of Lady Sheffield.

Looking towards the conservatory from the breakfast room

I had been informed that I was not to show too much zeal in displaying my property to the Queen, so as not to tire her. The hint was unnecessary, as I never intended to have taken her through any of the rooms except those known as my own apartment. Her Majesty looked with interest on the old English portraits in my Green sitting room, and at some of the curiosities in the Tower Room; and was so struck with the decoration, furnishing and arrangement of the rooms that she afterwards sent the superintendent of the furniture from Windsor Castle to inspect them. She gave proof of her memory and knowledge of genealogies when I showed her a large miniature picture, representing my Grandfather and Grandmother with their seven children, with whose intricate relationship and marriages she was thoroughly conversant. She told me that she particularly remembered my Grandfather, and on my expressing some surprise, seeing that he died in 1836, she said, with one

DÉJEÛNER DE SA MAJESTÉ

LA REINE.

Potage.

Comsommé à la Windsor.

Poisson.

Truite à la Norwégienne.

Entrées.

Cailles en Caisses.

Poularde à l'Algérienne.

Relevé.

Filets de Bœuf à la Chartreuse.

Rôt.

Canetons Garnis d'Ortolans.

Entremets.

Asperges en Branches.

Beignets à la Viennoise.

Petites Soufflés à la Royale.

A mis-spelled 'proof copy' (the only one to remain) of the menu of the luncheon for Queen Victoria

Baron Ferdinand's own sitting room (now known as the 'Baron's Room') in which he surrounded himself with pictures of pretty women. The two pictures to the left are by Reynolds (Perdita Robinson and Mrs Scott of Danesfield), on the right Mrs Jordan by Romney

of those charming smiles of which no one has the secret better than Her Majesty and her children, 'Why not? I was then eighteen years of age'.

After dinner rest awhile says the old proverb, and it evidently holds good in all ranks of society. The suite of rooms known as the State Apartments, on the bedroom floor, had been got in readiness in the event of the Queen wishing to seclude herself from the profane gaze. I conducted her upstairs, and in spite of the rheumatic affection of the knee from which she suffers, Her Majesty ascended the long flight with comparative ease. I then left her in the State Apartments, and during her absence smoked a cigar on the Terrace with Prince Henry of Battenberg, but had to throw away the fragrant weed unfinished, being bitterly railed at by my relations who said I should be reeking of smoke when Her Majesty came down.

On the previous day, a German curiosity dealer had been down to see the house bringing with him various things for my inspection, among them a diminutive French ivory fan of the last century, most beautifully set in diamonds. A more appropriate offering to the Queen could not have been desired so I begged Princess Louise to ask Her Majesty whether she would be pleased to accept it from me as a memento of her visit. At four o'clock I was sent for by Her Majesty to receive the fan. Were I of a shy disposition, a more embarrassing situation could hardly have been provided for me. The Queen was standing in the Small Green Boudoir—which I may incidentally mention I purchased some years ago in the rue de Richelieu at the Marshal de Richelieu's former residence, number 27—looking very majestic, solemn and severe; flanked on either side by her two daughters who seemed rather curious to observe how I should acquit myself of my task. But being neither shy nor embarrassed, I delivered a harangue worthy of an Elizabethan courtier, and having received the Queen's acceptance of the present, I knelt on one knee and handed it to her. It clearly gave much pleasure to Her Majesty as I could infer from the fact that, on my remarking that the initials of the lady for whom the fan had been made should be erased and replaced by those of Her Majesty, she seemed reluctant to part with it and replied that it would do very well as it was. I then bowed myself out of the room; and after an interval of a quarter of an hour, during which time Her Majesty's cap was re-exchanged for her bonnet, I was informed that she was ready to inspect the grounds.

The Queen's little pony-carriage had been sent down on the previous day to my stables. It is really like a bath-chair, and is drawn by a little pony which, as the Queen informed me, had first seen the light in the New Forest. The reins lay idly in Her Majesty's lap, while the bit was secured in the firm grip of one of the Queen's Highlanders, a brother of the deceased John Brown. I had ordered various pony-traps and carriages for the rest of the company; some of them, however, preferred following us on foot. We made at once for the Aviary, but the Queen's attention was diverted from its gaily feathered inhabitants by the conduct of her pony, which shied at the sight of the cockatoos and macaws which screamed and flapped their wings on their perches in the centre of the grass plot in front of the Aviary. The poor birds, however, meant no harm and were merely asking me for their usual piece of sugar. We next proceeded to one of the adjacent lawns, where my bailiff, Sims, and his foreman were ready for the fulfilment of the time-honoured custom of planting the tree—for which purpose a *Picea concolor* had been selected. I may observe that when, on the preceding day, I was on my way to Aylesbury to meet Princess Louise, I passed a dog-cart and my attention was involuntarily arrested by something peculiar in the appearance of the person who was sitting next to the driver. I had been requested to allow an artist from the *Illustrated London News* to take sketches of the proceedings at Waddesdon during the Royal visit, and my instinct told me that the gentleman in the dogcart was the artist in question. I was not mistaken, for after our carriages had crossed, feeling impelled me to turn round and I saw that the dogcart had stopped and that the gentleman was violently gesticulating to me to do the same. I did so and he entered my carriage, at once putting a series of questions to me as to how he could take sketches of the various incidents of the following day. I said to

Queen Victoria planting a tree at Waddesdon in May, 1890

The spade with which this act was performed

him—'You are quite at liberty to sketch any scenes you like, provided you do not permit yourself to be noticed'. 'Oh sir', he replied in a tone and manner the peculiar cockney vulgarity of which cannot possibly be reproduced—'I have been following the Queen about for ever so many years, and know exactly what I am to do. Where is the Queen going to plant the tree?' he enquired to my amusement. 'On one of the lawns' I answered, 'Why do you ask?'. 'Because', said he, 'I want to select a bush from behind which I can sketch the ceremony without being seen'. While the Queen was planting the tree, I could not refrain from investigating the shrubberies and there was the artist esconced behind a *Thuja gigantea,* adjusting the focus of a photographic apparatus on the *Picea concolor* and the august lady who was handling the spade. The tree planting ceremony over, we passed the deer pen which contains an Indian Black Buck, and Her Majesty was much pleased to behold a denizen of her Indian Empire. From thence we proceeded past the stables to the glass houses and I took advantage of the favourable opportunity then afforded me, of conversing quietly with the Queen, unheard by strangers, and broached subjects altogether irrelevant to the situation. The Queen entered freely into the conversation and I regret being too indolent to use my own pen, and unwilling to dictate the substance of our interview, the readers—if any readers there will ever be of this paper—will be debarred from learning its import. So much only can I say, that the various statesmen not only of Great Britain but of Europe, were freely canvassed.

Some of the flowering shrubs attracted a good deal of attention from the Queen, and she greatly admired the varieties of gorse and broom and a Japanese crabtree. So much so indeed, that my sister since received a note from Miss Phipps, asking for the exact botanical names of those plants. Mr Sander, the St Albans orchid grower, was in readiness at the entrance to the glasshouses, and I presented him to the Queen who addressed a few words to him, but he was so shy that he was unable to answer, and would have bolted straight away had I not held him back by the coat-tails. Sander was the only one of the many professionals I had employed in the creation of the estate selected for presentation to the Queen, an honour which he highly prized as he took good care to have it duly recorded and advertised in the press. I may mention that not only Sander but my butler and cook copiously dosed with champagne the *Daily Telegraph* reporter to whom I had given permission to come to Waddesdon, to secure their being mentioned in his report of the proceedings of the day. My poor gardener, to whom the opportunity was not afforded of plying the reporter with the same generous vintage, was ignominiously left out in the cold; and even the bouquet which I presented to the Queen—the work of his hands, and a more beautiful bouquet I have never seen, consisting of vandateres with sprays of odontoglossum pescatori—was described in the newspapers as having been made by Sander himself. *Surtout pas trop de zèle,* the words addressed by Talleyrand to one of his underlings, should have been remembered by my gardener, who was so anxious that the plants entrusted to his care should be duly appreciated, that he opened the doors of the stovehouses leading into the central corridor, instead of keeping them closed, which would not have prevented us from admiring the plants through the large glass panels of the doors, while keeping the heat from the central corridor, which, as it was, was so intense that we had to rush through it. The atmosphere of the orchid ranges was more endurable, where, oddly enough, the comparatively insignificant cyprepedium caudatum excited the greatest admiration from the Queen and her daughters. On concluding the inspection of the glass, the Queen re-entered her pony-carriage, we wended our way slowly up the hill homewards, and again I had the advantage of conversing with the Queen on matters highly interesting to myself. I left Her Majesty in the oriental tent on the tennis lawn in front of the house, where she partook of tea in the company of her family and my sister. About a quarter after five the Queen returned to the house, and having attended to her toilette in the small dressing room, she took her leave of the company. I shall never forget the manner in which the Queen bowed herself out of the house. The guests were assembled round the oval vestibule inside the front door: the Queen stood alone on the doorstep, and curtsied to the company in the most dignified and graceful manner—a marvellous performance. The procession returned to Aylesbury in the same order as it had driven thence. The stands along the road and at Aylesbury were, perhaps, somewhat less crowded than they had been in the morning, but the enthusiasm was as great as before. At the station, Her Majesty gave me her hand to kiss and made a few remarks expressive of the satisfaction she had derived from the visit—of which she gave further proof, subsequently, by presenting me with a small marble bust of herself by

Queen Victoria leaving Waddesdon

Boehm, with an appropriate inscription on the pedestal. The train steamed off, my cousin and myself drove home, thoroughly exhausted, but delighted that the visit had come to an end, and above all, that it had passed off so satisfactorily.

The result may be considered eminently agreeable in every sense of the word. That the Sovereign of this realm who, for the last thirty years, has lived in almost complete privacy, should have found my house an attraction so exceptional as to draw her from her seclusion, was highly gratifying to myself; but that gratification was enhanced by the fact that the Queen, as I have been informed by the Prince of Wales and every member of her household I have since seen, was thoroughly delighted with the arrangements I had made for her comfort, and with the place itself. That she lunched alone with members of her family, instead of lunching with us, has been commented on in society—but without reason. The proposal that she should do so emanated from me, as I was well aware, not only of her disinclination to take her midday meal in the company of strangers, but of the invariable rule, which she never breaks, of so doing.

Around the Queen of England there hangs an undefinable prestige, the result of a long and glorious reign; of singular domestic virtue; of an unblemished fame; of great political sagacity and unique simplicity of character on the one hand, and a supreme queenly dignity on the other. She, alone of all the Sovereigns of Europe, combines the charm of a woman with a legitimate consciousness of her position, and while ever ready to sympathise with the humble of her subjects and even to forget her position and her cares in the company of her chosen friends, maintains whenever she is called upon to do so, the most striking dignity. Her conversation may be sparse and her dress old-fashioned, but every word she utters bears witness to the fact that she is a lady in the true sense of the word, and her every attitude, whether walking, driving or sitting, is that of the first lady of the land.

This is all the more telling when we compare her with the other sovereigns of Europe and their consorts. The Emperor of Russia has only distinguished himself by his intolerance, his bigotry, his inaccessibility and his invincible objection to promoting any beneficial measures for

Baron Ferdinand in his sitting room with his dog 'Poupon'

his empire; while the Empress of Russia is only known to the outer world for her fondness of dress, and her daily increasing profusion of jewels. The Emperor of Germany is a clever young man, no doubt, but is a nineteenth century Hohenzollern, a restless fidget, a combination of autocrat and socialist, a German dreamer on the one hand, and an embryo Napoleon on the other: while his wife has only signalised herself by giving birth to a large family, by her tea-parties and her embroideries, her mystic aspirations and the almost countless number of her suite. The Emperor of Austria, a Hapsburg of the old school, is a well-meaning monarch, but narrow-minded in every sense of the term. During his long reign of forty-two years, his army has been beaten by that of almost every European country, and the laurels, borne by his effigy on his coins, were only won by his victory over his own Hungarian subjects in 1848. He may rise at five in the morning and work until five in the afternoon, and be animated by the most laudable intentions, but it would be better if he worked less and thought more—or at any rate, more intelligently. The King of Italy is a man, a soldier and a king, while his wife was

Writing table presented to Beaumarchais by his friends in 1781

once a very pretty woman and knows how to maintain her position. But, absurd as it may appear, for the King of Italy is a descendant of an old and illustrious house, Italy is but an upstart kingdom and its sovereign is not regarded as having the same prestige as his royal contemporaries, while his kingdom is honeycombed with revolutionary societies and undermined with revolutionary principles, and an Italian Republic may not be in the far distant future. It would be superfluous to mention the other minor sovereigns of Europe, most of whom are mere vassals or dependants of their greater neighbours, many of whose brothers and children marry actresses and dancers and who spend their time in going about from one continental country to another in first class carriages, dining in French cafés, and simply leading the lives of prosperous or adventurous citizens. Long may the Queen of England live for the benefit of the institutions, the security and satisfaction of her subjects! The day may may come when the Crown of Great Britain may be exchanged for the Phrygian Cap. May I not live to see it. From the political, as well as the social point of view, the results of the change could be but deplorable.

With the expression of these sentiments, I shall conclude this paper. Into whose hands will it fall? Who will be its first reader, and by whom will it be first opened? And will the thoughts and descriptions I have jotted down, afford him or her satisfaction or the reverse? Things to which we, the contemporaries of an event, whether significant or insignificant, attach importance, are nearly always viewed in a different light by future generations, and what may interest us may not interest them. I cannot look into the future, and in fact have only consigned to paper my thoughts on the Queen's visit to Waddesdon, not for any special reasons of my own, or for the gratification of my vanity, but because I have been pressed by my numerous friends to keep a record of an event, which in days far forward, may be regarded as one of some significance, and likely to arouse the historical, archaeological and social curiosity of unborn generations.'

The Prince of Wales' last visit to Waddesdon before Baron Ferdinand died did not end as satisfactorily as the Queen's. The Prince, one Monday morning in July, 1898, intent on having breakfast before catching a train to Windsor, left his bedroom and came down the West Stairs. Lord Warwick, who was also staying in the house, described what happened next in his 'Memoirs of Sixty Years'. He wrote:

Opposite One of the eighteenth century bindings of books by Padeloup collected by Baron Ferdinand

Overleaf Three of the bookplates in Baron Ferdinand's collection

Binding by Le Gascon, 1641

MEMOIRE
SUR LA
REFORMATION
DE LA POLICE
DE FRANCE

Bibl. hug
de Bassville
Rendés le livre s'il vous plait.

DE LA BIBLIOTHEQUE,
DE M. LAVOISIER.
de l'Academie Royale des Sciences,
regisseur des Poudres et Salpêtres
de France, Fer Général du Roy.
De la Gardette fecit

DULCES ANTE OMNIA MUSÆ.
DEUS NOBIS HÆC OTIA FECIT
C. S. IORDANI, ET AMICORUM.

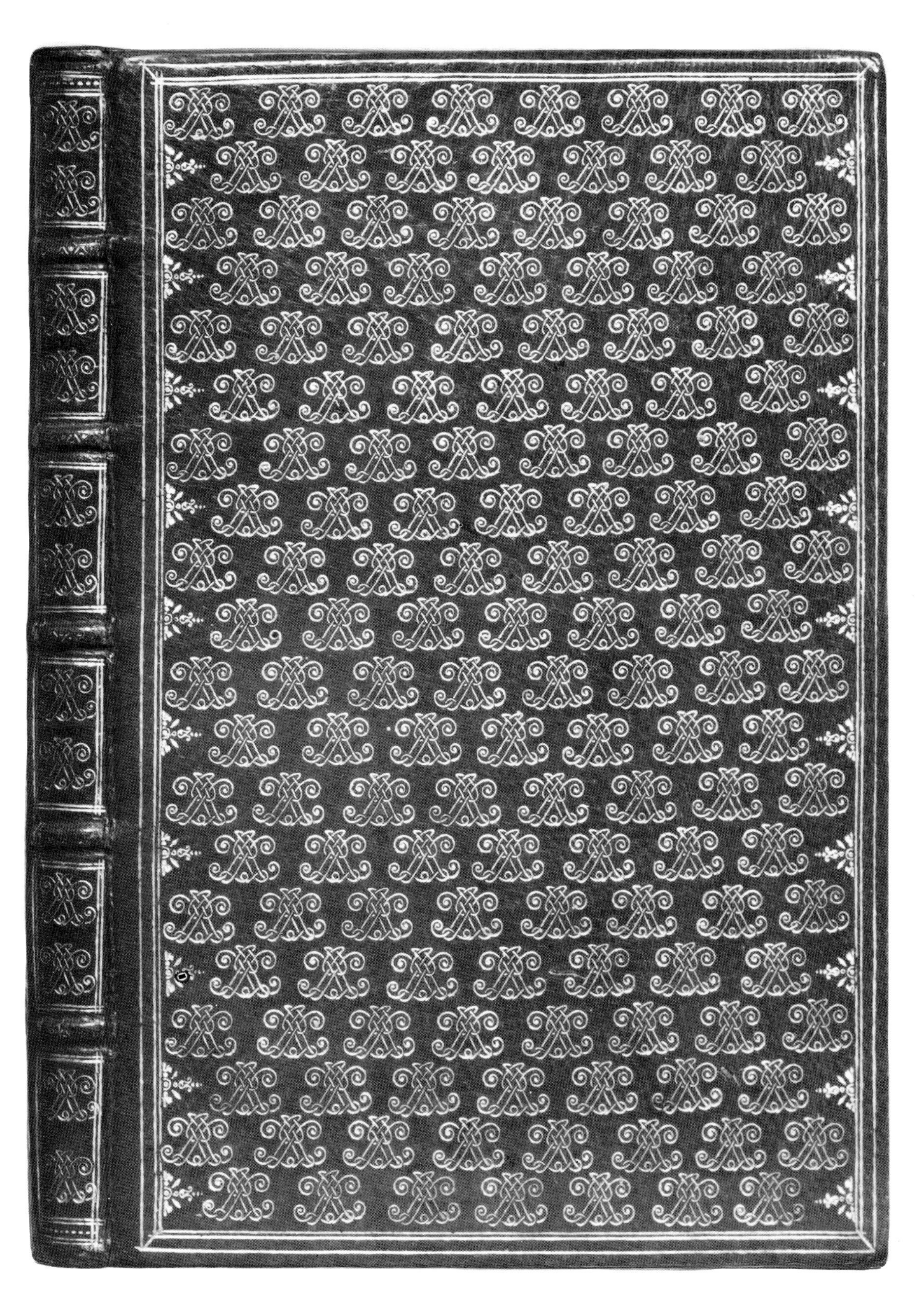

'I was out early and sitting on a chair in front of the house talking to one of the guests—I can't remember to whom. Suddenly the butler came out and asked anxiously if I knew where the Baron was. I replied I had not yet seen him, and asked if anything was amiss, as the poor man was greatly agitated. 'I fear' he replied, 'that the Prince of Wales has met with a bad accident. He slipped heavily on the spiral staircase, and is now sitting down there unable to move'. I hurried into the house, and found the Prince where the butler had left him, sitting on a step of the main circular staircase. He smiled re-assuringly at me, although I could see at a glance that he must be in great pain, and said: 'I fear I have broken something in my leg; my foot slipped, and as I fell I heard a bone crack'. Two servants came up at that moment bearing a long invalid chair, and fearing from what the Prince had said that he had split or broken his knee-cap, I tied his leg straight out onto one of the parallel carrying poles. Then the local doctor arrived, and the Prince was allowed to sit on a sofa with his leg down, to have his breakfast before leaving. I have always thought that but for the severe strain involved by his straightened leg the subsequent illness would not have been so long or so difficult—but I will not blame the doctor. The Prince was ever the kindliest of men, and his great anxiety was to reassure Baron Ferdinand, who was so grieved to think he should have met with a serious accident under his roof'.

Many years later, the Royal Bucks Hospital in Aylesbury began to wonder why they were 'Royal' and asked me if I could tell them whether they had received that distinctive title because the Prince of Wales had been taken there after breaking his leg at Waddesdon. I was almost sure that I had been told that the Prince had insisted on being taken straight back to Windsor, but I thought, before giving an answer it might be as well to check my memory. My investigations revealed an even more disastrous ending to the Prince's visit than that recorded by Lord Warwick. It appears the Prince was placed in a carriage at Waddesdon, with the carrying-chair, and driven to Aylesbury station. Then, as now, if one wishes to take a train from Aylesbury to Windsor the right platform can only be reached by traversing a high bridge over the rails which is approached, at either end, by steep turning stairs. The Prince, now a big heavy man of nearly sixty years of age, was safely carried from the carriage, into the station and up the stairs on to the bridge. But then his weight became too much for the carrying chair. It broke, depositing him unceremoniously and most painfully

The Grey Drawing Room. The portrait in the corner is of Lady Jane Halliday by Reynolds. The Savonnerie carpet was woven on a design by P.-J. Perrot for the dining room of Louis XV at the Grand Trianon in 1745.

in the middle of the bridge which from time to time, was engulfed by the acrid smoke of trains passing underneath it. It is hard to imagine how the Prince was eventually got off the bridge and into the Windsor train; doubtless, there were many willing hands, including Baron Ferdinand's, but it seems likely that the extra agony this final accident caused may have been just as responsible as the Waddesdon doctor's treatment—which Lord Warwick so doubted—for making the Prince's leg take so long to mend.

Baron Ferdinand died very suddenly in his bath, at Waddesdon, from a heart attack, on his 59th birthday. When the news of his death became known the Bucks County Council suspended its sitting and directed that a flag should be flown at half mast from the County Hall; the drivers of the hansom cabs and growlers which plied for hire in Piccadilly tied black ribbons to their whips and the Prince of Wales attended the memorial Service in the Central Synagogue which was held on the day Baron Ferdinand was buried beside his beloved wife in the Jewish Cemetry at West Ham.

His death in 1898 cut short the life of a man who still had much to contribute to the country of his adoption in the cultural, charitable and political fields. At Waddesdon his prediction that others might reap the chief benefit of his labour of love proved to be tragically accurate. He was widely loved, both in his family circle and by many friends in all walks of life. I think it was the fashion of the day for newspapers to print obituaries of length, giving complete details of every phase of their subject's life, but when, many years later, I found two huge volumes of cuttings from newspapers, of every shade of opinion and nationality, eulogising Baron Ferdinand for all he did and all he was, I could not help feeling that he must have been a most exceptional human being. To quote from one paper: 'Beneficence had been the business of his life'.

By his Will he left the contents of his London house in Piccadilly to relatives and friends. He bequeathed his collection of Renaissance objects in what he termed his 'new smoking room' at Waddesdon to the British Museum;* he made large bequests to hospitals and charities, particularly those concerned with the welfare of merchant seamen and their dependants, and, after making handsome provision for all those who had worked for him in Buckinghamshire and elsewhere, he left the Waddesdon estate to his sister, Alice.

A writing table inlaid with Sèvres plaques which was made by Martin Carlin in 1766.

* Where they are known as The Waddesdon Bequest. By order of the Trustees they have recently been beautifully re-arranged in a room of their own by Mr. Hugh Tait, who is also compiling a new and detailed catalogue of this bequest.

Miss Alice 1847-1922

BARON FERDINAND'S BEQUEST of Waddesdon to his sister may have caused some surprise. After all, it was only shortly before the Baron's death that Lord Meath, in the House of Lords, had had the temerity to recommend that the law should be changed so as to allow women to be elected to County Councils, on which, he thought, they might be helpful in such matters as the boarding-out of children. Although Lord Meath was instant to point out to their Lordships that he would utterly deprecate his proposal being used as the thin edge of any wedge which might one day enable ladies to sit at Westminster, (plainly, he said, they would be incapable of dealing with matters of *haute politique*) his suggestion was considered so foolish that he was quite unable to find another peer to second him.

The inheritance of Waddesdon was, of course, an entirely private family affair, but in the prevailing opinion of the day it seems that an estate of this kind was thought to call for a capacity in its owner which was judged to be the prerogative of the male sex alone. Miss Alice, grieving deeply for her brother, may well have felt daunted, but I am sure that no one who knew her at all well could have doubted the intelligence, humanity and administrative ability which would enable her to succeed him. The record shows she was well up to her task.

Miss Alice, the youngest of Baron Anselm's seven surviving children, was born in Frankfort in 1847. She spent her early childhood in Vienna to which her father had been sent to take charge of the family banking business in Austria. Even as a small child she must have had something about her. When she was eight years old, her grandfather died and, in the habit of the day, the entire family were gathered together to learn his testamentary dispositions. The way in which he had left his house, the Grüneburg and its large park, on the outskirts of Frankfort, must have been a matter of personal interest and conjecture not only to Miss Alice's father, but also to her three brothers. But when the Will was read it was learnt, to the

Miss Alice de Rothschild (1847–1922) in her early twenties

Lady Battersea (1843–1931)

bemused surprise of everyone, that he had bequeathed the Grüneburg, in its entirety, to Miss Alice.

When she was twelve years old her mother died, and she went to live in the Grüneburg with her much older sister, Mathilde who, like so many of the family, had married a Rothschild cousin—the Baron Willy. Lady Battersea, an English relative, writing of Miss Alice, described her at this time. She said: 'She spent rather a lonely childhood, owing to the fact of her being the junior member of the family. Following a suggestion of her English cousins, during a visit of their's to Frankfort, she came to England in the late summer of 1860, with her French governess, Mademoiselle Hofer, who became her life-long friend, and proceeded on a visit to her aunt, Lady de Rothschild. There, under the auspices of that beloved aunt she first learnt what country life and its duties implied. It was a happy time for the young motherless girl who shared a school-room existence with her cousins, soon to become her devoted friends. At that early age she already gave proof of very remarkable gifts, both mental and physical; indeed, her power of grasping the threads of an argument and of logical reasoning were unusual enough in one of her years to have aroused the admiration and astonishment of no less a personage than Matthew Arnold, who met her when staying at Aston Clinton as a guest of Lady de Rothschild. Alice was very proficient in all games of dexterity and skill; she was passionately fond of riding, and became as the years went on a fearless and well-known horsewoman. She always avowed that her visits to Aston Clinton had in a way prepared her for the great change that was about to come into her life'.

That change came when, having sold the Grüneburg to her sister and brother-in-law, the Baron and Baroness Willy, she determined to come to England permanently to be with her bereaved brother Ferdinand.

With Mademoiselle Hofer still at her side, she came to London and spent much of the winters with her brother at Leighton House. Here, as in London, Lady Battersea notes 'she proved a capable hostess to his many distinguished guests'—not an entirely easy thing to be at the age of 20 in what was still, to her, a foreign land. But she was determined not to be a foreigner for long and, in the following year, on reaching her majority, she became a naturalised British subject.

As the years went by she acquired—perhaps under her brother's influence—a great knowledge of works of art and showed a distinctive taste in their collection and arrangement. Miss Alice, I believe, may well have expressed her own ideas about the house her brother was planning to build and furnish

Miss Alice's elder sister, Mathilde, who married Baron Willy von Rothschild

at Waddesdon and possibly her ideas did not always entirely coincide with his. In any case, with her brother's encouragement, in 1875 she bought the neighbouring property of Eythrope and there set about building her own little Waddesdon. Monsieur Destailleur, working for her brother, was not asked to design her house for her; instead she chose an English architect, George Devey.

Eythrope had had a chequered history. It was an ancient property, first of the Dormers, then of the Stanhopes before it passed by descent to a French family, the d'Harcourts. It is said that the last Stanhope owner, being childless, sent for his French nephew and told him he would leave him the large house at Eythrope—with its renowned picture gallery—if he would promise him two things—that he would become a Protestant, and would spend six months of every year in England. The boy is said to have promised, but, the moment his Uncle was dead, reverted to the Catholic faith of his fathers, and never set foot in England again. At least it is true that for nearly a hundred years Eythrope House was uninhabited; then it was sold, not only the contents, but the fabric of the house itself, which was broken up into lots. It is said that Little Kimble church was built with material from Eythrope and that the very pretty front door of the County Museum in Aylesbury was once the door of Eythrope House. The d'Harcourts, however, retained possession of the land and it was from them that Miss Alice bought it, the only building then remaining being a ruined chapel which had once stood next to the vanished house.

Miss Alice decided not to build on the old foundations but

The Pavilion at Eythrope from the air, with the river in the foreground

instead set her new house a short distance away from them, in the middle of a meadow bounded by the river Thame. As the building of her house started Miss Alice fell ill—I imagine of some form of rheumatic fever, a complaint which was to bedevil her, on and off, for the rest of her days. Her doctor insisted, in the medical fashion of the day, that damp at night-time was the one thing she must avoid and told her that if she valued her health she must never, never sleep at Eythrope; it was so dangerously near water. This opinion must have been a severe blow to Miss Alice, but she was not one to disregard advice she considered expert. So Mr. Devey's plans were changed, and the fairy-tale, towered, pink brick house, named the Pavilion, was built to contain a sitting-room, a dining-room and a kitchen, but *no* bedroom, so that she should never fall into the temptation of sleeping there. The Pavilion was only four miles from Waddesdon and, in the following years, however many days Miss Alice spent at Eythrope, filling her house with works of art, organising her garden so that it should rival Waddesdon's, or entertaining her friends, she always returned to her brother's house at night.

An old acquaintance once described to me the usual routine of a summer day when visiting Waddesdon in the Baron's time. After a varied and leisurely breakfast a busy programme of inspection normally awaited his guests. The house-party might first descend the hill to the stables to admire or criticize the horses. Pausing, perhaps, to feed the Emus in their pen and braving the perfume of a grotto in which resided a mountain goat, they would then arrive at the glass-houses. Here they would wander through house after house of flowering exotic beauty. The Dairy was the next port of call, where those who wished to do so could sample the cream temptingly displayed in great bowls set out in a room embellished with decorative tiling. The Dairy 'Curio Room' would then be inspected. This housed Kändler models of Dresden animals and birds and ancient examples of faience and other curiosities which were then deemed 'rustic', but which are now thought to be some

The river Thame at Eythrope

The formal bedding on the South terrace at Waddesdon in Miss Alice's time

of Waddesdon's prize possessions. Toiling up the hill again presumably gave the Baron's guests an appetite for luncheon. Then, after a short rest, it would be time to go to Eythrope. A long line of open landaus would draw up outside the front door; Baron Ferdinand's guests would get in and, in a flurry of parasols and panama hats, would go clip-clopping through the park, over the road, and down through Miss Alice's long avenue of chestnuts. Then, I am told, it all depended on the weather, where they would have tea. If it was overcast they would drive straight to the Pavilion, but if the sun shone, they would transfer themselves into a large electric launch, manned by boatmen in straw hats, banded with blue and yellow ribbons—the family racing colours. Damp being only distinctly dangerous at night, they would then glide up the Thame to an enchanting tea-house Miss Alice had built on the river at the farthest point of her property.

But the weather can change at a moment's notice in England, as we all know. I had an old friend at Waddesdon who had worked for the family for many years. One day I asked him what his first job had been and he described it to me with relish and enjoyment. He said, as a boy of 12, he had been the cake-holder. He explained that on cloudy days, the delectable tea provided at Eythrope for the approaching guests from Waddesdon, would be set out in the dining-room of the Pavilion. Then, just as the landaus were arriving, the weather might change, the sun would shine, and it was realised that the guests might prefer to go up river. Happily the Thame does not pursue a straight course through the meadows, but winds its way. This made it possible for the big iced cakes, the ginger-snaps and wafer-thin sandwiches to be whipped off the table and packed into a pony-trap. This would be driven by a colleague straight across the fields to the tea-house at a speed which would enable the tea to beat the approaching launch by a short head. My old friend's task had been to stand in the trap, poised over the cakes, keeping them from over-setting and their fragile icing from damage, as they careered over the rough ground. Angel cakes, he remembered, had been particularly volatile and apt to bounce. As he recalled those long-gone summer afternoons he implied that those, indeed, had been the days.

The terrace at Eythrope: Baron Ferdinand seated 2nd from left: Miss Alice standing, far right

Some of those for whom those teas were made have also left us their impressions. In 1897, that great civil servant, Sir Algernon West noted in his diary:* 'On the 5th June, at the height of its glory, I went to Ferdinand Rothschild's at Waddesdon, and on Sunday to Miss Alice de Rothschild's fairy garden at Eythrope, both lovely; the only possible criticism that could be made were that they were too perfect—if that is possible'. He went on to record 'At Waddesdon J. Chamberlain said Mr. Gladstone was a bad judge of men; that he saw no difference between Harcourt, Bright and Childers. From a high mountain all things look equal. Chamberlain contended that it was an impossibility to be great and good—in reference to Napoleon. The essence of goodness was to be unselfish and indeed self-denying and thus to destroy greatness. Walked with Haldane, who said Chamberlain had strong Liberal leanings. Thought Rosebery very wise to wait. Would form a party of his own: E. Grey Foreign Secretary. Asquith not progressing. Mrs. Asquith apt to sacrifice the future for the pleasure of to-day; the result of superabundance of animal vitality and spirit. . .'

* *The Private Diaries of Sir Algernon West*. John Murray, 1922

The entrance corridor to the main part of the glasshouses

These small vignettes provided by Sir Algernon of some of the leading personalities of the time give the flavour of the opinion-forming gossip at political house-parties in the last years of Queen Victoria's reign.

Miss Alice never married. When she received her great inheritance she was a maiden lady, aged 51. To quote Lady Battersea again: 'At Waddesdon her rule was a very determined if also a generous one. Gifted with intellect and a firm sense of duty, also an unusually strong power of will and inflexibility of purpose, she pursued her way of life, managing her property, looking after every detail of her estate, undeterred by any opposition she might meet with. For some years her face and figure were well known in the villages of the neighbourhood, for she would drive herself about in a low phaeton, drawn by two nimble little ponies. She never changed her style of dress summer or winter, that of a tailor-made suit in soft grey cloth, with old-fashioned collars and cuffs, and her head covered by a panama hat. Those who met her walking in her garden remarked that she always carried a spud in her hand, with which she removed any offending weed from the carefully kept paths. No

A horse-drawn mower on the cricket ground at Waddesdon: at the back, the Pavilion from the roof of which Baron Ferdinand used to address his constituents

Formal bedding at Waddesdon

Opposite Miss Alice in old age at Eythrope

The Smoking room corridor hung with small arms collected by Miss Alice to replace some of the objects left by her brother to the British Museum

freaks or changes of fashion worried or affected her. She had never been good-looking, but had keen, bright eyes, a thoughtful brow, and something unusual and arresting in appearance and expression. She was most precise and punctual in all her habits, visiting daily her gardens, glasshouses and farm, her aviary of rare birds, managing personally every department of her property, and never resting until perfectly satisfied with what she saw. No detail, however small, escaped her notice. Her knowledge, indeed, covered a wide ground, for she was well acquainted with the art, literature and history of many countries. She was most interested in animal life, loving her dogs devotedly. Original in mind and speech, she had a great sense of humour, and could express herself both easily and with point in three languages'.

I first met her in 1913 and found that at the age of 67 she was a sparkling conversationalist and most entertaining, but she had one idiosyncracy which was rather unnerving. Whenever she said something amusing, as often happened, and one laughed, she would round on one, and ask with machine-gun speed 'Why do you laugh?'. Her health, since the first attack

Detail of a harp in Miss Alice's collection: French workmanship of the late eighteenth century

of rheumatic fever, had deteriorated and for some years she had been told that it would be unwise for her to spend the winters in England. So she had bought herself a villa at Grasse, in the South of France, where she spent the months from October to April, constructing what I believe was an outstanding garden which went half way up a mountain behind her villa. But Waddesdon was seldom out of her thoughts and a constant flow of instructions, enquiries and exhortations would flow from Grasse to Waddesdon throughout the winter months.

At Waddesdon she is still spoken of in terms of reverence, even awe, and anecdotes continue to be told of her which betray the strange mixture of alarm and yet real affection and pride in which she was held. She had almost impossibly high standards and would tolerate nothing but the best. Indeed, the phrase 'Waddesdon standard' became current in her day, and is still in use as typifying the degree of perfection which can only be achieved by intensive trouble-taking. But her real kindness is also well-remembered, both to individuals and to the neighbourhood as a whole. Her improvements to the amenities of Waddesdon village were countless and included schools, a nursing home and clubs for recreation. The more elegant of the clubs, which was furnished with a library of leather bound classics, was named the Institute and in those hierarchical days was reserved for the estate 'Heads of Department' and tenant farmers only. The other club, possibly jollier if less literate, was for the lesser fry of the village. The 'School Treats' which she continued to provide each year lost none of the glamour they had acquired in her brother's time. Her sense of piety and conservation induced her to take immense trouble to arrange the removal of a crusader's tomb from the now crumbling chapel at Eythrope to the safety of the nave of Waddesdon parish church.

In the Manor itself, one of her first cares must have been to re-adorn the Smoking Room and the long corridor outside it whose contents her brother had bequeathed to the British Museum. Being as passionate a collector as her brother she had already filled three houses—one in Piccadilly, her winter home at Grasse and the Pavilion at Eythrope—with enchanting pictures and furniture, mostly of the eighteenth century. I think she must have welcomed the opportunity given her by the bare walls of the Smoking Room to indulge her collecting instincts once again, and to some extent in a new field. She re-furnished the Smoking Room with many small pictures of the sixteenth and seventeenth centuries, Limoges enamels and Venetian and Bohemian glass. She hung the walls of the corridor outside it with small arms which she found and chose with the

Philippe Egalité, duc d'Orleans, at the age of 2, by François Boucher.

help of her friend, Sir Guy Laking, who was in charge of the Armour at Windsor and the Tower.

In the rest of the house she made very few changes, only adding one major picture and some snuff boxes. I believe she wished to change Waddesdon as little as possible and so preserve it intact as a memorial to her brother's taste and knowledge.

If Waddesdon's creation was due to Baron Ferdinand, its state of preservation is most certainly due to his sister. He was once described to me by an old friend who remembered him happily puffing a cigar all over his house, and I have no doubt he allowed the sun to shine in on his guests and light up the carpets, furniture and books he loved so much. Not so Miss Alice. In her day, smoking was most rigourously restricted to the Smoking Room and the continual adjustment of blinds which she enforced prevented all harmful rays of the sun from falling on textiles, marquetry and drawings. She laid down the most stringent rules about who should be allowed to touch china. No female hand was allowed to dust the decorative Sèvres vases in the various sitting-rooms; this was the responsibility of one particularly trusted man only. The Sèvres and Dresden china used in the dining room, however, was washed up by the Housekeeper and the Still-Room Maid, who did it in accordance with Miss Alice's simple but effective standing order: 'When touching china, *always* use two hands and maintain complete silence'. Visitors to Waddesdon to-day sometimes comment on the remarkable state of preservation of its contents which they find singularly unfaded, unbattered and unchipped. When they do so they are, unknowingly, paying a tribute to Miss Alice's constant and unwavering care.

There was only one part of Waddesdon in which, I think, she believed she could better her brother's administration; this was the garden. If the fruit, flowers and vegetables grown at Waddesdon had not proved absolutely perfect, or plentiful, Baron Ferdinand would not, I think, have been averse to making up the supplies he wanted from any convenient outside source. Miss Alice had other views. After her brother's death one of her first problems was to find a head gardener for Waddesdon who would be able to attain her more exacting standards. One highly recommended man after another was first engaged and then despatched as a disappointing failure. Having exhausted all obvious sources of recruitment without success Miss Alice then asked her trusted old French gardener at Grasse for advice. Without hesitation he told her she would not go wrong if she considered the promotion of a young Englishman, G. F. Johnson, who had been working in her mountain garden at Grasse for

Parade shield, probably made by Eliseus Libaertz of Antwerp for François I of France.

Hand mirror backed with a Limoges enamel plaque, by Jean de Court, depicting the Rape of Europa: sixteenth century

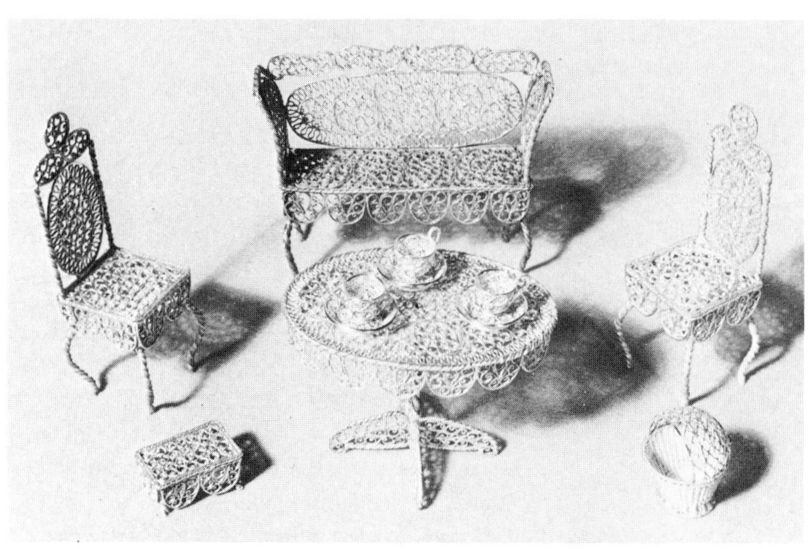

Eighteenth century Dutch dolls' house silver collected by Miss Alice

the past four years. Miss Alice took this advice, judging that the enterprise and determination already shown by Johnson in his career outweighed the risk of appointing someone aged only 26 to be in charge of the very large garden staff at Waddesdon.

Johnson's career had indeed been unusual. He was the son of a gardener who had done his best to dissuade him from following his own profession. Young Johnson, however, was determined to garden, and learnt his trade from Veitch, the great nurseryman, whose business was, in effect, a horticultural university. Through the friendship of his father with Baron Ferdinand's valet, he then secured a much coveted entry into the Waddesdon gardens. Having passed through all the departments there, he felt the need to learn the German language and asked the Head Gardener at Waddesdon to recommend him to his opposite number in Vienna where Baron Ferdinand's brother had a superb garden which was especially noted for its fruit grown under glass. This request was refused, and no introduction was given. Johnson, however, decided to take a chance; he took himself to Vienna, and was engaged to work in Baron Nathaniel's garden. After four years there he decided to learn French and again without introduction he reached Grasse in the South of France. He happened to present himself at Miss Alice's garden when she herself was there. His arrival caused a little commotion and Miss Alice asked what was happening. She was told that a young Englishman who had worked in the gardens of two of her brothers, in England and in Austria, was applying for a job with her. Not unnaturally, this made Miss Alice look upon him with some interest, and he was engaged on the spot. Not only did she appreciate his initiative in travelling the world, but even his extreme youth seemed to be an advantage; there was every chance that he could be trained up to fit her own sky-high standards.

Not long after Johnson's return to Buckinghamshire Miss Alice pointed out to him how desirable it was that the Head Gardener at Waddesdon should be married, and almost his first commission was to seek out a wife. Fortunately, Johnson had no objection to complying with this order and his admirable choice of spouse immediately met with Miss Alice's approval. He lived to celebrate 62 years in the family's service before dying in 1954 and throughout all those years he grew to perfection, first for Miss Alice and then for my husband, the special strains of flowers, fruit and vegetables she had sought out and collected from all over Europe. To this day I can remember the flavour of a variety of almost black strawberry, called I think 'Waterloo' with which she regaled us in 1913. Sadly, two wars later, this strain has now died out.

The private sitting room at Waddesdon allotted to Miss Alice by her brother, which remained unchanged until her death

I think Miss Alice considered it her duty to maintain the reputation for hospitality which had been established by her brother, so throughout the summer, when she was there, she continued to run Waddesdon on the same lines, and on the same scale. Many of his old friends—who were also hers—came to stay, as well as new ones. Her parties were not so large nor so numerous as his, and were noticeably less political. But politicians still came: Sir Willam Harcourt, the Chancellor of the Exchequer; Lord Rowton, Disraeli's trusted Private Secretary

Lancret. *Scene from the Italian comedy*

and biographer; and Mr. Winston Churchill again—no longer a youth with political aspirations, but now the Member for Oldham and with the charge at Omdurman and his escape from the Boers behind him. As the years went by she acquired many new friends while remaining faithful to the old: among her later acquaintances was Lord Kitchener who shared her own interest in the collecting of works of art.

There is no doubt that the friendship of the Royal Family for Baron Ferdinand also extended to his sister. During Queen Victoria's last years she too had sought the sun in winter, and when staying at the Grand Hotel in Grasse was a frequent visitor at Miss Alice's 'Villa Victoria'—so named by permission. Holidays in the South of France were taken rather differently in those days. In the evenings, the Queen would ask Miss Alice to come and sit with her, and on one occasion also invited Lady Battersea who was staying with Miss Alice. In her 'Reminiscences' Lady Battersea records: 'One evening the Queen sent for my cousin and myself. We found Her Majesty sitting in a

Venetian glass goblet

small room at the hotel, listening whilst at work, to Princess Beatrice who was playing duets on the piano with the Queen's maid-of-honour, Marie Adeane, H.M. beating time with her crochet hook'. Lady Battersea also noted that the Queen, when speaking of her privately, invariably referred to Miss Alice as 'The All-Powerful', and was astonished at her energy and capability, especially in the continual enlargement of her mountain garden which the Queen often traversed in her donkey-chair.

In the new reign Queen Alexandra was a guest at Waddesdon as was King Edward who came again to plant a tree in memory of his old friend, Baron Ferdinand. To the end of her days, Miss Alice was invariably invited to the children's garden-parties at Marlborough House; evidently, her hosts there knew of her liking for children who cannot have found her the formidable figure which Waddesdon legend has sometimes made her out to be.

The last big party she gave at Waddesdon, in 1913, was a dinner for all the officers of the Bucks Yeomanry. This was to celebrate the cessation of a running battle Miss Alice had fought with the British Army over the Yeomanry's temerity in riding over growing crops when on manoeuvres in the park at Waddesdon. So stoutly had this war been waged by both contestants that I understand it took the combined efforts of two Field-Marshals, the Duke of Connaught and Lord Kitchener, to settle the terms of peace. Typically, Miss Alice ensured that this dinner, to mark the end of hostilities, should be one of the most magnificent she had ever given.

In 1914 the real war started and the saddening changes it brought to the whole country also, of course, affected Waddesdon. Unmarried and childless, Miss Alice nevertheless worried greatly about the fate of her relations, all over Europe. She was particularly saddened by the death in action in Palestine of her English cousin, Evelyn, who she had hoped would succeed her at Waddesdon. No one was more jingo than Miss Alice, but she had the political foresight to gauge correctly the lasting consequences of a world war. But at the age of 68 there was little that she, personally, could do to further an Allied victory but to see that potatoes were grown in beds once filled with tea-roses and heliotrope, and arrange for the once immaculately kept lawns to grow much needed hay. Her chief worry, I believe, was to provide enough employment for the young wives of her erstwhile household, stablemen and farmers who were away fighting, and to find what means she could to comfort those whose husbands and sons would never return. During the winters Bournemouth became her refuge instead of Grasse, to which she only returned in 1919. For some years her health had deteriorated and in May 1922, while she was on her way back from Grasse to Waddesdon she died in a Paris hotel. From August 1915 until Miss Alice died, there are no signatures in the Waddesdon visitors' book.

James de Rothschild 1922-1957

I UNDERSTAND that in the last years of her life Miss Alice, realistic as always, refused to make any long term plans for the garden or the farms. Those in charge were repeatedly told 'that is for my heirs to decide'. She wanted them to be able to make their own choice of the manner in which the estate should be carried on. As my husband was her heir we appreciated this freedom enormously.

Both Baron Ferdinand and Miss Alice had enjoyed the company of their young nephews and great-nephews who were all often asked to stay at Waddesdon, so for a number of years my husband had known his great-aunt quite well. He and I became engaged to be married one Saturday in January, 1913. On the following day he came again to my parents' house in Carlton Gardens (which has now become the official residence of the Foreign Secretary) and from there we walked to Charing Cross Post Office which then, as now, is open for business at all hours of every day including Sundays. My fiancé said he was going to send telegrams to all his many relatives, announcing our engagement, and that if I watched him doing so he would give me a first lesson in who was who in his complicated family. We reached the Post Office and he began to write out the telegrams, giving me a short description of each intended recipient as he did so. When he came to the telegram to Miss Alice he said 'This one is important—and I bet it never gets there!' and explained to me that of all his family Miss Alice would be the only one to mind if she first read of our engagement in the newspapers. He had no reason whatever to think this telegram to Miss Alice would miscarry, but mysteriously, his light-hearted prophecy proved correct. Of all the telegrams sent that day the one to Miss Alice, through some unknown postal mishap, alone failed to arrive.

Although she felt the omission at the time, her vexation was short-lived and she was kind enough to ask us to Waddesdon soon after our marriage. In her remaining years I began to feel that I knew her quite well; I did not see her often, as the

James de Rothschild
(1878–1957)

first war followed almost immediately, and after 1916 she lived the secluded life of an invalid, but throughout all the period we were in touch by letter. Perhaps I felt I knew her better than I did, for I also heard much about her from her sister, Mathilde—my husband's grandmother—and also from my mother-in-law, her contemporary, who had been a close friend of her youth. But never, at any time, did it occur to me, any more than it did to my husband, that Waddesdon might, one day, be our home.

My husband, who was known to everyone as Jimmy, was born and brought up in Paris. He was a grandson of the founder of the French branch of the family. He was always delicate as a child, but at the age of three spoke French, English and German with the accent of a native in each tongue. He too, followed the family tradition in his youth, by making a collection of Greek and Roman coins, but these, like his stamp album, were put away with maturity. He ended his French schooldays—made nightmarish by the anti-semitism engendered by the Dreyfus affair—by being the head of his *Lycée*, Louis le Grand, and in an examination, the *Concours Général* which in those days extended to the whole of France, he again emerged top, with the title of '*caçique*'. When he was eighteen he was sent to Cambridge, where for three years his thoughts were concentrated not on works of art, nor on his books, but rather on hunting and steeple-chasing. He longed to remain at Cambridge for a fourth year, but his father agreed that he should do so only if he won a scholastic prize. With the remarkable concentration of which he was always capable, he switched his attention, for a few months, to intensive study and secured the Harkness Prize with his essay 'Shakespeare and his Day' which was subsequently published. After this year of grace he was sent to Hamburg to learn the rudiments of banking, but contrived, by enduring long night journeys, to spend his occasional free days hunting or steeple chasing in England. Following serious concussion he sustained through a fall at Cottenham, he emigrated under an assumed name to Australia, hoping to avoid entering the Paris branch of the family bank. For eighteen months he successfully eluded his family's attempts to find him and earned his living in various ways, starting as a book-maker's runner on the Melbourne race-course and ending as a cattle-hand on a northern ranch. Much to his annoyance, but to his parents' great relief, his whereabouts were traced by his English cousin Alfred, who prided himself on his world-wide connections. Thanks to this intervention and to his own feelings of remorse at causing his family so much anxiety, he met his parents in Ceylon and returned to France with them. His father thought perhaps a world tour with one of his Cambridge friends, Vere Ponsonby, might

James de Rothschild (2nd from right) in Palestine in 1918. On the left, Dr. Chaim Weizmann: 2nd from left, The Hon. William Ormsby Gore

soften the transition from roughing it in Australia to life in a Paris bank. This intuitive idea proved a good one; the two young men went literally round the world: Canada, the United States, China and India were included in their itinerary. In China he had the astonishing experience of dining with the famous Empress Dowager, an occasion made all the better for Jimmy by his always adventurous taste in food. He ate all the local delicacies, including 100-year old eggs, with relish. Vere Ponsonby was far from sharing his pleasure in this respect: I sympathise with him as I also much prefer roast chicken and a normal boiled hen's egg to any other form of food. Their visit to India coincided with Lord Curzon's Durbar—another flamboyant and memorable occasion. But the Paris bank awaited him, and in this he worked hard and took a prominent part until the 1914 war started.

His experiences in the war were varied: he started as a *poilu* in the French army and was seconded to the British army with the rank of '*Interprète Stagiaire*'. Many of Jimmy's peace-time friends were on the staff of the British 3rd Corps, to which he was attached and so he was invited to join the mess of the Corps' C.O., General Pulteney. Here the red trousers of Jimmy's *poilu* uniform and his non-commissioned rank caused some hilarity, although he was ultimately taken seriously enough to be awarded the D.C.M. In 1915 he was badly injured near Bailleul when a large lorry in which he was travelling overturned, pinning him beneath it. Fortunately a British platoon came by, led by an officer who stopped to enquire

The author's father and mother, Mr and Mrs Eugéne Pinto

what had happened. An explanation was given with the comment that the figure whose head, buried in the mud, was just protruding from the side of the lorry, was that of a dead man. The officer stirred the mud with his boot, thus revealing the face of the body, and then exclaimed 'My God! It's Jimmy Rothschild! Dig him up'. It still took some while for this order to be carried out, and during that time Jimmy could hear, but not see, other passers-by on that shell-torn road. He recognised two English voices as belonging to acquaintances of his peace-time days. The first voice—that of a General—asked:

'Is there anyone under there?'

'Yes' replied the General's A.D.C.

'Do you know who it is?'

'Yes, Jimmy Rothschild'

'Is he dead?' asked the General

'Not yet' came the reply.

Jimmy said that the cheerful tone in which this 'Not yet' was pronounced always made him feel slightly less than friend-

Baron and Baroness Edmond de Rothschild by Bakst

ly whenever he met the A.D.C. in after years.

He had received multiple injuries, including a broken pelvis, and was despatched to Paris in great pain. Within a few months he tried to resume his interpreter's duties with the 3rd Corps, but his health had been shattered and he was forced to retreat to a spell in the Ministry of Munitions in London. However, his health eventually improved sufficiently for him to return to active service and he spent nearly all 1918 in Palestine where, among his other duties, he raised a Jewish Battalion for service under Allenby. Three of his recruits were named Ben-Gurion, Ben-Zvi and Sprinzak: I don't know how useful they were as infantrymen but more than 30 years later the first became the Prime Minister, the second the President and the third the Speaker of the Parliament of the State of Israel.

This was Jimmy's first visit to Palestine and while he was there he was able to see for himself the colonies which his father had founded, of which he had heard so much. As long ago as 1882 his father, moved by the plight of Russian Jews at the height of the pogroms, had begun his colonisation work in Palestine. By 1918, some of the innumerable difficulties of establishing preponderantly intellectual Jews in an uncultivated desert, or in malarial swamps infested by mosquitoes, had been overcome. Jimmy was captivated by the courage, persistence and ingenuity which had created the existing settlements, with their orchards, oranges, grape-fruit and vines in the midst of a desert landscape and vowed then to do all he could to help his father continue his work, and to further the Zionist cause, which he saw as the one hope of his tortured co-religionists in Eastern Europe.

After the war he had the misfortune to lose an eye while playing golf at Deauville and this proved a lasting handicap: at the end of his life he was almost blind.

In 1919 he applied for British naturalisation, some three years before we were overwhelmed by our totally unexpected inheritance of Waddesdon. I say 'overwhelmed' in no sense of ingratitude, but as our friend, Lord d'Abernon said, when he heard of our good fortune, 'Waddesdon is not an inheritance, it is a career'.

In 1922 I had reached the mature age of 27 and had been a married woman for nine years. In childhood I had had a wonderfully care-free existence: no boarding-school; no exams; a bi-lingual father who always spoke French to me, but who did not, alas, endow me with his adventurous spirit; and a mother who was as enchantingly pretty as she was angelic in character. They made sure that I learnt the rudiments of golf, croquet, lawn tennis, bridge, bézique, riding and waltzing, but

I never had any experience whatever of country life. All our holidays were spent in a small house in Brighton. When Jimmy asked me to marry him I had only just been promoted by my parents to dine with them at 7.45 followed immediately by bed.

Quite apart from emotional feelings, the experiences of the few weeks of our engagement can never be forgotten. The failure of the telegram to reach Miss Alice was not the only complication to arise. Jimmy had telephoned our news to his parents in Paris who had no inkling of his budding romance. The line was not clear and in any case the name of Dorothy Pinto conveyed nothing to them. Their anxiety was great and they telephoned to their cousin Alfred in London, hoping to get more detailed information. Unfortunately his accuracy for once failed him and he reported that Jimmy was engaged to a most charming and beautiful actress, Miss Dorothy Minto, who was a star of the musical comedy stage.

The effect on my future in-laws was devastating; their views on mixed religious marriages were rigid and they had thought they were shared by their eldest child. Mercifully, later and more accurate information freed them from anxiety and within four days my father, mother, Jimmy and I set off to see them.

My total lack of imagination fortunately spared me any anticipation of the ordeals which lay before us. Straight from the Gare du Nord Jimmy and I were conveyed in his family's electric motor to his paternal home in the Faubourg St. Honoré, next door to the British Embassy. To Jimmy's embarrassment, the household took the view that our arrival was a momentous occasion; the lodge gates were flung open and we drove into a brilliantly illuminated courtyard and entered the house by the imposing front door, instead of by the customary cosy little side-door which I used ever after.

We were received by my prospective in-laws on the first floor, to the accompaniment of the shrill barking of a dachshund and a Skye terrier, both quite out of control. Fortunately, Jimmy's parents' smiles of welcome obliterated the mounting terror of the dogs as they swirled round my legs.

There followed, that evening, a small dinner party—not at the Faubourg's usual hour of 8.30, but at 7.45, to suit my father who always maintained that 7.46 was too late to begin eating. Sir Frank Bertie, the British Ambassador, was the only other guest, but after dinner all members of the Rothschild family in Paris were invited to come and have a look at the prospective bride—an interesting ordeal for me.

My father had two sisters and a brother living in Paris, and they all wished to give dinner parties for us. It was most kind,

Above Caricature of Mr. & Mrs. James de Rothschild by Sem

Opposite James and Dorothy de Rothschild at Wisbech in the 1929 election

but the existing French custom enjoined that engaged couples, after dinner, should be ushered into a different room from the other guests, and should stay there throughout the evening, with the door left wide open to ensure propriety. The element of the ridiculous in this situation made it hard for us to accept it gracefully.

Trousseau hunting filled the days, and at the end of an exhausting week we were invited to stay with Jimmy's cousins at Ferrières, a huge house in the country modelled on Mentmore. There a large house-party was invited to meet us. Unfortunately, my mother was unaware that in France the principal guest was expected to give the signal for the end of the evening and bed—she was more accustomed to the English habit of depending on the hostess for this relief. Far, far too late, a solution to this impasse was found and, dropping with fatigue, we thankfully got upstairs. On our return to England I then faced a further round of introductions to Jimmy's huge family here. This included a visit to Lord Rosebery, to whose charm I fell an instant victim, but whose personality was distinctly alarming until one got accustomed to his brilliant banter.

Looking back on those hectic days before our wedding on February 25th, it is difficult to realise that most of those hurried introductions led ultimately to many friendships which have been one of the delights of my life.

After our honeymoon spent hunting at Pau and touring Spain we settled down—if that is the word—to a pattern of life which consisted of continuous travel. Just before we married, Jimmy had bought a house in London, in Park Street, and in Paris we lived in his bachelor flat in the Champs Elysées. As he was still a member of the French branch of the family bank, our days were divided between his work in Paris, and his racing in England. We also went further afield. I was taken to stay with his wonderful grandmother, Baroness Willy, the sister of Baron Ferdinand and Miss Alice, who lived in Frankfort. Our first visit covered the period when she and I both had birthdays in March, she became 81 while I achieved 18. She was not only brilliant intellectually, but also endowed with that rare quality of understanding that made her the confidante of all the members of her family. She shared the linguistic talents of her brother and sister and, in addition, was an accomplished musician—a pupil of Chopin, and a composer herself. At Waddesdon there is a complete collection of the music she wrote, mostly songs which were sung by such famous artists as Mme. Patti. When I knew her she was the widow of the most religious member of the Rothschild family and although she survived her husband by twenty-three years,

'The Pink Boy'—
Gainsborough's portrait of
Master Nicholls.

she never forsook the exacting Orthodox life to which he had accustomed her. We spent Passover with her in 1913, with Jimmy officiating as closely as he could in the tradition of his grandfather. As I was the youngest person present it fell to my lot to ask the ritual questions in Hebrew—another experience I shall never forget. Even when we were in London, the change from childhood's regular routine to the whirl of married life could not have been greater. I found myself a member of a huge new family, with a brilliant husband who had many friends in all walks of life, particularly in the to me unknown worlds of politics and racing.

But no sooner had I become used to this existence than the 1914 war came. I found myself, bereft of the company and guidance of my husband who, when leaving to join the French army on August 1st, insisted that I should remain in England. At least this meant that my parents would not be bereft of both their children during those horrible times and I was able to share with them the anxiety for my brother who had joined the Coldstream. To our joy he did manage to emerge alive in 1918, although not entirely unscathed and with an M.C.

In London, in 1915, I found much friendship in the world of Liberal politics and, having made the acquaintance of Dr. Weizmann, I was also introduced to the hopes which I shared and still share of a Zionist future for Palestine in which my father-in-law was primarily interested. I became the post office which transmitted the views and news of Dr. Weizmann to Baron Edmond and vice versa.

When Jimmy returned to England and worked in the Ministry of Munitions while his injuries were healing, we were together again until he was well enough to join the army once more, and went off to Palestine. This time he agreed that I might go to France where I remained until the end of 1918—a strange experience, but one which enabled me really to get to know my parents-in-law, a memory I shall always cherish.

It was my hope when peace came and Jimmy returned to England, we should lead a more normal existence at last. But our first days were disrupted by the worry and pain occasioned by Jimmy's loss of his eye, and then in 1921 we started to travel again. First we went to the United States and to Canada on behalf of the Zionist cause, and then, after hardly a pause, we went to Palestine. Here we had the unusual experience of being the guests of the High Commissioner, Sir Herbert Samuel, simultaneously with Mr. and Mrs. Winston Churchill and the Emir Abdullah, while the Emirate of Jordan was being planned.

Gainsborough's portrait of Lady Sheffield.

I have only given this account of my early days in order to show that although by 1922 they had had a certain variety, nothing in my upbringing or experience had prepared me for life in the English countryside or, indeed, at Waddesdon.

It was with feelings of apprehension that we faced this fateful new future which had so suddenly opened before us. Obviously, we had to take the plunge and visit Waddesdon at the earliest opportunity, but we could not rid ourselves of the feeling of being interlopers taking over what had been a closely guarded preserve. Jimmy felt strongly that he wished to avoid any impression that might be given to Miss Alice's mourning household of a brash new heir arriving with a swagger, and decided that it would be more modest if we travelled from London by train. As our own motor met us at Aylesbury station to drive us the six miles to Waddesdon I never quite understood the point of this manoeuvre, although I shared the feelings which prompted it.

One of the more alarming consequences of our inheritance was the prospect of finding myself in charge of a large household staff. But Miss Alice had been a shrewd judge of character and she could never have chosen more wisely than in Mrs. Boxall, her housekeeper, who received us on our arrival. White-haired, but with a young pink and white complexion, she had an encyclopaedic knowledge of all the arts of conservation on which Miss Alice had so much insisted. In the following months it was she who told me of Miss Alice's rules for handling china, and it was she who explained how textiles should be treated in a perfectly run house. I was let into the secrets of the great cupboards in the North and South Linen Rooms and was shown the enchantingly pretty patterned linen covers which Miss Alice had had made for every chair in the house. In her philosophy, as in Mrs. Boxall's, tapestry and silk upholstery should only be allowed to be visible when there were guests in the house.

To my great relief I found the various heads of department would relieve me of the responsibilities of recruitment. It was only in the dire event of one of the 'heads' themselves leaving that we would be expected to find and engage their successor.

Mrs. Boxall reigned supreme over all the women in the house, as did the Steward over the male staff. The living quarters of the men were as far removed as possible from that of their female colleagues. Indeed, there was no direct route from the top floors of the batchelors' wing, in which the men lived, to the main part of the house. Nevertheless, I came to understand that these stringent precautionary measures were not entirely successful, and that an ingenious if unorthodox means had been evolved of at least gaining the housemaids' sitting-room.

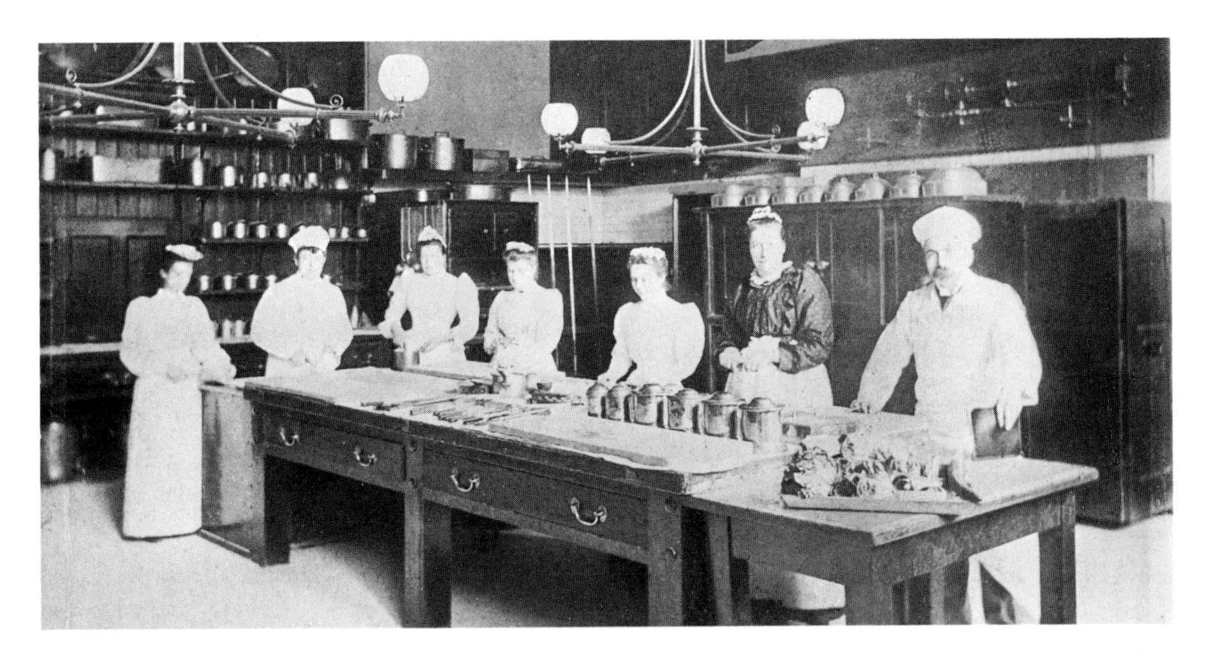

The kitchen staff at Waddesdon, c. 1910

The third department in the house, beyond the control of either the Steward or the Housekeeper, was the kitchen. Here a French Chef held undisputed sway, even over the Italian Pastry Cook who operated in a separate room. One of the walls of the main kitchen was entirely taken up by great coal-fired ranges and ovens. Another longer wall was covered in shelves which bore row upon row of shining copper pans. Variously shaped for every culinary purpose, and in every size, each of these bore a monogram—F. R. on the older ones, and A. R. on the more modern.

In these gleaming surroundings the Chef was aided by five assistants, the more senior of whom wore a coloured blouse; all the others were clothed in white from head to toe. Not only were the Chef and all his assistants talented and dexterous but, it seemed to me, they also appeared to be possessed of immense physical strength. Some of the coppers needed two people to carry them, even when they were empty, and it must have required a Hercules to close or open some of the great oven doors. Of all the changes in daily living which have come about in my life-time I think the greatest may be in the preparation and cooking of food. When I compare what was done in the Waddesdon kitchen when I first knew it with the simplicity of heating up a pre-cooked meal from a freezer, it hardly seems possible that both methods are equally successful in warding off hunger—if not of satisfying taste. The only thing which seems to have remained constant is the preoccupation about getting fat.

The still-room, as in other houses where one existed, did

not come under the Chef, but was part of the Housekeeper's kingdom. Although both the kitchen and the still-room produced food, their work was divided by an exact, well-understood, but seemingly inexplicable line of demarcation. Many years later, I asked a beloved ex-still-room maid to remind me of the work of her department. She gave me a mouth-watering description of the scones, jams and tisanes which had been made in the still-room and ended by saying 'And, of course, we washed and prepared the parsley for the sandwiches—but naturally, we did not make the sandwiches themselves; that was kitchen work'.

By the end of 1922, the Pastry Cook had departed, and by what would now be called 'natural wastage' the numbers in each department were diminished, but the internal structure and discipline of the house remained.

Out of doors, neither Baron Ferdinand nor Miss Alice had thought it necessary to employ an Agent—a superior being who would have been in ultimate charge of everything, both in the house and in the surrounding estate. I think they had preferred to deal more directly themselves with the chiefs of all the separate entities. These included not only the Home Farms, the tenant farms, the garden and the stables but also the Forestry department, which tended the woodlands and the fences, and the Works staff which maintained the farm buildings and the many cottages and village houses in which the employees of the estate lived.

Relations with the tenant farmers were conducted by Mr. Sims, who had once been in charge of the tree-planting in the Baron's day, and who had since been promoted to Farm Bailiff. As such he was, apparently, responsible for supplying us with a list of the type of poultry each employee would prefer as a gift at Christmas time. We were somewhat startled by our first experience of this list; presented without a heading or any explanation, its first line read: 'Myself—a Goose'.

In those days, before the complexities of insurance contributions and V.A.T. had even been thought of, there had, it seems, been no need for an estate accountant. We found that everyone on the estate, both indoor and outdoor, was paid by the family lawyer who, once a fortnight, drove the six miles from Aylesbury—at first in a horse fly but latterly in a more modern conveyance—bearing with him a Gladstone bag stuffed with the necessary money.

Overwhelmed as we were by our new surroundings, our instinctive wish was to make as few alterations as possible. But one or two changes in the house had to be tackled immediately. Baron Ferdinand, ever an enterprising man, had

Part of the greenhouse range at Waddesdon

been one of the first in the country to convert the lighting in his house from gas to electricity. He did this in the days when, if you wanted such a new-fangled invention, you had to make the electricity yourself. His installation, dependent on a power house secreted in a grove of chestnuts by the back door, was plainly insufficient to deal with more modern needs and appliances.

We decided to re-wire the whole house to cope with the stronger supply we hoped to introduce and then found, to our intense surprise, that the drainage was also suspect. Seemingly Waddesdon's drains had been installed without the meticulous care which had been lavished on all the other components of the building. The suspicion that we have today that the Prince Consort's early death from typhoid was due to defective drainage at Windsor Castle was a theory unknown to Baron Ferdinand or Miss Alice and to many of their contemporaries: if they had had an inkling of it, I can well imagine the speed with which they would have taken steps to improve the drainage in their own houses. As it was, the whole system had to be renewed, and while this was being done we took the opportunity to install one or two more bathrooms. There were already some in the house, as both Baron Ferdinand and Miss Alice had catered for the more modern notions of some of their guests, but to the end of her days Miss Alice, like some others of her age, had preferred a hip bath.

In the event, we also found we were obliged to make considerable changes in the garden, principally in the glass-houses, which must have been as extensive as any in the country. It was in their management, I believe, that Miss Alice had had such difficulty in finding a head-gardnener competent to meet her needs. The houses were divided into four sections—first for display *in situ,* in what was known as the 'Top Glass' which, in turn was fed by the growing houses which also produced the flowers used for indoor decoration as well as the many gifts of malmaison carnations, orchids and other delights with which visitors to Waddesdon were often sent home. Thirdly, there was the colossal Fruit Range, and finally the heated frames in which were grown the early vegetables before the outdoor varieties were ready.

Mr. Johnson, whose career I have already mentioned, was responsible for all this as well, of course, for the herbaceous borders, the rose garden, the rock garden and the 'bedding out' round the house which, as contemporary photographs show, was of unbelievable elaboration. During his many years at Waddesdon Mr. Johnson managed to hand on at least some of his almost unique knowledge to whole new generations of gardeners, but learning from him was certainly no sinecure. I heard later from some of those who had done so that whenever, in the course of one's work, one happened to come within his view, it was essential not to be seen with a cigarette in one's mouth and—if one was to escape his wrath—also to be seen moving at the double: it was not only speed, but also the most

Cyclamen grown for market in glasshouses previously devoted to semi-tropical plants

Daffodil Valley: Chestnuts and Sycamore on the left: Wellingtonia on the right

minute attention to every detail that he demanded from those who worked under him.

We came to the sad conclusion that the beautiful Alamandas, Bougainvillia and Gloriosa Rothschildiana which ramped up the central sections of the 'Top Glass' would have to be scrapped and that the exotic species in many of the other houses must also go. Their place was taken by commercial cyclamen grown on a vast scale; they, too, had their beauty especially when massed together in great sheets of colour when awaiting the lorries to take them to Covent Garden. One exception was made in the general holocaust of plants which required great heat to thrive; these were the anthuriums which continued to be preserved for a number of years. Greatly daring, we decided to exhibit the anthuriums at one of the Royal Horticultural Society's shows at Vincent Square, where they were awarded a Gold Medal. That accolade only underlined the probable quality of all the other exotic plants we had so reluctantly abolished. But the huge fairyland of semi-tropical colour so enthusiastically created by our predecessors had ceased, in the 1920's, to be a viable project for any private garden to harbour. In the Fruit Range Miss Alice's carefully selected figs, peaches, nectarines and grapes continued to flourish. I am thankful to say that in newer and much more modest quarters a few of their descendants are still alive to-day.

The only change we made in the garden at Waddesdon which might be called an improvement was to enable the flowering season to start in the early spring. Miss Alice had always been obliged to miss this enchanting moment in England, owing to her rigid time-table. Our most notable success was the planting of what is now rightly called Daffodil Valley, just below the Aviary, which is one of the out-door delights to greet our visitors at Easter time.

Never can any man have had less incentive, or need, than Jimmy to make a personal collection of works of art. Quite apart from the unexpected inheritance of Waddesdon, he would, in the nature of things, one day inherit a share of his father's possessions. Baron Edmond was one of the most notable collectors of his time, and indeed some of the loveliest

Limoges panel attributed to Jean de Court. *Juno and the Three Furies.* Second half of the sixteenth century

Limoges ewer

George Belcher's cartoon of James de Rothschild racing

The Ascot Gold Cup of 1909

Opposite James de Rothschild leading in *Bomba*, the winner of the Gold Cup at odds of 33–1

furniture, drawings, manuscripts, Limoges enamels and Renaissance jewels which are now at Waddesdon, as well as paintings by Watteau and Rubens, were bequeathed to Jimmy by his father. Born in 1845, the youngest son of a youngest son, Baron Edmond had been only 23 years old when he inherited from his father, the first Baron James, many outstanding works of art, and throughout the course of a long life he had never ceased to add to them. He was only nine years old when he first began to gather together the astonishing number of engravings which, on his death at the age of 89, he left to the Louvre. He studied these engravings with passion, and knew them so well that even when he was almost completely blind, he could describe the detail of any one of the thousands he owned, and the differences in the 'states' of the same composition. He maintained that these engravings were the source of much of his knowledge of his other works of art, and whenever something in his house was to be constructed, from a cornice or a moulding, to a doorway or a frame, he used his engravings as an infallible reference and pattern.

It is not difficult to understand, therefore, why most of Jimmy's personal additions to Waddesdon were outside the house. His improvements on the estate were varied; they included a number of modern cottages and additional holes to the 9-hole golf course Miss Alice had laid out in the park. Jimmy continued to enjoy playing himself despite the loss of his eye on the Deauville links. The Waddesdon course was helpful during a house-party but was mainly used by players from the immediate locality.

Jimmy also built a stud farm to house his brood mares. This was set on a hill with sweeping views of the Vale of Aylesbury from its surrounding paddocks. Racing had been one of his principal delights from boyhood and lasted all his life. He won two Gold Cups—one at Ascot, and one its war-time equivalent run at Newmarket in 1917—as well as many other good races, including the French Grand Prix and two Cambridgeshires, but except for one victory in the One Thousand Guineas, the Classics eluded him. The Derby winner, Gainsborough, was one of the most famous stallions in that era and one of the jokes I remember was that if my husband had had rather fewer Gainsboroughs on the walls of his house, and rather more in his Stud, he might have done better. But the few major successes he had on the Turf over a long period were no gauge of the amount of pleasure he derived from racing. He brought off one, I think, unprecendented coup, which I remember vividly. He won the Jockey Club Stakes—a distance race—and the Cambridgeshire—a much shorter one—with the same horse,

Milenko, in 1921, well within a period of two months. It was one of his more unlikely ideas to succeed; the general experience being that it is in any case difficult to train a horse within a short time to run first a short and then a long distance course, but to do it in reverse order was next to impossible.

Perhaps because of his appearance and personality even his most minor exploits on the race-course always appeared to be newsworthy. He bought a mare called Tishy from Sir Abe Bailey which had the doubtful fame of having crossed her legs when running as the favourite in the Cesarewitch. Jimmy had faith in her, however, and she subsequently won a small race for him—not a feat to make race-course history—but the following day almost every newspaper contained a cartoon of some sort celebrating Jimmy and Tishy's mini-victory.

One of his earliest failures was with a horse of his which he fancied tremendously, named Snow Leopard. The day following the race in which all Jimmy's hopes had been misplaced on him, he was re-named Slow Leopard, much to the amusement of the race-going public.

He always said that the first race he had ever witnessed had been his undoing; this was the Epsom Derby of 1898, when the winner, Mr. Larnach's Jeddah, priced at 100 to 1, had been selected by Jimmy for his very first wager. From that day on his support was always attracted by an outsider. A caustic friend said that many people were known to back outsiders, but Jimmy alone appeared to attempt to breed from them.

Always delighting in the unlikely and unorthodox and loving any upset of the accepted norm in his recreations, he was nevertheless one whose judgment and wisdom were indisputable in the more serious matters of life.

Between 1922 and 1939 we gradually accustomed ourselves to the joys and problems involved in making our home at Waddesdon. Among the joys was that of finding ourselves in the proximity of other family houses. I think the fact that Tring, Aston Clinton, Ascott, Mentmore and Halton were all within riding distance from Waddesdon may well have influenced Baron Ferdinand in his selection of the land.

In our day, Halton had already been sold to the Air Ministry, but all the other houses were still lived in by cousins, and could be reached by no more than half an hour's drive. We only once went to Aston Clinton, to see Lady Battersea, one of Sir Anthony de Rothschild's two daughters. As both she and her sister, Annie Yorke, had country houses of their own, and were only able to spend one month a year together in their father's old home, Aston Clinton was sold soon after we came to

Waddesdon. The house was for a time a preparatory school, and after various other transmutations, it was finally destroyed by fire. But its gloriously wooded park has survived and is now a centre for youth activities and sport, in the care of the Bucks County Council.

Tring Park remained the home of Lady Rothschild, her son, the second Lord Rothschild and her daughter-in-law Mrs. Charles Rothschild, two of whose brood of four children have gained distinction—Dr. Miriam Rothschild in the entomological world, and her scientist brother, Lord Rothschild of Think Tank fame. Tring Museum, with its great collection of butterflies, moths, fleas and other insect curiosities, which was founded by the second Lord Rothschild, still flourishes as a section of the British Museum, but the house itself has become a ballet school. In our day, however, the links between Tring and Waddesdon were very close and enjoyable. The same can be said of Mentmore and Ascott. In 1922, the ex-Prime Minister Rosebery, the widowed husband of Hannah de Rothschild, still lived at Mentmore. In 1923 he gave it to his son, Harry, Lord Dalmeny and following this transfer it became a centre of hunting activity. Its new owner was Master of the Whaddon Chase and locally the many female followers of this popular hunt became known as ' The Harriers '. Lord Rosebery's famous Crafton Stud continued its triumphant influence on the breeding of race-horses and I need hardly say it was the subject of intensely interested conversation between the owners of Mentmore and Waddesdon.

Mentmore now stands empty, but Ascott still remains, having been given, like Waddesdon, to the National Trust. In 1922 it was Mrs. Leopold de Rothschild who lived there with her son Anthony, and many an hour we spent there enjoying their outstanding hospitality. Anthony's son, Evelyn and his wife and family now live there.

After the modernisation of the electricity and the drains we made very few changes in the house at Waddesdon. The main exception was in Miss Alice's private sitting-room on the first floor. It was undeniably a most lovely room, literally crammed, in the Victorian manner, with beautiful furniture, china, pastels and drawings. Its Savonnerie carpet, on which it would have been unthinkable to tread with muddy shoes, had been made in the seventeenth century for the *Grande Galerie* of the Louvre, and was hardly a surface on which one could chuck untidy books and newspapers. But we needed somewhere in which we could tackle the affairs of daily life without being inhibited by the beauty or fragility of our surroundings. So this room was completely emptied; bookcases were put all round the walls;

a plain carpet was laid on the floor and comfortable leather chairs and sofas installed. Emptied of its silks and drawings there was no need in this room to keep a constant and watchful eye on the position of sun-blinds which were here, in fact, abolished. For us it became a blissful snuggery.

The other unchanged rooms in the house were by no means unwelcoming or unused. Waddesdon gave us, as much as to our predecessors, the opportunity to be hospitable. As in earlier days, many of those who now came to stay were politicians, but the House of Commons had changed very much since the 1880's and no comparison can be made between the importance and effectiveness of any meeting of our guests and of those invited by Baron Ferdinand some fifty years earlier. He had been an influential member of the governing Liberal party, whereas Jimmy, also a life-long Liberal, found himself an adherent of a party in opposition which, after a flicker of revival in 1929, steadily declined in numbers and power from that date onwards. For this reason, if for no other, I do not think that in our time the confabulations of leading politicians at Waddesdon can have led to spectacular results on the political life of the country.

In my recollection, I like to think our friends, including even such dominant personalities as Mr. Asquith and Mr. Churchill, regarded Waddesdon as a place where they could relax from their labours and indulge in such pastimes as golf, bézique, bridge and Mah-jong—the most popular games at that time. Any political discussion was largely confined to the period at the end of dinner when, in the English fashion, the ladies retired from the dining-room and the men remained, unencumbered by femininity, to settle down, maybe, to serious talk. However useful these masculine exchanges of view may have been to the participants, I chiefly remember them for the unconscionable length of time they seemed to go on.

In our day Waddesdon was once again honoured by a visit from the reigning Sovereign. The attendant difficulties and dilemmas of this occasion have now been transmuted into pleasurable recollection, but every detail remains vividly in my mind. Even so, I cannot hope to rival Baron Ferdinand in giving an account equal to his of the reception of Queen Victoria.

Unlike Baron Ferdinand who had a whole year in which to prepare for his august visitor, we had comparatively little time. The first intimation was conveyed to me at one of the Spring Meetings at Newmarket in 1926 when the Princess Royal told me that Queen Mary would like to visit Waddesdon, and that the moment Her Majesty had in mind was the afternoon of a not far distant Sunday. It so happened that this particular

The East Gallery in Baron Ferdinand's day

The East Gallery in 1978

Sunday came just after the Thursday on which a huge Liberal Fête was to be held at Waddesdon and I immediately pictured what Aunt Alice's feelings would have been at the prospect of the Queen seeing Waddesdon marred and besmirched by the inevitable damage and litter left behind by a crowd of some thousands of people. I therefore pleaded for another date, but no other was available.

So we made what arrangements we could for the prospective damage and mess resulting from the Fête to be cleared up quickly and ordered a beautiful cedar sapling in the expectation that Her Majesty would agree to commemorate her presence by planting it in the time honoured way. Her visit was timed for 3 o'clock and was to include tea.

Everything seemed in order; the political Fête duly took place and an army of helpers moved in to try to obliterate its traces.

Late on the Friday evening we were visiting the Stud when a telephone message was brought to us. It came from Buckingham Palace from the King, asking if he could accompany Queen Mary on the Sunday, and could they come to luncheon?

In a flash I realised the difficulty of dealing with this change of plan in the short time left to us and of securing guests and food for a luncheon party in the country at 24 hours' notice. I also became uneasily aware of my ignorance of the conventions which might rule the reception of a reigning monarch in one's own home—was it for him, for instance, to rise and thus signal the end of luncheon, or was this still the duty of the hostess? Thanks to much telephoning, the provision of food and suitable guests was resolved the following morning, but on seeking advice from Peggy Crewe (a mentor on many problems in my life) I found my ideas about tree planting were not hers. It seemed to me a simple matter that King George should now be asked to plant the cedar, rather than Queen Mary. Peggy said that this was out of the question: it was unthinkable that the King should not be invited to plant a tree and it would be exceedingly rude if the Queen was not also asked to do so: two trees must be provided. I protested that only one was available and that however much she knew about Court manners, she was plainly deficient in her grasp of arboriculture: suitable saplings, I pointed out, did *not* grow on bushes. However, she was adamant, and so I sped to the garden to consult Johnson. He was as resourceful as ever, and calmed my agitation by showing me, just next to the spot where it was planned the cedar should go, an old and fairly rare tree of a species which never exceeded four feet in height, even

A chair from a set of mid 18th century French furniture which is covered in Beauvais tapestry.

GILLE·LAÎNE
A PARIS

when fully grown. This he thought could well be dug up and then after suitable titivation, could be returned with ceremony to the hole from whence it came, with no-one being any the wiser. I thankfully agreed to this proposal.

Conversation during luncheon was fascinating. The King remembered with the utmost clarity the occasion of his first visit to Waddesdon when, as a very young man in 1889 he had helped to entertain the Shah of Persia. His account of the varied incidents of that memorable party and the character and appearance of all his fellow guests, was enthralling. At the end he somewhat sadly remarked that he and Ralph Nevill were the only survivors of all those who had been at Waddesdon on that occasion.

Happily, it was a very fine day and after luncheon we went out onto the terrace and stood there for a few moments before moving off to the tree planting. Johnson, in order that the King and Queen should see Waddesdon at its best, had conceived the idea that our appearance should be the signal for a distant tap to be turned on which would operate all the jets of the fountain on the South Terrace. These were rarely made to play, and now they failed in their duty. Instead of emitting graceful cascades of glistening drops high into the sky, they produced a sluggish minimum of water accompanied by a series of gurgles and plops of a distressingly suggestive nature. For several minutes we all stood solemnly listening to these gurgitations: then the Queen was the first to disolve in laughter and thus released the pent-up giggles of everyone else present. The tree-planting and the rest of the visit was conducted in a spirit of hilarity.

My memories of trying to arrange any agreeable house-party at Waddesdon are also vivid and are tinged with anxiety from start to finish. During the initial period of invitation one composed the perfect party which one learnt from experience would so rarely end up as planned. For excellent but varied reasons some guests would begin by accepting and then chucked; others refused for the date on which they were invited but wondered if they could not come on some other day or days, invariably awkward for oneself. And when the party did assemble I understood all too well Baron Ferdinand's anxiety about his guests' plans and wishes. Presumably we knew in advance who preferred talk to bridge and the relative skills of players of card games, but the plans for the following day always depended so much on the weather—who wished to play golf? Who would be cajoled into visiting the garden or the Stud? Or who might be bent on some intellectual excursion

French clock, c. 1750, decorated with Meissen birds and a figure of Harlequin playing the bag-pipes.

to Oxford? Or who might have business at near-by Chequers? Preparations for all these possibilities were easier if made in advance.

In recent years the appreciation of the arts seems to have grown into a popular fancy. A mass of sight-seers gyrates discerningly round houses 'open to view' and innumerable societies devoted to various aspects of the arts appear to flourish. But in the hey-day of our time at Waddesdon things were very different and any interest in works of art seemed to be a rarity among our guests. Occasionally some of them conscientiously toured the pictures but more often it was the view out of the window which caught their eye: china, furniture and carpets were never objects of interest. However, I do remember very clearly one remarkable morning when Brendan Bracken and Leslie Hore Belisha sat, intensely absorbed for at least an hour, each gazing at one of the two big Guardis which hang at either end of the East Gallery. Solemnly, from time to time, they exchanged seats, in total silence.

I don't think any of Baron Ferdinand's more discerning guests visiting Waddesdon in our day would have noticed much difference in the arrangement of the rooms. The only major change was floral; instead of palms pervading the house,

The two Guardis bought by Baron Ferdinand in 1877 round which the East Gallery was constructed

we substituted flowers, or flowering shrubs—a concession to modern taste.

In my memory the years between 1922 and 1939 form a somewhat blurred jig-saw of trying to fit in too much in too little time. My husband's health continually troubled him which made all plans uncertain. As I remember it, we were never able to spend much consecutive time at Waddesdon, but were constantly doomed to flit to London where Jimmy had a mass of committees to attend, mostly concerned with charities and Palestine, or to Paris to visit his parents, to whom we were both devoted. These journeys were interspersed with others to the variety of race-courses at which devotees of the sport like to be present, whether they have a horse running or not. At that time, too, social life had revived and we received many invitations which necessarily implied at least one night away from Waddesdon.

In any competition for points indicating preference for a neighbour at a dinner party, Jimmy would have ranked high. His very real interest in the lives and opinions of everyone he met stimulated conversation and seemed to draw from his neighbours a brilliance and expansiveness which made them feel they were having an unusually good time. He would not,

I think, have been awarded similarly high points at the bridge table. As a player of the cards few could surpass him but his insatiable inclination to try to bring off the seemingly impossible was also a feature of his game. So much so, that I remember one disgruntled player declaring that whenever fate gave him Jimmy as a partner, he could never be sure who was on his side and who was not.

In all his accomplishments he tended to be unexpected. He was always assumed to be a compatriot by Frenchmen, Germans and Englishmen to whom he spoke in their mother tongue and in Hebrew, Spanish and Italian he was by no means tongue-tied. In other languages which he knew less well his marvellous ability to imitate the correct cadence and emphasis in the spoken word always made him sound all right, even if his vocabulary was small. Yet, most surprisingly, he was completely tone-deaf musically. On many occasions, particularly later in life, when attending parliamentary constituency affairs, his failure to recognise the National Anthem in a suitable manner gave me many bad moments if I was too far away from him to take remedial action.

In 1928, in the midst of our days of constant movement, there came a deputation from the Liberal Party Committee of the Isle of Ely, asking Jimmy to be their candidate at the next General Election. The sitting member for the Isle was a Tory, but previously, from 1906 until 1917, it had been held in the Liberal interest by Jimmy's cousin and great friend, Neil Primrose, who was killed in action in 1917. Ever since his Cambridge days, Jimmy had nursed an ambition to become a Liberal Member of Parliament, and this opportunity to contest a seat which, in the past, he had enjoyed helping his cousin to win, was a temptation he could not resist. He won the seat in the 1929 General Election and held it until 1945. So a new and very demanding element entered our lives which reduced even more the ration of time we could spend at Waddesdon.

Nevertheless, Waddesdon remained the anchor of our lives and even provided the scene for some of our major political efforts to propagate Liberal doctrines to mass audiences. The first was the giant 'Liberal Fête' already mentioned, held on the cricket ground where there was a pavilion with a flat roof from which Baron Ferdinand used to address his constituents. Our star speaker at this first Fête was Sir John Simon who attracted a large audience; but this was, perhaps naturally, exceeded by the numbers who, at a later date, came to listen to the Party's leader, Mr. Lloyd George, who spoke at another mass rally. Optimistically, we hoped this one might be an historic occasion and were delighted when Sir John Lavery

The author speaking at a political meeting in the Isle of Ely in 1931 accepted our invitation to immortalise it in paint. Although we were wrong in our assumption that that afternoon might have a bearing on the political situation of the day, I am glad that Sir John Lavery's picture of the platform party still hangs at Waddesdon.

Jimmy was an assiduous Member of Parliament and spoke on a variety of subjects—both on those which were of particular interest to his East Anglian constituents, and on topics of international concern. I shall always regret that one day in 1944 I was kept in Aylesbury by my war-time employment and so could not be in the House when he rose to make an impromptu intervention in which he thanked the British people and Government for their treatment of the German Jewish refugees from Hitler who had managed to reach this country. His fellow members were so moved by what he said of the sufferings of his co-religionists in Europe that when he had finished they all rose to their feet in mute expression of their sympathy: an almost unknown happening in the House.

Late in 1944, Mr. Churchill offered him the post of Under-Secretary to the Ministry of Supply, which he held until May 1945. Alas, by then, a new anxiety governed our lives; the sight in his one remaining eye began to fail.

But I have run ahead of time: in 1935 both my parents-in-law had died within a year of each other and a proportion of their possessions had devolved on my husband. A year later an avalanche of wooden crates containing furniture, pictures, china and *objets d'art* of all kinds descended on us in a house already full of appropriate beauty. I shall never forget our embarrassment on surveying this problem. In the event, incorporation proved much easier than I had expected, as fortunately the tastes of my parents-in-law and of the previous owners of Waddesdon were in such harmony that the difficulties of rearrangement were greatly minimised.

We had just got all the things from Paris settled in their new quarters when the war clouds appeared in 1938 and, at the time of Munich, the contents of the house were dismantled and put in the cellar for safety. In that year they did not remain below ground for long, but we began seriously to think of what to do should war really come.

Our first idea was a hospital and we invited an official from the Ministry of Health to 'case the joint' with that end in view. His verdict was disappointing: 'the most unsuitable house for a hospital which could be imagined'. We came to understand that *boiserie*, even if covered up, would be a first-class harbourer of germs, and so we had to give up that idea. After many consultations, the only function it was deemed we could

The children having their afternoon rest

usefully attempt, was to harbour children from the perils of air attack on London. In the event, three separate organisations from Croydon, caring for one hundred children in all, and all under five years of age, were selected for Waddesdon. We were greatly relieved to hear the children would be accompanied by their attendant nurses and their own furniture.

By Easter 1939 one of the most odious consequences of Hitler's rule over Germany had a direct impact on life in Waddesdon village. His anti-Jewish drive was making existence in Germany intolerable for all Jews—neither age, youth nor any previous outstanding service for Germany made any

Sitting on the stairs on which King Edward VII, when Prince of Wales, broke his leg in 1898

difference. Our young cousin, Lord Rothschild was active in trying to arrange for the evacuation of Jews from Germany and he told us of the plight of a Jewish Orphanage in Frankfort a/Main which urgently needed to be moved to England. It was run by a most capable couple, Dr. and Mrs. Steinhardt who also had two young daughters of their own and an adult sister-in-law. The whole group numbered thirty; the ages of the orphans varied between six and twelve.

Luckily a large house in the village had been built and planned by Miss Alice as a maternity home to be run by two nurses who had looked after her admirably during one of her illnesses. By 1939 both nurses had died and the house was available for the Orphanage, and just big enough to house the refugees. They arrived for Easter and remained in this house called 'The Cedars' until all the children had grown up and found careers for themselves all over the world. It says much for the understanding of the village, and for the tact of the newcomers, that this little orphanage was welcomed with open arms. The children were all educated either in the village school or in the Grammar School in Aylesbury. They learnt English astonishingly quickly and were integrated into the life of the village almost immediately. They were not only quick to learn but also proved their worth on the playing field: football came naturally to them and one boy even represented Aylesbury in a boxing contest.

They are now scattered all over the world, in England, Israel, Canada and North and South America. Their careers are diverse; one is the Assistant Agent to a big estate in England; another, also in England, is a Master baker. One is the head green-keeper at the Caesarea golf-course in Israel and others are lawyers, writers and industrialists in a variety of countries. During the war they were unfailingly helpful: the Waddesdon village Salvage Collection record reached dizzy heights thanks to the regularity of their assistance and their persuasiveness.

Three days after the declaration of war, our 100 'underfives' with their escorts and furniture duly arrived. We had been given four days' notice to prepare for them, but thanks to the rehearsal at the time of Munich, this went much more smoothly than could have been hoped. With the exception of three rooms on the ground floor, all the others were stripped and emptied, as were all the bedrooms on the first floor. We ourselves were evacuated to the Bachelors' Wing. There we and our household occupied the first and second floors and we shared the kitchen with the children.

The first few days were naturally somewhat chaotic, as the children came from three separate establishments in Croydon. Their three staffs were unknown to each other and unaccustomed to co-operation, being used to their own routines. It took a little time to persuade them to combine their hours for food.

Ultimately the Croydon contingents were recalled in 1942 and found other quarters which suited them better than those we could offer. They were immediately replaced by the Ministry of Health which sent us 100 children all belonging to a single unit in the care of Miss Ridley who was the epitome of calm kindness and understanding of both young and old.

The picture of life at Waddesdon during the second World War was little different from that of any other rural area which was in a relatively targetless zone. Our only strange distinction was that throughout the war, although subject to 'black-out' like everyone else, a beacon blazed throughout the night on top of the Manor, to prevent aircraft crashing into it as they came in to land at Westcott airfield, just to the north. But the war, of course, affected everybody's life in one way or another. Even those who were not fighting or making things for offensive or defensive use, were jolted out of their routine. Apart from the children in the Manor, many other evacuees were housed in the village. In addition, the garden bothy became a temporary shelter for 'expectant mothers', and the Village Hall, no doubt much to its surprise ,was occupied for nearly two years by families whose numbers at times rose to nearly one hundred persons: they slept there, and were fed there from a canteen in an adjoining room where a team of women from the village cooked for them seven days a week, and week after week, and month after month.

Then in 1941, Waddesdon Park became one of the biggest petrol dumps in the country. Naturally, there was not a drop for us, and it was hard not to feel covetous: there was not a sizeable tree within our boundaries which did not have a concrete platform and a Nissen hut full of petrol drums nestling beneath it.

I was the local WVS Organiser and mercilessly badgered everyone in the neighbourhood to collect salvage or make camouflage nets, in addition to trying to cope with all the bits and pieces connected with those elastic words 'Evacuation' and 'Civil Defence'.

There was one other occasion in which Waddesdon's protective capacity was tested for yet another purpose. This need arose in 1944, during the Doodle Bug period which, in its early stages, caused considerable damage in London before brilliant counter-measures were invented.

Lady Reading, Chairman of WVS, whose Headquarters in Tothill Street were situated in rather an obvious target area close to Westminster, Downing Street and Buckingham Palace, became anxious for the safety of the very mixed but precious stores housed on the premises. These included a huge variety of invaluable gifts from the USA; emergency supplies for the bombed out; canteen equipment and a stock of stationery which, at that time of paper shortage, was particularly prized.

Lady Reading asked me if I could still find a cranny at Waddesdon where these miscellaneous objects could be stored away. Fortunately, the stables were largely filled with varied junk which could be exposed to the weather. Maria Brassey was the WVS member at Tothill Street in charge of all stores;

Lady Reading having accepted our proferred hospitality, despatched her in a 3-ton lorry, brimming over with its load. She continued to drive it down several times a week, until even the Waddesdon accommodation could take no more. At the time this invasion did not seem specially notable, but good fortune sometimes reaches one unannounced. The driver of that appallingly noisy lorry has since become an invaluable friend who has proved, ever since 1944 that a ready wit, a sense of humour and a temperament that nothing daunts can help in trials and tribulations, and they have engendered a sanity which might well have deserted me but for her companionship. When I was confronted with problems and complications, she developed a special capacity for coping with them which was as astonishing as it remains welcome.

The wonderful moment when war in Europe came to an end brought WVS the most enchanting of all jobs they had been asked to undertake. It was decided that many of our prisoners of war, as they were liberated, should be flown from the German camps direct to Westcott airfield. Most of those arriving appeared with their uniforms in tatters, or at least well below the army standard of smartness. The Army therefore decreed that none of the returning prisoners should be allowed to leave the airfield for their own homes until they had been newly kitted out. New uniforms themselves were supplied by the army, but would not be complete until they had had sown on to them the regimental or corps insignia, medals or stripes of rank proper to each man. I was asked 'Could the WVS come and sew?' Throughout those days and warm summer nights women were gathered in from all the surrounding villages. They sat at trestle tables on the airfield, sewing away for dear life, often by the light of hurricane lamps, so that each man could go to his longed-for home at the earliest possible moment. As they sewed, they talked to the men whose uniforms they were embellishing, in the first enchanted hour of their return.

A shockingly untimely attack of chicken-pox deprived me of this personal pleasure but I was nevertheless kept busy in my bed, arranging on the telephone the many rotas of sempstresses and their transport to their enviable duty.

I think Miss Ridley's Nursery, which had succeeded the Croydon contingents, were sad to leave Waddesdon and we were really sorry to see them go. There are two images of the children's stay with us which will always remain in my mind: the first, seeing them being carried down the winding staircase to their prepared beds in the basement during an air-raid warning—all so orderly and quiet and, to a strange degree, so natural. And then the Christmases the children spent at Wad-

The carved panelling of the Grey Drawing room which came from the Paris house of the duc de Lauzun that later became the Convent of the Sacré Coeur

desdon. The house never looked so attractive as when they all assembled in the East Gallery, and the door of the Breakfast Room was suddenly flung open revealing a huge lit-up Christmas Tree, with a live Father Christmas to greet them and hand out gifts. This imposing personage was none other than my beloved maid, Eliza Kimber who, sweltering in the appropriate beard and robes, undertook this exhausting role for the duration.

After the 1945 General Election, when Jimmy lost his seat for the Isle of Ely in the House of Commons, he went through another period of poor health, partly due to injuries from an accidental fall he had had during the election campaign. There was, however, one advantage in this phase of our existence—we were able to spend much more time at Waddesdon and could take stock of our surroundings.

We had been immensely fortunate that nearly all the contents of Waddesdon had escaped irretrievable damage during the war. There were only two near misses. In the first week of the war we had put all the pictures in the cellar in specially fitted wooden cases made by our house-carpenter, Mr. Chapman. Fortunately, after a fortnight, he thought he would open one or two of the cases just to see that the pictures inside were all right. To his horror, in case after case, he found a blue haze creeping over the surface of each canvas or panel. Expert consultants told us that the only hope was to remove all the pictures from their damp confinement in the cellar and expose them to fresh air. Luckily, the Grey Drawing-room was still available; racks were made and installed there, and the pictures hoisted into them. There were three pictures by Watteau which never quite regained their former condition, but all the rest responded to the fresh air treatment. We comforted ourselves with the thought that the danger of Hitler's bombs falling on Waddesdon was less than the known peril of Waddesdon damp. However, when we received an invitation from the National Gallery of Ottowa, we availed ourselves of their kindness, and thankfully sent them four pictures for the duration of the war. In Ottowa they were admirably housed and exhibited in safety and returned to us, when peace came, in excellent condition.

The other misadventure occurred on the very last day of the war. In the general relief and excitement a tap was left running in a bathroom on the first floor, and the resultant flood cascaded down into one of the three rooms we had retained for the storage of furniture. A stream of water fell plumb onto the pictorial marquetry of the writing table given by his friends to Beaumarchais in 1781, and spread from there to a pile of books which were also stored in the Baron's Room. The results were alarming, particularly to the table, but this was found to be reparable through the skill of Messrs. Hatfield's *ébénistes*.

Following the departure of the children we were confronted with the problem of what to do with the house. Shortages of every sort in the post-war period included a shortage of personnel and the idea of re-instating Waddesdon for us two old people seemed out of the question. But something had to be done: we could not leave all the contents of the house in a few rooms, stacked up to the ceiling. It was, in fact, quite difficult to enter the Morning Room it was so congested; only a mouse had managed to do so, and had established a tiny trail right across the room, getting what nourishment it could on the way.

It was then that the solution of the National Trust began to germinate in my husband's mind and I cannot say how thankful I am that it did. But before the Trust could even be approached there would have to be something visible to show

Girl at a window by Gerard Dou, bought by Baron Ferdinand from the Six van Hillegom Collection in 1897

them, so we decided to unpack everything in store and reinstate the ground floor rooms.

On examining these rooms, now clear of the cots and miniature tables and chairs to which we had become so accustomed, we found that they did, indeed, bear some scars of war. However these, needless to say, were all well below waist level. The Red Drawing Room whose walls were covered in silk, had been the children's dining room, so may have been specially vulnerable to sticky fingers; its walls had also been a tempting background for coloured chalks. Anyone who has had the experience of trying to remove the traces of coloured chalk from any surface—from natural fibre to marble—will know what a frustrating occupation it can be. But the worst damage to the red damask came from the sunshine that had poured into that room unimpeded, and rotted its lovely panels into rags. It would clearly have to be replaced.

We searched high and low for a material with a pattern which would suit the dimensions of the room, realising as we did so, ever more clearly, the degree of perfection achieved by Baron Ferdinand in his choice of materials. Nothing we could find equalled what was now in tatters, and we were fortunate in eventually discovering that Messrs. Hammond employed a superb weaver aged 81 who could faithfully reproduce the the Baron's wall-covering. Messrs. Hammond found this commission so unusual that, with our gratified consent, they affixed a brass plate to the wall, under the new silk, on which were inscribed the names of all those who had worked on the weaving and on the cutting, sewing and application of the new silk to the walls. The final name on this plate was that of Mrs. Green, our housekeeper, the very remarkable successor to Mrs. Boxall. Perhaps in some future age, this plate will be revealed and will become an object of interest to some art historian. But however assiduous a researcher he may be, I feel sure that he will never be able to recreate in his thesis the personality of Mrs. Green. Red-haired, formidable, an unmistakable member of the old school, but with a heart of gold, she was altogether wonderful, both to us and for Waddesdon. It is difficult to separate her name from that of her boon companion, Mabel Chatfield, the Linen Maid, whose character can only be described as angelic. Whenever Mrs Green and I, in our household perplexities, had a divergence of opinion and she wished to be assured that her own view would prevail, her final and nearly always winning thrust of argument was to restate her opinion and add 'And Mabel thinks so too'. I believe if they had known the house better Messrs. Hammond would also have added Mabel's name to that plaque as well as that of the other pillar of war-time Waddesdon, Mr. Tissot, who had cooked every one of the meals eaten by the children in that very room.

It was curiously difficult to replace the furniture as it had been before the war; I kept on getting mixed up in my mind with the arrangement before and after my parents-in-law's possessions had appeared from Paris. Moreover, although the exact angle and spacing of furniture can make or mar a room, much of the furniture at Waddesdon is heavy enough to prohibit many experiments to find out the best arrangement. I remember my joy when I suddenly realised that the carpets still bore the slight marks of flattened pile made by the legs of tables and cupboards which had stood on them before 1939. No longer was replacement a question of 'fish and find out'; one had only to search for those slight indentations on the carpet, retrieve the piece of furniture which corresponded to them and lower it gently into place.

Negotiations were started with the National Trust and we decided to transfer ourselves to Eythrope which Miss Alice had left to my husband with the Waddesdon Estate. As we had no use for the Pavilion at Eythrope in 1922, it had been let to Mrs. Somerset Maugham who, unlike Miss Alice, had a need for bedrooms and bathrooms. She therefore added what became known as the 'Maugham Wing' and lived there until the war. It then had other tenants, but now it was vacant again, although in great need of repair.

In the immediate post-war years London and many other cities needed rebuilding and in order that the whole construction force of the country should concentrate on repairing bomb-damage, the ordinary private householder was restricted to doing building and decorating work of only £25 in value each year, unless he was given a special licence. For some time it seemed most unlikely that we should ever receive a licence, but then the roof of the 'Maugham Wing' fell in and so demolished the only bedrooms the house possessed. As this made it uninhabitable, a building licence was forthcoming in the mid 1950's and the work could be started. But all this had taken a long time and on May 7th, 1957, Jimmy died, before Eythrope, which is now my home, was ready for occupation.

During his last years, when he was out of the House of Commons and struggling against blindness and ill health, Jimmy had never ceased to work for the causes he had supported throughout his adult life. To the end of his days he remained a convinced member of the Liberal party and was constantly in touch with its leaders. He kept himself remarkably well-informed about world politics, but his most constant preoccupation remained the fate and development of the State of Israel. He consistently advocated the possibility of including Jewish Palestine in a larger configuration—in fact, the British Empire—and thus, in some measure, securing a lasting peace in the Middle East: but only shortly before his death the Foreign Office was still brushing any such proposal aside. This is not the place to refer to his specific achievements in Israel; they are dealt with in detail in Simon Schama's *Two Rothschilds and the Land of Israel.*

After Jimmy's death a number of people wrote to *The Times* about him: most of them were far more capable than I of putting their memories into words. One of them wrote:

'Young men and women had only to spend a few moments with him to forget his age and distinction and to treat him as a stimulating and provocative contemporary. They would not have guessed that when he was a young man he left Paris and spent a year in Australia, under an assumed name to find out what it was like not to be called Rothschild'.

The author of another contribution was particularly apt in describing Jimmy's character. He wrote:

> 'James de Rothschild was at all periods of his life a man of striking distinction and charm and spirit, with a most brilliant and penetrating wit, a rich and eccentric fancy and ideas of great sweep and originality. His conversation was entrancing, fed by a prodigious memory and an all-embracing curiosity and a fabulous insight into human motives and character; an acute sense of the comical and incongruous; a love of life, of paradox, of anything new and original; an often diabolical ingenuity in argument which he could conduct in three languages with which he appeared to be equally familiar. He was a most fascinating and indeed magnetic figure to his friends.
>
> Violently proud, morally fastiduous, with a deep natural piety, he was devoted to the tradition of his family, his faith, his race and his adopted country. He was first and foremost a *Grand Seigneur*, formidable, imperious, disdainful, contemptuous of danger; civilised with extreme independence of character and judgment, and with a deeply imaginative and unswerving loyalty to the political causes he served, especially Liberalism and Zionism, to both of which his life was devoted ... His broken health forced him towards the end to lead the life of a semi-invalid, but his vitality and vast interest in people and events remained unimpaired. Conversation with him obliterated all differences of age and reputation. The combination of paternalistic and benevolent schemes, of

The Earl of Crawford and Balcarres, Chairman of the National Trust from 1944 to 1965

romantic loyalties, gaiety, the verve, the high originality, the style of life and utterances belonged to a world of which he was one of the most noble and attractive survivors'.

The day after Jimmy's death a popular newspaper sent one of their reporters to Waddesdon. He spent his time sitting in one or other of the village public houses, offering each habitué, as he entered, a glass of beer and £10 down for any story he cared to tell about my husband. I am told that all the reporter received were stony stares, and that he eventually retreated to London without a story of any kind, and with all his money intact. The beer drinkers of Waddesdon were, it seems, at one with *The Times* which, in its official obituary, had described Jimmy as 'an ideal landlord, a squire of the best type'.

Quite apart from my personal feelings, the sudden change for me from an existence which had been totally free from taking decisions of importance, was traumatic. My husband had indeed been the guiding light in all sections of my life, and now the struggle began to try to take the decisions which he would have taken and to act in accordance with what I thought would have been his wishes.

He had intended to make Waddesdon over to the National Trust in his life time; now it came to them by bequest. I understand the Trust had some hesitation in accepting it not only because the house was relatively modern, but also because it was built and furnished in the French style. At least one influential member of the National Trust, the late Lord Esher, declared quite plainly 'I hate French furniture', and for some days Waddesdon's fate hung in the balance. I think in the end Lord Crawford, who was then Chairman of the National Trust, persuaded his colleagues that perhaps the contents of the house might compensate for the drawbacks of its foreign style and relative modernity. In any case, it was realised that thanks to the endowment my husband had bequeathed with the house, its maintenance would not cost the Trust anything.

Curiously enough an argument did arise with the Treasury over the endowment. Like all those settled on houses bequeathed to the National Trust, it would be exempt from death duty. But the Treasury held the view, at first, that the endowment for Waddesdon was bigger than would be needed for its upkeep, and thought therefore it should be taxable. Fortunately, the Treasury changed its mind and experience has shown very clearly that the amount needed to maintain Waddesdon had been correctly gauged by its donor, but only thanks to wise subsequent investment.

If it be true that the best way of keeping grief under control is to be forced to be very busy, the Estate Duty Office of the Inland Revenue must indeed be the widow's best friend.

In this century, whenever someone dies, a valuation has to be made of all their possessions so that the Estate Duty Office can assess the amount of death duty payable. Any of their possessions, however, which are judged to be of a standard which would be acceptable to a national museum can be classified as being of 'National interest' and, if the new owner agrees to keep such objects in good and safe condition, no duty is payable until such time as a decision is taken to sell them. When Miss Alice died in 1922 a probate inventory had been made of all the contents of Waddesdon and Eythrope which filled five sizeable volumes, and many of the objects listed in them were of 'National interest'. It was now my task to find, identify and make available for the inspection of museum officials all those things which we had agreed in 1922 to keep in good and safe condition.

Most of the objects Jimmy had left to the National Trust were relatively easy to identify by comparing descriptions in the old inventories with what was now visible in the newly arranged ground floor rooms. But the arms collected by Miss Alice to replace some of the objects left by her brother to the British Museum presented far greater problems. At a guess,

I could distinguish a halberd from a rapier and, perhaps, an arquebus from a pistol, but my lack of knowledge was total when it came to identifying, say, 'A pillow sword enriched with gold azzima' or 'A main gauche with chased drooping quillons'. In the end I was forced to disregard these cryptic descriptions in the old inventories. I counted all the cutting instruments I could see, all the fire arms and all the powder flasks and, when these were found to tally in number with those listed in 1922, I left it at that. Fortunately, the Estate Duty Office and the National Trust, the new owner of the arms, pronounced themselves satisfied.

My lack of specialised knowledge also bedevilled the identification of garden statuary. We had so often walked by marble figures and vases thinking how beautiful they looked dappled with the play of light and shade through the trees. But now I was confronted with the problem of deciding whether a large nude marble lady peering from her leafy bower was indeed 'Pomona—18th century', 'Flora—probably Venetian', or 'Ceres—19th century'. I learnt the hard way that it all depended on what produce she happened to be carrying. A similar state of indecision seized me when confronted by large muscular stone gentlemen. I took it that if they were clasping rather agitated females they were probably the *Rape of the Sabines* or *Pluto carrying off Proserpine*, but

Dutch musical box surmounted by a flute player: late eighteenth century

Waddesdon seen through the North Fountain and framed by an avenue of oaks and cedars, *Atlantica glauca*

if they were not, who was to say which was Hercules and which was Samson?

The upper floors at Waddesdon were the most difficult of all. The contents of all the rooms which had been cleared for the children were either still packed away higgeldy-piggeldy in any attic cupboard or cranny which could be made to hold them, or else had come out of the main store rooms into unaccustomed and unlikely places. Daily, hugging the old inventories—or as many of them as I could carry—I tramped the house, trying to find and identify, and incidentally make up my mind what would be best for me to take to Eythrope, all of whose contents had been in store at Waddesdon ever since the Pavilion had been let. I remember particularly searching for a 'National interest' object described in 1922 as 'A musical box—probably Dutch'. Vainly I searched in every cupboard and drawer for any small box-like object. Memory plays strange tricks and I cannot now recall what it was that one day inspired me to consider a ten foot high carved wooden statue on a plinth, of a young man playing a flute. Had he, perhaps, the musical connection we were seeking? Investigation proved that there was indeed a mechanism for making music in the plinth, and that this was, at last, the long sought musical box. Because of its vast size, it had been left undisturbed throughout the war and stood where I had always remembered it in a corner of the long bedroom corridor.

This was the season of lists. Every evening they had to be compiled for the National Trust; for the Estate Duty Office; for the various museum experts who would be coming to check all the 'National interest' objects; for the packers who would be removing me to Eythrope as soon as it became habitable. There were even yet more lists to be made in connection with, for me, a most untimely County Council election in which I had to defend my seat.

Finally everything, as I thought, was located, labelled and entered on the appropriate list. But I had reckoned without the impeccable precision of the Estate Duty Office officials who compared the many sheets I sent them with the probate lists of 1922 which they had on their files. Their reply to my final definitive effort on their behalf, instead of acknowledging in any way the hours of work it represented, merely stated that I appeared to have omitted two items which had been recorded in 1922. The first, they said, was: 'Fountain composed of three groups of tritons, nereids and marine monsters' and the second—'Small tapestry cushion with motif of heraldic lion'. Happily repairing these omissions did not mean much more searching. The North Fountain, at the end of the approach to the house, was so large that it had been overlooked and the tapestry cushion had been duly found, but through a typing error, had been left off the list.

At this time too, Mademoiselle Denise André arrived at Waddesdon to inspect all the things bequeathed to the National Trust and repair and clean them in any way necessary so that they might be handed over in tip-top condition. The André family had played a part at Waddesdon since the days when old M. André, Mademoiselle André's grandfather, had helped Baron Ferdinand with the decoration of his 'new smoking room' in the 1880's. Monsieur André *grandpère* had been the head of the family firm in Paris which was famous for repairing works of art of all kinds. Their secrets of how to clean safely, or mend invisibly, objects made of porcelain, ormolu, stone, wood or tortoiseshell were known, it seems, to few others. The grandson of the founder—Mademoiselle André's brother—had unhappily, died young, leaving a number

Late 16th century Bohemian glass beaker painted with the 'Ages of Man'.

Overleaf 6-fold Savonnerie screen woven on designs by A. F. Desportes between 1720 and 1740.

xxx · iar · ein · man
xl · iar · wolgethan
xxx · iar · nimmer · weis
xc · iar · der · kinder · spott

of small children, and it was left to his sister and his widow to carry on the firm until the children became old enough to play their part. Mademoiselle André, living in Paris, and working in museums and great collections throughout Europe, was the most cultured and charming of human beings, and had magic in her fingers; it was a delight to watch her handling any work of art. She also had one unexpected talent—an extraordinary sympathy with animals of all kinds which every species reciprocated.

When Mademoiselle André came to Waddesdon which, except for the war years, she did at regular intervals, the crustiest old parrot in the aviary would start dancing on his perch and the shyest inmate of the deer pens would come galloping at her call. To the discomfort of late sleepers, a cockatoo, rightly named Denis the Menace, who should have lived in the aviary but who was more often at liberty, would fly to the house in the early morning when Mademoiselle André was present and would sit on a chimney, screaming down it, until such time as she opened her window, and invited him in to have breakfast with her. But her greatest love affair was with Jumbo, a guard dog who lived in a large kennel by the back door. She always spoke to him in French, addressing him as 'Joombeau'. Together they would go for walks while she told him the latest news of poodles and bull-dogs of her acquaintance in Paris.

Jumbo died not long after my husband's death and I fear that at that time none of us thought of letting Mademoiselle André know of this sad event, which she only discovered on her next visit. The distress she felt made her guilty—I am sure for the first and only time—of expressing her ideas in what was, perhaps, a less than tactful order. I could not be at Waddesdon the day she arrived on this occasion, but on reaching home the next morning I sought her out and I remember her running towards me, crying as she did so: *'Ah! Madame, comme c'est triste! Pas de Joombeau! Pas de Monsieur de Rothschild!'*

Mademoiselle André, alas, is now also dead. But before she left this world she handed on to her nephew Jean-Michel her knowledge and her expertise and he, with Pierre Klieski and other talented colleagues, continue to come to Waddesdon for the National Trust and take those stitches in time which, it is hoped, will preserve old works of art for the enjoyment of many future generations.

The front door at Waddesdon.

The National Trust

My husband's bequest to the National Trust consisted of the house; 120 acres of surrounding land; the contents of the eleven ground floor rooms and all the arms and the garden statuary.

Lord Crawford immediately proposed that a National Trust Management Committee for Waddesdon should be formed and was kind enough to suggest that I should be its Chairman. One of the most sensitive features of the National Trust's policy is that, so far as possible, the family of a donor should either be encouraged to continue to live in the house, or help to keep it in the tradition to which it had been accustomed.

It may perhaps interest some people to know what preparations we thought it necessary to make at Waddesdon before it could be opened to the public.

We were somewhat harassed at the time by one of the national newspapers which kept on printing paragraphs asking why my husband's bequest was still invisible to the public, some months after his death. It was even suggested that there must be some mysterious circumstance which still kept the contents of Waddesdon hidden. The only mystery lay in the newspaper's lack of comprehension of what had to be done before we could open the house. It was still alive with museum experts who came on behalf of the Estate Duty Office whenever their ordinary work allowed and they were constantly running into valuers who were assessing all the more mundane furniture and things such as sheets and saucepans, bedsteads and hoovers, on which duty would be payable. At the same time the house was full of workmen because the Management Committee's first job was to make the house and its contents as secure as possible. As I was about to move to Eythrope it was obvious that others would have to be found to live in the Manor at Waddesdon permanently. The problem was how to ensure a comfortable family life for a number of resident wardens in a house which was in no way designed for that purpose. The answer was to carve out individual flats, each with its own front door, and complete with bedrooms, sitting-room, kitchen and bathroom. This was a very big conversion

The author, photographed at Eythrope, by Bern Schwartz in 1977 job which naturally took time; it was brilliantly carried out by our ingenious architect, Mr. R. J. Page.

It also took time to recruit the wardens and several of those who agreed to come could not leave their previous jobs immediately. Perhaps thanks to the comfortable modern flats which were made for them, the house has been fully manned since 1958 and most of our wardens remain with us until they retire. Some of them then find accommodation in Waddesdon village and continue to help by lending a hand from time to time.

The vital need was to find people able and willing to take on a great variety of tasks. Security was one thing, but keep and cleanliness came next on the list of essentials. Mrs. Green and Mabel Chatfield had more than reached the age of retirement and when I left, they decided they would also leave. How on earth could they be replaced?

As so often in my difficulties I turned to Lady Reading for advice. Her response was immediate. I was bidden to luncheon to meet the head of the WAAF. On learning of my problem she told me of Miss Gwyneth Morgan who, during the war, had been in charge of a large WAAF camp in Wales. Since leaving the service she had been living in another house, recently bequeathed to the National Trust, where she had been helping the widow of the donor who, for personal reasons, wished to pack up and move to another house. In doing so, it appeared, Miss Morgan had won the praise and gratitude of all. Now knowing what such a feat implied, I was most anxious to meet one who appeared to have experience both in taking charge of others and in handling works of art. I made Miss Morgan's acquaintance and took to her at once; I was indeed glad when she agreed to come to Waddesdon as its housekeeper.

Mrs. Green was exceedingly doubtful of anyone lacking a life-time's education in 'private service' being able to look after the contents of Waddesdon satisfactorily. It was not quite a case of 'Mabel thinking so too' but very nearly. However Miss Morgan arrived some months before Mrs. Green and Mabel left. They told her all they knew and initiated her into the so-called mysteries of 'the Waddesdon standard' and how to attain it. To their surprise she was so intelligently capable of absorbing their tuition that, when the day came, they left with lighter hearts and higher hopes for the future of Waddesdon than they had ever thought possible. For some years Miss Morgan demonstrated her ability to recruit willing helpers from the village; train those who had not worked in the house before, and maintain the 'keep and care' in the tradition established by Miss Alice. When the time came for Miss

Morgan to wish to retire she handed this tradition on to her immediate successor, and so far the chain has remained unbroken ever since.

The choice of a Director to be in over-all charge at Waddesdon was one of the most important decisions the Management Committee had to take in 1957. We interviewed twelve candidates who came with their wives to look and be looked at. We chose as Director a nationally known figure with a great artistic reputation. Unfortunately it soon became clear he was not really interested in the period or taste of the contents and decoration of Waddesdon and he and the Management Committee found themselves in constant disagreement. It was with mingled disappointment and regret that we accepted his resignation not long after the house was opened to the public. Looking back on this unhappy time, when sympathy between us seemed impossible to attain, I feel sure that his love of modern art, of which Waddesdon was devoid, would have always made it uncongenial to him.

After a few months experience we believed we understood what would be the most desirable qualities in an administrator at Waddesdon. He should possess such things as a flair for man and woman management; an understanding of the best temperature and humidity for pictures and furniture; an ability to spot a leak in a roof or a boiler; even a comprehension of the part hoggin can play in avenues over which coaches thunder. He should also have rather more than a nodding acquaintance with the mysteries of composing annual estimates. In our search for such a paragon we turned to the Army and were extremely fortunate. First a Brigadier set a pattern of good management and when, ten years later, he retired, he was followed by a Colonel; both proved to have all these abilities as well as many other virtues.

Maybe it is coincidence, but Brigadier N. S. Cowan and Colonel A. R. Waller, both regular soldiers who had had distinguished military carreers in war and in peace, developed an intuitive feeling and love for works of art although in their previous lives they had had nothing to do with their keep or arrangement. Happily they both also proved to be admirable PRO's—a talent not to be ignored in the management of National Trust properties. Last but not least, both came accompanied by the most charming of wives who, each in her turn, has taken in her stride the duties of 'instant hostess' to visiting experts and has provided that oil and comfort which is so needed when some crisis hits the lives of those who inhabit a closed community. Their handiwork is also in evidence at Waddesdon. Mrs. Cowan evolved at lightning speed

Madame de Pompadour, signed and dated J.-B. Lemoyne, 1761

Opposite The Blue Sèvres room. The lacquer and ormolu mechanical clock in the form of a birdcage, which includes a musical box, was made in Switzerland, c. 1780

the tented ceiling of the display of materials in the 'Store Room'—a problem which had defeated both our architect and decorator; and Mrs. Waller's talent for cleaning the miniature silver on display is only equalled by her intimate and soothing influence on the birds in the aviary.

It had always been Jimmy's special wish that the general appearance of Waddesdon would give visitors the impression of an inhabited private house rather than a museum. It had indeed been a most convenient setting for a house party of a couple of dozen people but it was another matter to adapt it for the hundreds we hoped might visit us simultaneously once the house was open to the public. All the sitting rooms

The 'Store Room'

Opposite Two terra-cotta figures by Clodion. Late eighteenth century

had comfortable armchairs made by Howard, a fashionable upholsterer who, alas, vanished after the first world war. Now that we hoped each room would be filled with many visitors a choice had to be made; there would not be room for beautiful 18th century chairs, the modern armchairs and the public, and it was the comfortable chairs and sofas which had to be sacrificed. Old photographs taken before they were removed show how immensely liveable the house looked, even if a little more crowded. There was one other obvious difficulty in keeping things as they were—the Savonnerie carpets; they looked beautiful in many of the rooms, but how could we keep visiting feet from treading on them? We solved this problem by stretching in front of them thin coloured cord supported on slim stands only about one foot high. This is what Monsieur Pierre Verlet of the Louvre calls *'protection symbolique'* and so far it has worked admirably.

Circulation was also another matter to be considered. Inevitably at Waddesdon there would be no way of avoiding one line of arriving visitors meeting another line going away, until we could arrange for some of the first floor rooms to be opened and thus provide a circular tour and an unencumbered exit. There are many methods of showing visitors round a house, some more agreeable than others. Freedom to roam with information available whenever it is desired is delightful but costly to administer. Waiting for some twenty people to collect and then conducting them round, opening and locking all doors as the party progresses, is economical and secure, but not quite so pleasant. But there are many ways which can be devised between these two extremes in different houses. At Waddesdon, on each open day, we find it necessary, in addition to the resident staff, to have some forty extra people on duty inside and outside the house.

Most sightseers expect to be able to buy a guide-book of some sort: getting one written, illustrated and printed introduced us to the problems of book production about which we were to learn much more when the detailed catalogues of the contents of the house began to be published some years later.

Before the house was ready for opening we plied the National Trust with innumerable questions of a practical nature—what would they suggest we should prepare in the way of parking

Waddesdon during the 'open' season

facilities, food, lavatories and litter bins? As far as the last were concerned we received an answer which surprised us. The ideal, apparently, would be to keep the garden looking like a private one rather than a public park furnished with expectant receptacles for refuse. In some magical way this has also worked so far—no litter bins mean no litter.

All these preparations took almost a year to complete. I was obliged, because of the Probate, to continue to live at Waddesdon for nearly all that time, so there was no need to engage any but a skeleton staff before I left. This meant that a large part of one year's income from the endowment was available to cover some of the cost of the structural alterations.

Just before we opened the then Minister of Works came to Waddesdon for a preview. After a careful tour, he very kindly told us not to be disappointed if the attendance of visitors dropped dramatically following the interest a new venture always attracted. I am thankful to say that the reverse has happened. After a rather shaky start when fewer than 30,000 came, the number of our visitors increased year by year until in 1974 there were some 103,000. In the last four years our figures have fluctuated just below or just above the 100,000 mark, and with this we are content. We have discovered how helplessly dependent we are on the weather, particularly on Bank Holidays; in the last few years they have been capable of producing snow, thunder and intense heat.

In one way we may well have disappointed our visitors. In our over-riding anxiety to protect the contents of Waddesdon we made a rule, and have kept to it, that children under the age of 12 should not be admitted to the house. I believe we are almost alone in trying to enforce this, but as I have explained, the house is arranged as nearly as possible as if it could be inhabited at any moment, and this necessarily means that there are many precious china and other fragile objects within easy, breakable reach. The visual result, we believe, greatly enhances the pleasure of visitors. But it takes a good hour to go round Waddesdon and for small children it is no pleasure to be kept under tight control for such a time; and a struggle between conscientious parents and fractious, thwarted children is a risk we are not prepared to take. Children are most welcome in the garden, the aviary and the tea-room—as they will be in a special outdoor play ground which is now being planned for them, which we hope may provide distraction for them while their parents are enjoying a tour of the house.

Once Waddesdon was opened, it settled into its summer and winter routines—both equally busy, but quite different. From Easter until the end of October all efforts are concentrated on

The State bedroom, now transformed to show examples of Sèvres china of every colour in the house. The Savonnerie carpet was made for the Grande Galerie at the Louvre, c. 1681. The Beauvais tapestry on the sofa is mid-18th century

Overleaf A lace fan which belonged to Baroness Ferdinand

Three eighteenth century fans from Baroness Edmond's collection

seeing our visitors get everything they want; a convenient place to park; an enjoyable tour of the house; any information they ask for; guide-books, postcards or catalogues; and a good tea. Naturally the provision of all these things implies a large staff and the Manor has become, to some extent, the Waddesdon village industry. Neighbours who have an interest in the arts form a changing rota of guides; they have all been subjected to a rigorous training which enables them to answer intelligently questions about any object in the house. We rather pride ourselves that they can do so in at least four European languages. As the guides' work is necessarily seasonal, we try to hold their interest during the winter by arranging lectures for them by experts or by planning special visits to other collections. When the house is open it is not only the guides who are on duty: the bus plies to and from the village bringing in sellers of postcards and garden produce; makers and servers of tea and, most numerous of all, the 'sitting wardens'. These merely sit in each room the public go through, guarding its contents. They seldom have to prevent attempted theft, but are often called on to frustrate a desire to touch.

Before we opened we were told horrifying stories of other houses where it was said china vases had to be filled with

lead or sand, or even bolted to the furniture on which they stood, to prevent their being rushed at and up-ended by enthusiasts who were anxious to see what marks the china bore. We have, I believe, found other means of protection and, in the event, have been free of such dangerous '*connoisseurs*'. But, as in all other houses, we have had to take precautions against the unconquerable urge of all females to touch materials which appeal to them. It appears to be an unbreakable law of nature that if a woman sees any pleasing stuff, particularly velvet, she must inevitably stroke it with her fingers. Doubtless she will assume that such a caress from her will do no harm, but when thousands of women think so, one after another, the result can be disastrous even to the most stalwart textile. We have found the answer is to sheathe all easily touchable materials in the finest possible net up to a height beyond which a woman's hand is unlikely to stray. If fine enough the net is either invisible, or at most gives the faintest misty tinge to the material underneath it, but it does deter and preserve.

The application of net is a winter job, as is so much else. As the last visitor leaves on the last day of October the packing up begins. China, snuff boxes and other small objects are put away; everything that can be be covered is swathed in a linen *housse* or in white or black tissue paper which prevents colour fading or metal tarnishing. The weight is taken off great curtains by propping them up on chairs and every object in the house is allowed to relax comfortably in a state of hibernation. But this is not true of its human inhabitants—for them the winter is a truly busy time.

One seems to find a small factory in operation at every turn in the house between November and March. Garden seats are being oiled or painted; chandeliers are being laboriously cleaned and the lighting of pictures examined and improved. The Dining Room is cleared and filled with long trestle tables at which work a marvellously gifted team of sempstresses which the bus now carries to and from the village. They not only reline curtains but also undertake much more complicated preservation work on various textiles in the house.

In these days when so many people are anxious to save their houses and their precious contents from the necessity of sale by showing them to the public, one is apt to forget the unavoidable back-room work which must be undertaken. A private householder can, perhaps, put off to some convenient time the repairs for which his house and possessions may stand in need, but if one is aiming to attract visitors who pay, and who look at everything with minute attention, every sign of deterioration

The dining room at Waddesdon in winter, converted into a sewing-room

must be spotted as soon as possible and repaired, if it can be, in the few winter months before a new season begins.

Quite apart from the vulnerability of the roof, which owing to its exposure to the elements, is generally expected to need repair from time to time, there seems to be nothing in any house which is not liable to call for attention. Everything from electric wiring to clocks, and from furniture to drawings is lamentably subject to slight disintegration which only constant supervision and care will halt.

Apart from the André family we have enjoyed the help and counsel of many outside experts. Mr. John Fowler gave us his invaluable advice over the re-instatement of the first floor of the West Wing: both the Victoria and Albert Museum and Mrs. Finch at Hampton Court have performed miracles with textiles whose repair was beyond our capabilities and the watchful eyes of Professor Rees-Jones of the Courtauld Institute and Miss Seddon have detected any trouble with the pictures which they have then arranged to put right. In recent years all the Savonnerie carpets and screens have been cleaned—probably for the

Repairs being done to the roof of Waddesdon

first time since they were made more than two hundred years ago—by Mr. Maurice's firm in Wigmore Street, and the brilliance of their original colour has now been restored.

We decided early on to improve the circulation in the house by opening some of the rooms on the first floor. They were all still in their war-time condition and, having been used as dormitories for the children, were in considerable need of 'refurbishing'.

We were told that any self-respecting stately home always provided a view of at least one bedroom and, if possible, a bathroom as, apparently, an added attraction. So we started on what proved to be an extensive programme, partly rehabilitation and partly improvisation, which eventually provided, as part of the visitors' tour, eleven other rooms for display. This took many years to complete.

Fortunately, there was no lack of material to be shown on

this floor. In addition to the furniture for the bedrooms which had been stored away, we had two other sources of supply from France. Part of Jimmy's inheritance from his parents had not reached us before the war started and having remained in Paris fell a prey to the Germans. Some of it had been taken by Goering for his own use, but luckily this particular batch had never been unpacked and had remained in the cases in which they had been put for transmission to Germany. These included my parents-in-law's incredible store of textiles of all kinds, and of all centuries, which they had found on their many travels and which Baroness Edmond had treasured in case any of the contents of her various houses needed repair or replacement. Then there were many works of art which had been officially recuperated; mostly from the Austrian salt-mines, by the allied team led by Mr. Rorimer of the Metropolitan Musem in New York which had been given the task of tracking down and retrieving as much allied property as possible, as soon as the war ended; their success in doing this, though not complete, was considerable.

One way and another the rooms on the first floor were repainted and became filled, some with beautiful things, some with objects with an interesting past history and some with relics of former glory.

We thought more than two bedrooms would bore even the most domesticated of our visitors and so decided to turn the rest into exhibition rooms, more or less in the museum manner. Some structural alterations were needed but these only became a major operation in the West Wing. Here, Mr. Page most ingeniously converted four bedrooms, two bathrooms and two large corridors into four exhibition rooms which Mr. Fowler, with impeccable taste, provided with curtains and carpets which do much to mitigate any museum atmosphere. There were many individual collections made by different members of the family, through the years, which we were able to show here: Miss Alice's Dutch dolls' house silver; my mother-in-law's lace and her eighteenth century buttons and seals and part of my father-in-law's famous collection of drawings. Here too, the lovely embroidered Chinese wall-hanging with which my husband had returned from his world tour in 1904 at last found a place in which it could be seen.

The smallest of these rooms, which has become known as 'Rothschild Corner' contains intimate relics connected with the family as well as early photographs of those who visited the house throughout the years. My wedding dress, made in 1913 by the famous Callot *Soeurs* can be seen here: today I can hardly believe how I ever got into it. Among other mementoes of the

Overleaf Lace from Baroness Edmond's collection. Two borders of seventeenth century Venetian needle-lace and a detail of a large stole, Brussels bobbin-lace about 1860

Buttons depicting winter scenes from the collection of Baroness Edmond

family are the results of one of my father-in-law's archaeological 'digs' in Palestine in the 1890's and commemorative scrolls in Hebrew given to Baron Ferdinand and to his successors: these frequently tax the translating powers of our guides.

Four other ex-bedrooms have completely changed their appearance. One which used to be a round chintz room in a tower has become an exotic tent containing show cases in which is displayed a complete turquoise Sèvres dessert service which in former days we cheerfuly used on grand occasions, confident that it would survive our use and the washing-up by Mrs. Green and her companions. Another bedroom contains examples of Sèvres china of the many different colours the house contained. Yet another is now called the Music Room because, to our surprise, we found there were enough old musical instruments scattered round the house to fill one room. At the other end of the house Miss Alice's collection of arms still remains on the first floor of the Bachelors' Wing, but the Billiard Room has lost its table to the one-time Still Room where it is still used and is popular among the snooker-playing residents of the house. The Billiard Room now houses some of the mediaeval illuminated manuscripts collected by Baron Edmond as well as the Savonnerie carpet which had adorned Miss Alice's private sitting room.

All this conversion of the first floor does occasionally bemuse some of our visitors who have been heard to express surprise that a house of this size should apparently have had only two bedrooms.

There also had to be some reconstruction out of doors. Waddesdon had always been most carefully maintained, particularly by Miss Alice, and we had done our best to follow her example. But I must confess there was one big exception to our endeavours and that was the aviary. Enchanting though this building is, it never figured prominently on the repainting list and during the war and the following years, it lost all priority. The result was that in 1957 it was in deplorable condition. The National Trust felt strongly that the aviary should be preserved and insisted on its repair as soon as this was feasible. No short cut towards this end was possible. The aviary's elaborate trellis work and curlicues are all made of cast iron and workmen with the necessary skill to replace the many gaps where the iron had perished through rust were not easy to find. But they were discovered eventually, and it was even perhaps fortunate that it took seven years to complete the repairs, so that the cost of putting the aviary back in order again could be spread over a number of years.

Sometimes the old days at the Manor have overlapped with

The Music Room. The portraits of Dr Clerke Wilshaw and his wife, Rebecca, on either side of the fireplace, are by Thomas Hudson. The picture on the right, the Daughters of Lady Boynton, is ascribed to Richard Cosway.

the new, and we have had visitors, grown men, often with wives and families, who are anxious to find and point out to their relatives the rooms in which they slept during the 1939–45 war. It is sometimes hard to reconcile their memories with what is now visible, but invariably they remember the big circular staircases down which, in their infancy, and in droves, they were urged to crawl backwards, on all fours, as the safest means of making the descent.

Some years after their retiremnt Mrs. Green and Mabel came to stay with me and we made what became an annual visit of state through the house at Waddesdon. Mrs. Green's eye-sight by now was most indifferent, but she still had a wonderfully erect carriage and, beautifully dressed, she advanced like a ship in full sail through all the rooms at the Manor. The 'sitting wardens' were each in their place. In their youth and before marriage, many of them had worked in the house under Mrs. Green's care, but many others had not, and were what she would regard as newcomers to the village. To those in the latter category Mrs. Green's progress must have been rather startling. Moving with ceremonial tread, she halted as she came level with each 'sitting warden', bowed over to peer narrowly in her face, then seeing someone she did not recognise, clearly pronounced the single word 'No', and then moved on again. When however, she found on investigation a face that was familiar to her she enquired with impeccable memory 'Well, Violet, how are you?' or 'Now Annie, how have you been getting on?' and generally received in reply an exact account of the children and grandchildren who had been born since they had last seen Mrs. Green. Other visitors, overhearing these conversations, appeared to be puzzled that these mostly grey-haired guardians ended every sentence they addressed to Mrs. Green with the word 'Ma'am'. Times had indeed changed.

The decision to publish a comprehensive Catalogue of the contents of Waddesdon was one of the first to be taken by the National Trust when it became the new owner. I can say with my hand on my heart that we took up this task with enthusiasm. Looking back over the last twenty years I can see that at the time I had not the slightest realisation of the problems that lay ahead. We proceeded with energy and the first steps were easy, thanks to the guidance of Sir Anthony Blunt, who until recently combined the arduous duties of being Surveyor of the Queen's pictures and the Director of the Courtauld Institute. Putting his great knowledge at our disposal, he agreed to become the General Editor of the series, and found the eminent experts, both British and foreign, to write the text of each volume. The photography of all the objects to be catalogued was another winter job which took an inordinate amount of time: for many winters Mr. Eost and Mr. Macdonald, the expert photographers of the Victoria and Albert Museum can have had few Sundays free from the claims of Waddesdon. My ideas on the complexities of producing colour illustrations, as on all other preliminaries to publication, were of the haziest, but I clung to the idea that whatever malign fate might conceivably overtake Waddesdon, a published account of its contents would remain and would preserve for all time a record of the taste and knowledge of some remarkable collectors who had all been members of one family.

The Aviary, restored between 1958 and 1965

I now have a much better comprehension of the many detailed problems which pursue those who aim at perfection in the technicalities of publication and my admiration for those who solve them is unbounded. Like them, I have learnt patience. If the leading expert in any particular field of artistic knowledge is engaged to write a book, he will inevitably have many other commitments which may well claim priority. And tragedy has struck our hoped-for schedule; two of our authors have died before their work was completed. But thanks to Sir Anthony's persuasive powers and remarkable capacity for work, both in discussing every detail with our authors and in translating various foreign texts into English, the volumes continue to appear.

Happily, Waddesdon was large enough when the flats for its present residents were constructed to include two additional ones for visitors. Throughout the years these have been used by the various authors of the catalogue who come to stay, when their time permits, and study the objects of their work, sometimes for days on end. They are aided by Miss Rosamund Griffin who, as the Keeper at Waddesdon, not only instructs the guides on whom the public depend for information, but has the care of the condition of all the works of art. Joining the staff in the earliest days of the National Trust era she now has the greatest and most intimate knowledge of the date and history of every object in the house. The cataloguers' debt to her knowledge, and to her prowess as a calm and charming amanuensis and proof-reader, is rightly acknowledged in the foreword to every volume of the catalogue which has so far been published.

I believe Waddesdon is now inhabited by many who have as great a feeling of affection for it as any of its previous private owners. Those who live there now have to combine a capability in many professions, and be at the same time administrators, art historians and conservationists, as well as public relation experts and shopkeepers. I feel sure that Miss Alice would approve the standard of care which is still exercised and that Baron Ferdinand, that most gregarious man, would be pleased with the great number of our visitors. I hope, too, that they would both have been in favour of my attempt to follow

Baron Ferdinand feeding one of his birds

their hospitable example by giving a party to celebrate the hundredth anniversary of Baron Ferdinand's purchase of the estate in September 1874. Exactly one hundred years later Waddesdon was thronged by the visiting public until late in the afternoon, so the party could not be held there; instead, it took place in a huge marquee on the lawn of the Pavilion at Eythrope. At this dinner, followed by the traditional fireworks, some four hundred people were united: members of the family; all those who worked on the estate and those who worked for the National Trust; and many others who had contributed in a wide variety of capacities to the life, embellishment or maintenance of Waddesdon throughout the years. In proposing the continued well-being of the estate, the tenant farmer whose family had had the longest tenure of their land said he remembered his father telling him to stick to Waddesdon as it was a good place in which to work. It was music in my ears to hear him say that he would still give the same advice, and for the same reason, to any young relative to-day.

Writing in 1897, Baron Ferdinand said: ' Art is a small factor in history, perhaps only an incident in it, yet it follows history in all its stages. So long as the Church and the Throne were the primary forces of civilisation it was the aim and the ambition of the artist to devote his genius to the adornment of Churches and Palaces, which he filled with all that was noblest and richest in art: but when the growth of democracy destroyed the spell of the old influence it set the artist adrift and carried away, scattering broadcast, the old artistic accumulation of ages. A new centre of attraction has been formed on the ruins of the old, produced by the very action of democracy. If the artist no longer gravitates towards the Prelate and the Prince, he now pays homage to the People, whom he idealises as an entity, competing for their patronage in academies and exhibitions, while the artistic productions of the past turn to the same magnet and pass into the hands of the People '.

Even Baron Ferdinand could hardly have foreseen the extraordinary growth of interest in the artistic possessions of this country which has come about since he wrote those words; but it is my great hope that he and both his successors would be pleased that Waddesdon has become one of the ' new centres of attraction ' of which he wrote. The very evident pleasure of our visitors seems to confirm his judgment: pleasure gives pleasure and to me it is an exceptional privilege and delight to witness it at Waddesdon year after year.

Appendices

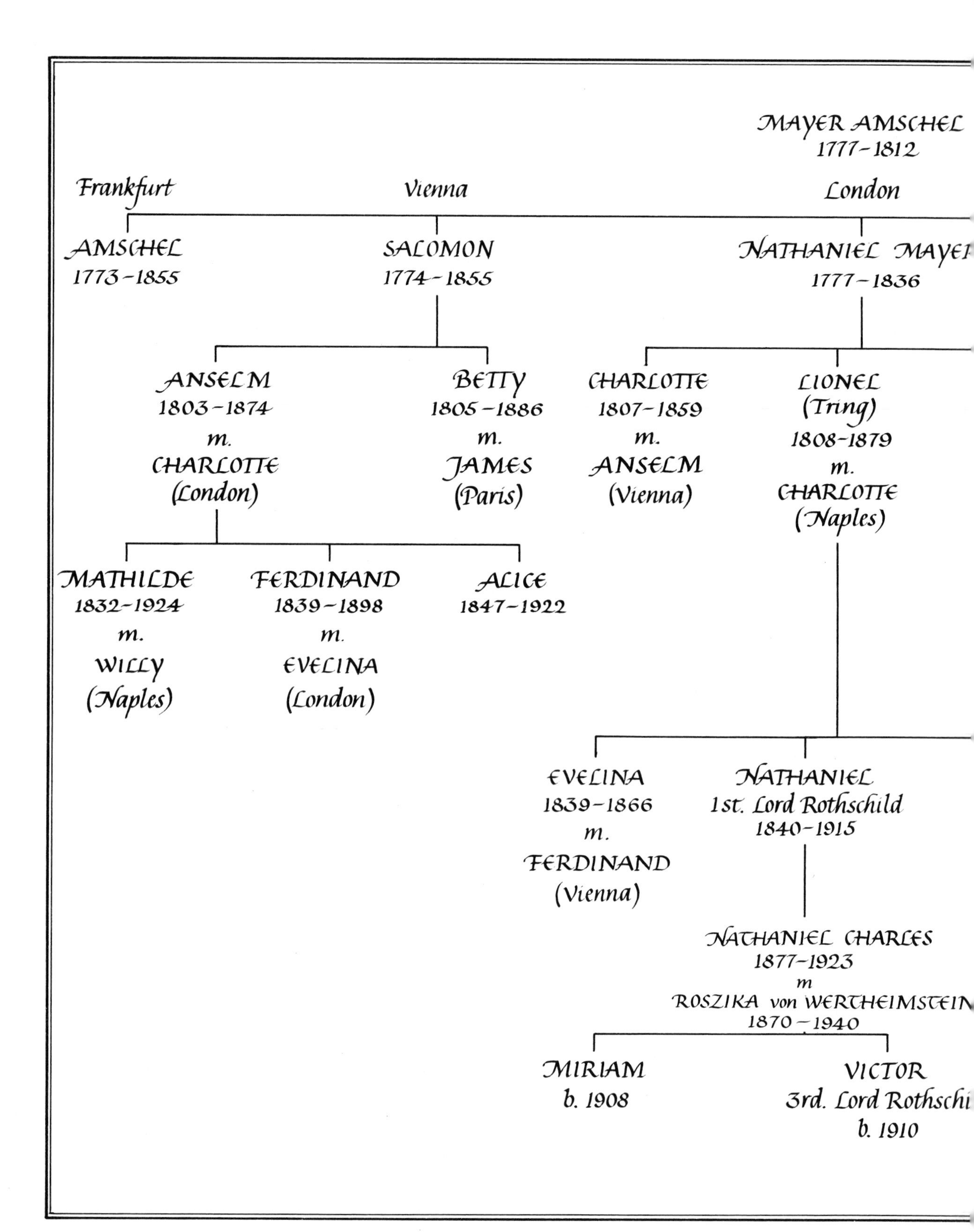
MAYER AMSCHEL
1777–1812
Frankfurt
Vienna
London
AMSCHEL
1773–1855
SALOMON
1774–1855
NATHANIEL MAYE
1777–1836
ANSELM
1803–1874
m.
CHARLOTTE
(London)
BETTY
1805–1886
m.
JAMES
(Paris)
CHARLOTTE
1807–1859
m.
ANSELM
(Vienna)
LIONEL
(Tring)
1808–1879
m.
CHARLOTTE
(Naples)
MATHILDE
1832–1924
m.
WILLY
(Naples)
FERDINAND
1839–1898
m.
EVELINA
(London)
ALICE
1847–1922
EVELINA
1839–1866
m.
FERDINAND
(Vienna)
NATHANIEL
1st. Lord Rothschild
1840–1915
NATHANIEL CHARLES
1877–1923
m
ROSZIKA von WERTHEIMSTEIN
1870–1940
MIRIAM
b. 1908
VICTOR
3rd. Lord Rothschi
b. 1910

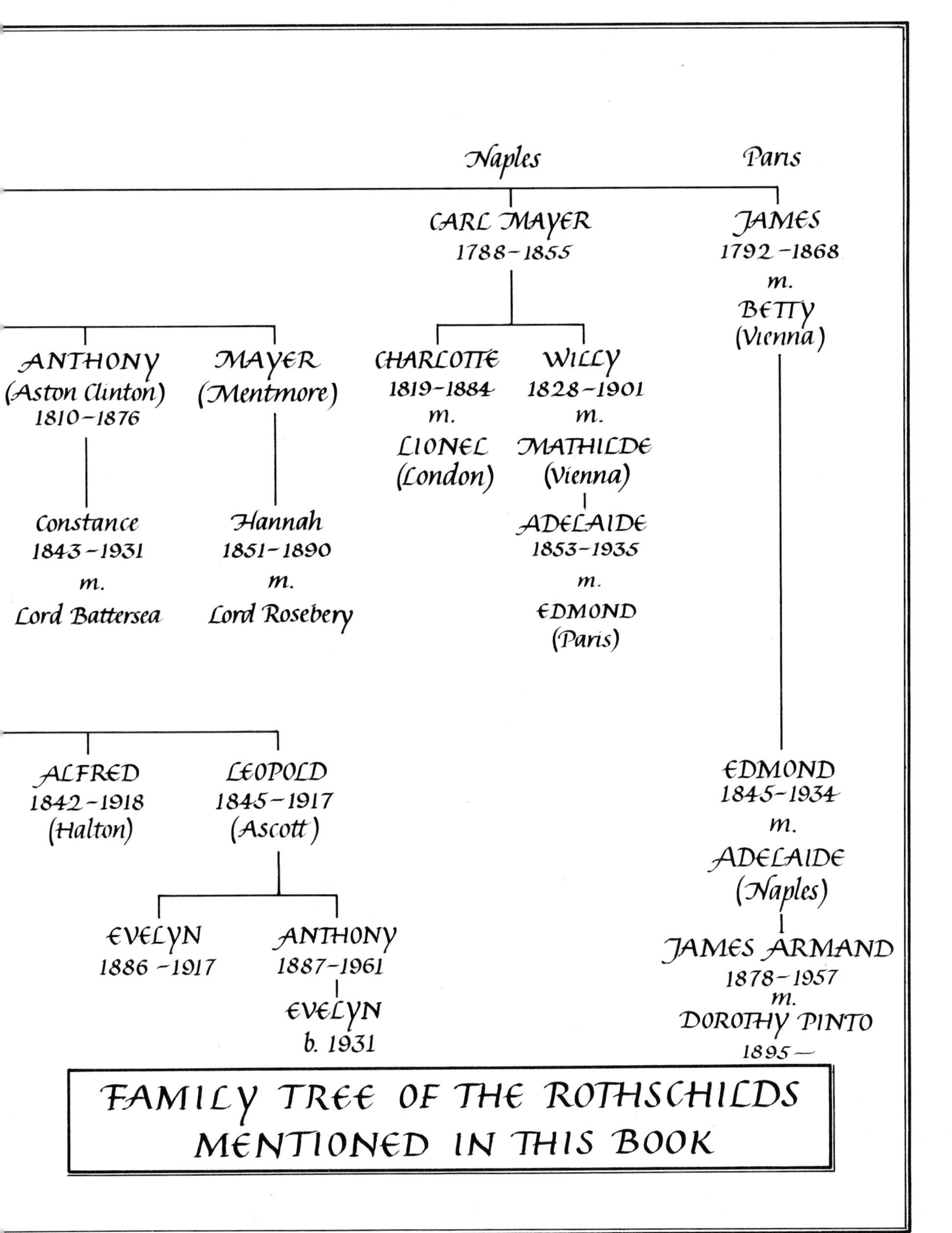
Naples
Paris
CARL MAYER
1788–1855
JAMES
1792–1868
m.
BETTY
(Vienna)
ANTHONY
(Aston Clinton)
1810–1876
MAYER
(Mentmore)
CHARLOTTE
1819–1884
m.
LIONEL
(London)
WILLY
1828–1901
m.
MATHILDE
(Vienna)
Constance
1843–1931
m.
Lord Battersea
Hannah
1851–1890
m.
Lord Rosebery
ADELAIDE
1853–1935
m.
EDMOND
(Paris)
ALFRED
1842–1918
(Halton)
LEOPOLD
1845–1917
(Ascott)
EDMOND
1845–1934
m.
ADELAIDE
(Naples)
EVELYN
1886–1917
ANTHONY
1887–1961
EVELYN
b. 1931
JAMES ARMAND
1878–1957
m.
DOROTHY PINTO
1895–
FAMILY TREE OF THE ROTHSCHILDS
MENTIONED IN THIS BOOK

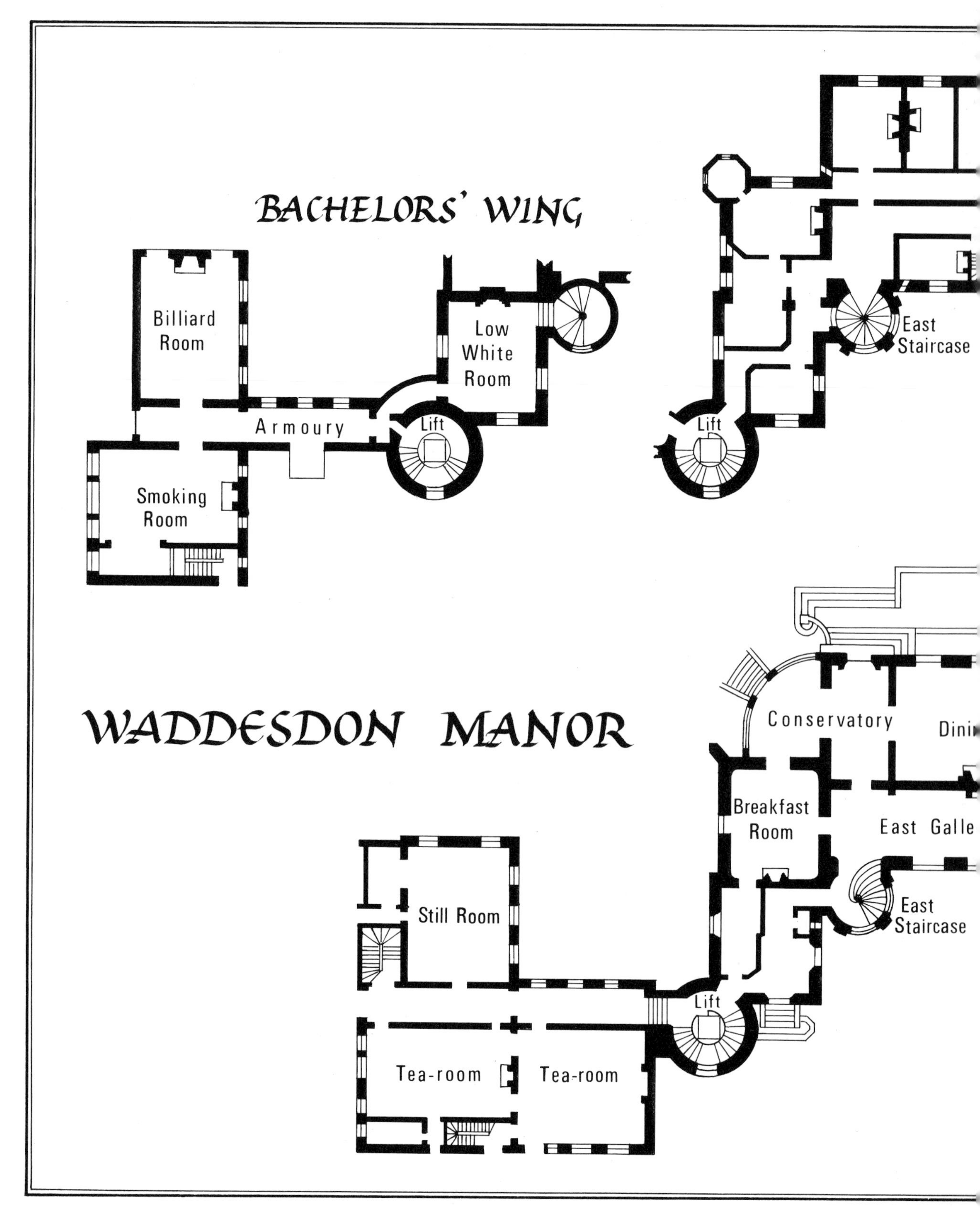
BACHELORS' WING
Billiard Room
Low White Room
Armoury
Lift
Smoking Room
Lift
East Staircase
WADDESDON MANOR
Conservatory
Breakfast Room
East Galle
Still Room
East Staircase
Lift
Tea-room
Tea-room

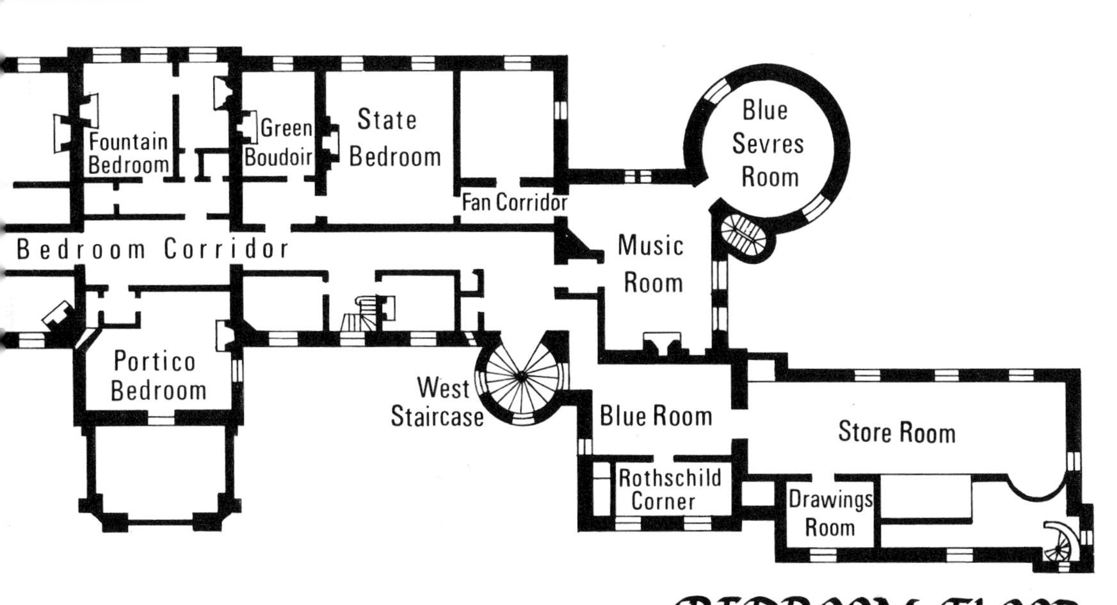
Fountain Bedroom
Green Boudoir
State Bedroom
Blue Sevres Room
Fan Corridor
Bedroom Corridor
Music Room
Portico Bedroom
West Staircase
Blue Room
Store Room
Rothschild Corner
Drawings Room
BEDROOM FLOOR

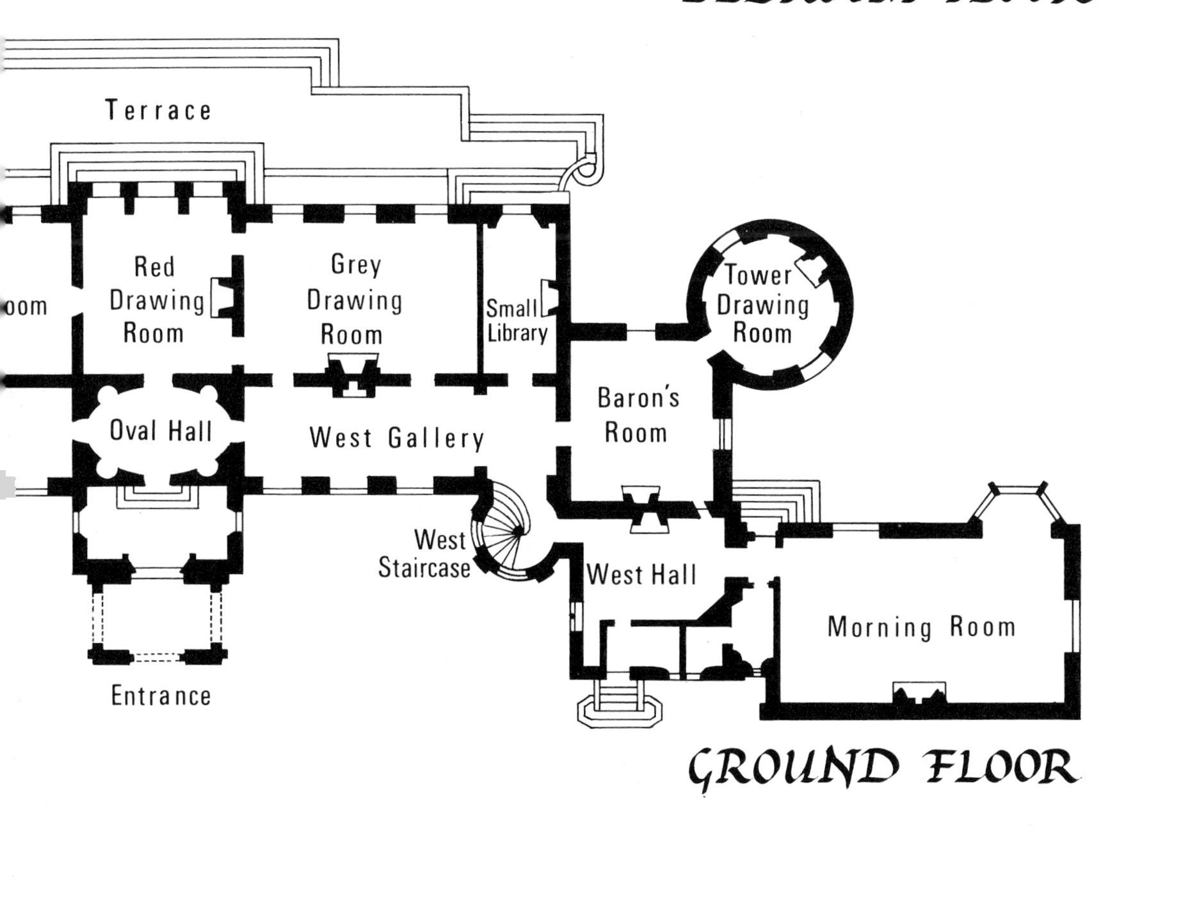
Terrace
oom
Red Drawing Room
Grey Drawing Room
Small Library
Tower Drawing Room
Oval Hall
West Gallery
Baron's Room
West Staircase
West Hall
Morning Room
Entrance
GROUND FLOOR

Index

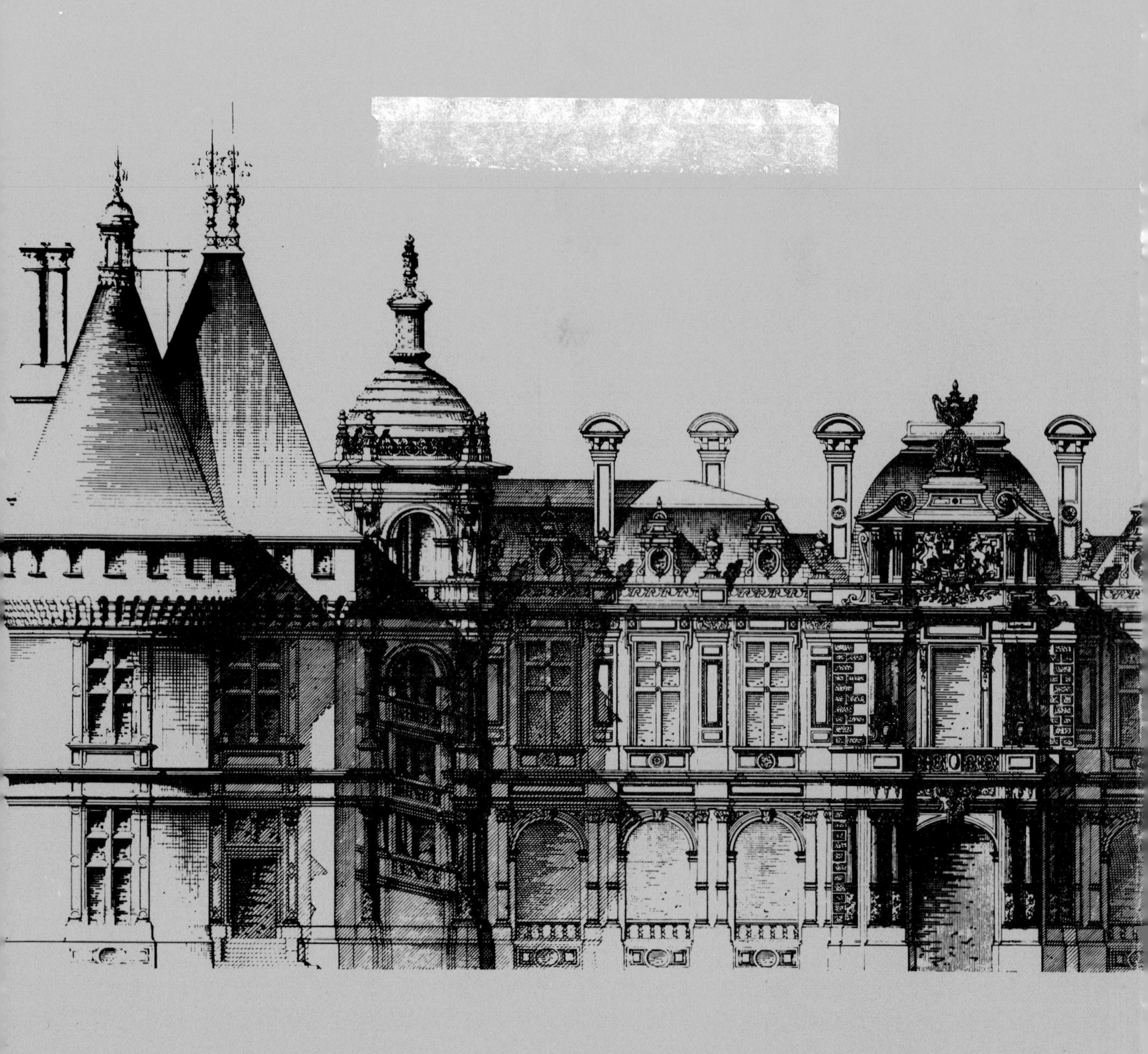